D1084805

UNACCOUNTABLE ACCOUNTING

UNACCOUNTABLE

New York, Evanston, San Francisco, London

1817

ACCOUNTING

ABRAHAM J. BRILOFF

HARPER & ROW, PUBLISHERS

Grateful acknowledgment is made for permission to quote from the following:

The material found on pages 63-65, 135-147, 193-203, 228-251 originally appeared in *Barron's* on July 15, 1968; December 2, 1968; January 11, 1971; October 25, 1971, respectively. Reprinted by courtesy of *Barron's National Business and Financial Weekly*.

Do You Sincerely Want to Be Rich? by Charles Raw, Bruce Page and Godfrey Hodgson. Copyright © 1969 by Times Newspapers Ltd. Reprinted by permission of The Viking Press, Inc.

"Blow to Confidence," by F. J. McDiarmid, *Barron's*, May 12, 1969. Reprinted by courtesy of *Barron's National Business and Financial Weekly*.

"How's That Again?" January 15, 1971, *Forbes Magazine*. Reprinted by permission of *Forbes Magazine*.

STANDARD BOOK NUMBER: 06-010471-6

LIBRARY OF CONGRESS CATALOG CARD NUMBER: 71-156509

Designed by Sidney Feinberg

For

Edith, Leonore and Alice

To

University Distinguished Professor
        Emanuel Saxe

Contents

Acknowledgments

No book is created parthenogenetically, as though it came forth full bloom like the goddess Athene from the forehead of Zeus. This is all the more true in this case, where the work is in good measure the result of a cumulative experience over the past third of a century—especially of the past decade. So it is that I have built up a huge roster of acknowledgments—only some of which can be presently brought to mind for inclusion in these few pages.

First, to Dean Emeritus, now University Distinguished Professor and, most important to me, beloved friend, Emanuel Saxe. He started it all as my teacher almost two score years ago. It was he, as I said in dedicating my previous book, "who by precept and practice has demonstrated that a path to the *summum bonum* passes through accountancy."

Moving closer in time, to describe the "critical path" leading to this writing as I now discern it, my appreciation to Stanley Sanders who, after reading my critical, but yet rather academic, article on pooling of interests accounting in the July, 1967, *Accounting Review,* invited me to deliver a paper on that subject before the New York Society of Security Analysts the following January.

Then there is Professor Michael Schiff who, in a Spring, 1966,

Journal of Accounting Research article set a new standard for accounting criticism. He there showed that it is entirely respectable and responsible to take as a frame of reference an accounting aberration perpetrated by a still very much alive major entity, to actually name names, and for him to survive the resultant obloquy.

Now my gratitude flows to my friend Phil Copelin who, in late 1967, while I was developing my thoughts in anticipation of the January, 1968, talk confessed to me that he, despite his sophistication in the realm of business and finance, just could not comprehend the current Litton financial statements. On looking into those statements I felt, along with Keats, "like some watcher of the skies when a new planet swims into his ken." Immediately close by in the heavens were the statements of Gulf and Western. These, then, gave me the primary frame of reference for my address before the security analysts. From there the pace escalates, probably at a geometric (sometimes exponential) rate.

Thus, there is David Norr, most competent and conscientious certified public accountant and chartered financial analyst, the chairman of the meeting, who forwarded a copy of my talk to Nicholas Molodowsky, the late, great, intrepid editor of *The Financial Analysts Journal.* How he did it, I don't know, but that mid-January speech found its way into the March/April, 1968, issue of the *Journal.*

This led to the invitation from *Barron's* which provided the "muscle" for what would otherwise have been the jeremiads of an academician. I am so very grateful to my friends there—Robert M. Bleiberg, Alan Abelson, and especially Steven S. Anreder—for their confidence and sincere friendship from which I have benefited so much over the past four years. I know they took important risks (one article alone brought forth $165 million in lawsuits—joining *Barron's* with me as co-defendants); that they are still my warm friends is so very gratifying.

The transition from articles to book, while considered in passing moments theretofore, was triggered by Dr. Harvey H. Segal, who was then an editor at Harper & Row. This led to the most agreeable relationship with Tadashi Akaishi, Susan Albury and John Gordon at Harper's. Each of them did much more than an author might expect of his publisher.

Coming closer to home, my affectionate appreciation to the Briloff girls, Edith, Leonore and Alice, each of whom through typing, indexing, footnoting, contributed importantly to bringing this book to fruition. And then there is Maxine Redford, my most conscientious secretary, to whom I owe special thanks. How she kept her cool, typing insertions to material that had not yet been written, and then, somehow, having it all come out reasonably logical and straightforward, is a phenomenon which is beyond me to comprehend.

Having thus noted my most sincere appreciation for their important, in fact indispensable, contribution to this work, I want to emphasize what should be self-evident: the responsibility for any aberrations is entirely mine.

Preface

A half dozen years ago Justice William O. Douglas described the vital role which the accounting profession should be called upon to play in the effective "functioning of our capitalistic society . . . rooted in full confidence in those to whom power is delegated [which, in turn] requires a functioning system of checks and balances." He recognized the substantial burdens he was putting on the profession, but, he added:

> . . . our economic society is in urgent need of this service. If the accounting profession does not respond effectively to the challenges presented, there may be little alternative but to have possibly a new profession fill the breach.

Since Mr. Justice Douglas thus wrote we have witnessed a most serious failure on the part of the accounting profession to "respond effectively to the challenges presented." That failure could be evidenced by the profession's abdication of responsibility for full and fair visibility and accountability regarding the conglomerate craze which convulsed the American economy in the decade of the sixties; in the accountings for the high-flying industries of that decade (the franchisors, computer lessors, land developers), and in the distorted accountings in other, more particular, instances. That failure has led to the identity crisis in which the accounting profession presently finds itself.

In this narration we will meet up with a bevy of old friends, and some new ones, including (in alphabetical order, and not in order of appearance or importance): City Investing, Commonwealth United, Great Southwest, Gulf and Western, Investors Overseas Services, Kaufman and Broad, Leasco, Liberty Equities, Ling-Temco-Vought, Litton, Lockheed, Major Realty, Memorex, Mill Factors, National General, Occidental Petroleum, Penn Central, Performance Systems (the erstwhile Minnie Pearl), Telex, U.S. Financial, U.S. Home, the prestigious Wall Street houses, Westec and Yale Express.

More generally, the American Institute of Certified Public Accountants, the profession's principal organization, is criticized for permitting inordinate power to be concentrated in so few hands. As a consequence, the Institute is failing in the profession's essential self-regulatory responsibilities, especially when it comes to disciplining those within the "inner circle." This failure or "cover up" might well cause the Institute to become something of the "defendant of last resort" (paralleling the plight in which the New York Stock Exchange found itself in 1970).

So it is that this work is not a psalm of praise for the profession. But then, neither should it be read as a song of despair. To the contrary! The primary objective of this book is to reemphasize the Justice's challenge and to move the profession's commitment to yet a higher plane—a quantum leap which is essential to the fulfillment of the new dimensions of corporate responsibility which can already be seen taking shape. Thus, we hear demands on the corporations and their auditors from various sectors of our society for forecasts and projections, for the measurement and disclosure of social costs, social benefits, opportunity costs; there is the movement for "fair value" accounting. All point to a drastically different profession of accountancy, and radically different standards governing the conduct of our major corporations.

A glorious challenge is being laid before the "Consciousness III" generation of accountants and corporate managements—

those who will be called upon to implement these dramatic proposals, and possibly even more inspired and ambitious ones which might evolve. Through such an implementation the intrepid accountants and managers should help assure that the modern corporation will help in the fulfillment of Man's objectives, rather than the other way round. They will, of course, require the understanding and active cooperation of their contemporaries in the disciplines of the law, ethics, sociology, economics, finance, and public policy—in fact, none is outside the ambit of disciplines required to comprehend the nature, function and structure of the evolving corporation.

This book, then, is for all of them, as well as for the "consciousness II" investors who may wonder why they were so "unhappily hooked" in the great bear market of 1968-1970, and are determined to prevent the past from being prologue to an even greater devastation tomorrow.

ABRAHAM J. BRILOFF

New York
June 20, 1972

Chapter 1

2 Plus 2 Equals . . . ?

T_{HE} owner of a closely held enterprise was desirous of going public, whereupon he turned to a prominent underwriter for help. The underwriter reviewed the financial statements and told the owner that his company was first-rate and he would help; however, it was necessary to give the financial statements the appropriate "image"—hence, the company would now have to be audited by one of the "Big Eight" firms.

The owner didn't know what was meant by the Big Eight, but the underwriter gave him a list of the eight firms comprising this inner circle, namely (in alphabetical order): Arthur Andersen; Ernst & Ernst; Haskins & Sells; Lybrand, Ross Bros. & Montgomery; Peat, Marwick, Mitchell; Price, Waterhouse; Touche, Ross; and Arthur Young.

The next day the owner called the underwriter to tell him that it was all arranged—the books would henceforth be audited by one of the Arthurs. The underwriter was impressed—how did the owner go about his task? Did he really study the quality of each of the firms or did he just spin the bottle?

The owner assured the underwriter that a most careful and objective study was made. As the partner of each firm was interviewed, he was asked, "What does 2 plus 2 equal?" Each of the respondents replied "Four, of course"—that is, all but the one

from the lucky Arthur firm. His answer, after some serious re-
flection, was, "What number did you have in mind?"

This apocryphal tale will gather credibility as our saga un-
folds. We will soon see how 2 plus 2 need not equal 4, if the
managerial-accounting game plan calls for a lesser or greater
number to come forth. Those who prefer to ignore this possibility do so at their economic peril.

We will see that the optimum response to the 2-plus-2 query
can change according to the prevalent style or mood of the
market place. Thus, we will soon see that when the Twiggy
look was the vogue during the decades of the '40s and '50s, the
accountants were able to oblige, in good conscience and with
expedition, by providing managements with income-statement
and balance-sheet depressants such as last in, first out inventory
(LIFO) metaphysics and abstractions; depreciation deductions
far in excess of those allowed by the Internal Revenue Service;
immediate write-offs of copyrights, film properties, and other
long-term assets; peremptory expensing of research and development costs; the accrual of pension costs beyond their economic
reality; carrying investments in various subsidiaries, especially
those in foreign countries, at only nominal sums. As a consequence of these accounting practices (and there were a great
many others which had a corresponding effect), corporate managements felt more secure: they had "a nice conservative balance
sheet," with huge pools of suppressed liquidity and values, to
help tide them over difficult days. Further, by these suppressions and write-offs they were able to minimize taxes and resist
pressures from labor and shareholders for increases in wages
and dividends respectively.

It was this condition which gave rise to the quip, "A balance
sheet is very much like a bikini bathing suit. What it reveals is
interesting, what it conceals is vital."

In the early '60s, however, or possibly even at the end of the
preceding decade, the styles changed. No longer was Twiggy
the rage, and the bikini became old hat—the mood favored the

full bosom (and we will see how this brought us closer to the big bust). Once again the accountants were able to respond, as good and loyal couturiers, armed with flexible tape measure, to make 2 plus 2 equal "what?"

First we were able to help by permitting the new breed of management to relax the old corsets, and then with the women's lib vogue to discard them altogether—revealing corporate voluptuousness in full splendor.

And then when the prurient (as distinguished from the prudent) investor cried for more, the couturiers were able to provide the padding and falsies to generate even greater excitement. It may, of course, be a mere historical coincidence that this evolved with the hot-pants era—when it became fashionable to expose assets with ever greater daring to produce the highest levels of excitement and exhilaration.

But you might ask, what about the pressures from government, labor, and shareholders for increasing shares of this newly exposed felicity? As it happened this was also the era when our tax laws and practices introduced so many tax-avoidance gimmicks that the government frequently considered itself fortunate if it got enough from many corporations to pay the cost of mailing the tax forms to them. Further, my colleagues have evolved a body of schizoid precepts whereby we are able to show huge profits to the public, while showing correspondingly huge deficits to the Internal Revenue Service.

As to labor: their negotiators soon became sufficiently astute so as to permit them to look behind the books. Besides, they became increasingly interested in what they wanted, rather than the employer's ability to pay—leaving it to the employer to tack on the added costs (plus an added profit margin) to the selling price.

And the investor was conditioned to believe that only widows, orphans, and numbskulls sought cash dividends. In view of the tax cost incurred on the receipt of dividends, the "sophisticated investor" avoided dividends as he would the plague.

Once again, accounting was able to oblige. Corporations were taken off LIFO, one way or another; depreciation and pension costs were cut back to irreducible minimums; research and development, sales, and training expenses were capitalized rather than written off; income of various kinds was anticipated, or "front-end loaded"; also, as we will see, there was "dirty pooling" and "polluted purchase," and again there were many more kinds of padding that we were able to introduce to maintain the big-bosom look.

Then during 1970 and into 1971 the padding started falling out, frequently showing the corporation as embarrassingly emaciated. This became known as the era of "big-bath accountings," when the accountants scrubbed the corporations clean, wrote down the excessive carrying values of assets, eliminated the previously inflated income, and the like. What's remarkable about all this is that my colleagues only very rarely manifested any embarrassment at this new intimacy—they just don't feel called upon to demonstrate how and why this padding and dirt are permitted to accumulate in the first place—necessitating the trauma of the big bath.

These charges preceded a *New York Times* Market Place column for May 4, 1971, captioned "Full Disclosure: Fact or Fancy?": "Is it possible for a company to follow acceptable accounting methods and still bring about a picture so colored as to completely mislead the shareholder?"

The article reported on an accounting symposium where a leading securities analyst leveled just such an indictment against the independent auditors for our major corporations.

Moving to the vigorous defense of the profession, and thereby putting the issue in clearer focus, the general counsel for one of the giant accounting firms reiterated a statement he made earlier, that management takes the initiative in looking for flexibility (or "creative" accounting) under existing rules. The independent auditors, he said, cannot qualify an opinion so long as those initiatives are consistent with generally accepted accounting principles.

The counselor thereby unwittingly supplied the underlying theme for this book, namely, the exposure of flexible and creative accounting; and the demonstration of risks the reader of financial statements is running if he infers from the independent auditor's certificate that the auditor is asserting that the statements are fair and true.

But now the reader is forewarned—this is not especially a book on accounting; not even on the understanding and interpretation of financial statements. Instead, what I will describe is the environment in which the public accountant pursues his profession—an environment characterized in good measure by major publicly owned corporations. These corporations are, presumably, responsible to a wide spectrum of "publics," those of management, shareholders, labor, government, customers, and consumers, all the neighbors in the communities where the corporations exist and to which they relate. Further, as concern for ecology and the well-being of consumers intensifies, this responsibility will extend to the total society and environment. And because our corporations are moving aggressively toward a multinational complexion, responsibility and accountability are destined to become universal.

Visibility and Accountability

My principal thesis is that such an expanded and expanding environment demands of the corporations, and those who exercise the power and control over the corporations' resources, a full measure of visibility and accountability—qualities which, ostensibly, should be assured by the independent certifying or attesting auditors of these corporations. I believe these standards to be inadequately implemented by the accounting profession as presently structured; this book will consider in some depth a number of areas where financial statements deviated seriously from an objective standard of fairness, and where despite these most serious aberrations the statements were deemed by the auditors to be "fair in accordance with generally accepted accounting principles (GAAP)." We will see that this "fair" versus "GAAP-fair" is a most invidious distinction.

The disclosures of these aberrations are not intended as muck-raking or scandal-mongering expeditions; instead, I will be describing a pattern of financial-accounting presentations which were certified by the auditors as fair in accordance with GAAP but which, when probed, proved to be eminently unfair. The complaint, then, is rooted in the likelihood that GAAP may be unfair; though much of what I will describe might better dem-onstrate that GAAP is capable of being unfairly applied, not that it is inherently unfair.

This dichotomy of "fairness" and "GAAP-fair" has con-fronted the accounting profession (as well as the corporations for whose historical narratives the accounting profession is sup-posed to be responsible) with the challenges of "crisis in confi-dence," "credibility gap," and "creeping irrelevance." The conduct of the American corporation is being challenged by its adversaries, and at least questioned by its friends. One might then expect the implementation of procedures for assuring the corporation and its management the highest degree of visibility and accountability—so that all who are entitled to know will know, and thereby be able to make rational decisions. This expectation notwithstanding, the situation is very much other-wise.

By way of illustrating this frontal attack, *The Greening of America* casts American corporations in the role of the ultimate enemy of the people, against whom new generations will be constrained to battle, eventually to overcome through some form of nonviolent revolution. In that work Charles A. Reich indicts the corporation for mankind's "lost self," thus:

> What kind of life does man live under the domination of the Corporate State? It is . . . a robot life in which man is deprived of his own being, and he becomes instead a mere role, occupation, or function. The self within him is killed, and he walks through

the remainder of his days mindless and lifeless, the inmate and instrument of a machine world.

This critical judgment follows Reich's study of the pathology of the "Corporate State," with its powers of amalgamation and integration, its principles of administration and hierarchy, its autonomy and alienation, the uncoupled "new property"—that is, shares in the hands of disembodied shareholders—and the systems of power and status, all enshrouded by law especially benign to the vested interests in the Corporate State.

That Professor Reich's "Consciousness III Revolution" may already have begun might well be substantiated by the Ralph Nader–inspired "Project on Corporate Responsibility," especially its "Campaign to Make General Motors Responsible"—a battle which may have been lost but which may yet be followed by an ultimate victory in the "greening" revolution. Similarly, the Corporate Participation Act introduced by Senator Edmund S. Muskie is a straw in the wind.

The Medical Committee Case

More immediately we have the decision of the United States Circuit Court of Appeals for the District of Columbia in the so-called Medical Committee Case. The court there held that Dow Chemical Company was obliged to include in its proxy material a shareholder's resolution which would ban the corporation's manufacture of napalm.

A *New York Times* Washington dispatch datelined May 10, 1971, carried the headline "S.E.C's Staff Tells Fund to Hold Social Issues Vote." The article advised that "Mutual funds will apparently be required, in the future, to let their shareholders vote on whether fund managers should consider the social policies of corporations before investing in their stock." Reporter Eileen Shanahan was referring to what she said was "a recent decision by the [SEC] staff . . . concerning some proposals involving social policies that two shareholders of the Fidelity Trend Fund want to bring before the fund's . . . shareholders' meeting." According to one staff member, says Miss Shanahan, "the change in the position taken by the S.E.C.'s staff was the result of intense internal discussions at the agency, following the Court of Appeals decision in the Dow case."

Whether this reported change of position will be affected by Attorney General John Mitchell's appeal of the Dow decision to the Supreme Court is not entirely clear. To the extent the Circuit Court's views and/or the SEC's Fidelity Fund position become effective, the shareholders, if they are to be an "enlightened citizenry," will have to be informed regarding such matters (based on Miss Shanahan's inquiries) as to "whether any government agency had brought a proceeding against [a corporation] for failure to comply with laws or regulations concerning air, water or noise pollution. . . ." Also, "On the issues of minority hiring . . . information about the company's employment practices and its compliance. . . ."

I don't know what, if anything, will come from Miss Shanahan's predictions regarding this brave new world at the SEC; the Medical Committee issue, however, was tossed into the discard, at least for the present, by a January 10, 1972, decision of the United States Supreme Court. The Court determined that "Events have taken place . . . which require that we dismiss this case on the ground that it has now become moot." Among these events was Dow's acquiescence "in the Committee's request and included the proposal" in its 1971 proxy material. Mr. Justice Douglas's lone dissent concluded with the lament: "This case now joins a growing list of monuments to the present Court's abdication of its constitutional responsibility to decide cases properly within its jurisdiction."

For another straw in the wind I turn to Barry Commoner's *The Closing Circle*. When discussing "The Economic Meaning of Ecology," Commoner begins by observing that "Until recently, the role of environmental factors has been given only slight consideration in conventional theory." To the extent the term "externalities was used, it was to express what once appeared to be a rather rare departure from the basic economic process—exchange." But then "with the recent advent of environmental problems, which generate very large negative externalities, economists have begun to pay much more attention to this hitherto minor facet of economic theory."

This change in economic conceptualizing will, I predict, be mirrored by vital changes in our profession's theory and practice. As a consequence our traditional frame of reference—the entity with its historical cost and exchange-transaction presumptions—will be radically expanded. We will be compelled to integrate into the entity's cost structure the cost of these "environmental externalities." The impact of such a change would extend beyond debits and credits; it would go to the heart of critical investment decisions. Commoner refers with important praise to the conclusions of K. W. Kapp that when one considers

> . . . the neglected aspects of unpaid social costs it becomes evident that the social efficiency of private investment criteria . . . is largely an illusion. For if entrepreneurial outlays fail to measure the actual total costs of production because part of the latter tend to be shifted to the shoulders of others, then the traditional cost-benefit calculus is not simply misleading but actually serves as an institutionalized cloak for large-scale [spoliation]. . . .

Clearly, when this changing economic theorizing takes hold, we will be required to "factor in" the ecological or environmental costs into the cost and pricing patterns of the corporation for which we are accounting. This will demand something of a quantum leap beyond the accounting profession's traditional narrow assumptions of the entity and the exchange transaction.

Add to this conjection the surmising by SEC Chairman William J. Casey. Speaking before the National Industrial Conference Board in 1971 he expressed his belief that "the time has come to take a broader view of what is pertinent to investment values and the obligation to convey economic reality as management knows it to stockholders and investors."

Implicit in this broader view would be a reexamination of

"the question of the inclusion of projections, forecasts and appraisals in our disclosure framework."

Clearly, we have a brand new ball game coming up.

Questions from Our Friends

Even the corporation's friends are asking hard and critical questions regarding the conduct of these entities. Thus, Ralph S. Saul, President of the American Stock Exchange, commented on the shift from industrial capitalism to financial capitalism, with a change from "concentration on producing goods and services to an increasing concern with earnings per share, price/earnings ratios, and financial results, almost independent of the process of production and consumption of industrial products and services." This shift has, as a consequence, seriously influenced or confused the goals of corporate management; it has imposed new decision-making demands on the corporate chief executive. These new attitudes of investors toward the corporation produce executive-suite nightmares.

Then too we have the question "Is the Corporation Dead?" raised by Dan W. Lufkin, head of a leading Wall Street firm. In answering the rhetorical question, Lufkin first alludes to the fate of Willie Loman a score of years ago, and then proceeds to predict that the youth of today (more so, those of tomorrow) will not accept such a fatalistic response to the hierarchy of the business world. Instead, the "greening generation" has identified the corporation with the military-industrial complex.

But, as Lufkin points out, armament manufacturers have always been a target for the idealists of every society and every generation; hence, antiwar sentiment alone cannot explain the deep and widespread concern and discontent prevalent today. He continues:

> Its source is far closer to home—in the air we breathe—the water we drink—the land we live on. It is where quantity of production meets quality of life that the battle line against the modern corporation has been drawn. A decade ago, this conflict was

dramatized by one lonely David ranged against the Goliath of organized industry. Today, consumerism is a rallying cry for millions—and no corporation has yet proven immune to the slingshots of its dedicated enemies. Every day's headline or television news program brings new evidence of corporate complicity in the rape of the environment and the destruction of the good life. From detergents to DDT; from mercury in the water to fly ash in the air; from oil spill in the Pacific to fish kill in Lake Erie— the American industrial giant seems to stumble from disaster to disaster. The cigarettes it produces by the billions cause cancer; the breakfast foods it seductively urges upon small children are apparently without total nutritional value; its automobiles turn the atmosphere into a lethal fog and its waste matter threatens to transform the pleasant land into a junk yard.

In seeking the source of the problem, the young people believe they have found it in the profit-oriented corporation. Rich, successful, geared to mass production and mass distribution, the corporation makes a tempting target.

In the future, as Lufkin sees it, "cost effectiveness . . . must be measured in terms of total impact." This will mean that corporations cannot measure results solely in terms of earnings. A corporation will be held accountable for the larger implications of its business activities; its internal environment; its concern for employee welfare; its ecological relationship with the communities in which its plants and offices are located; its responsiveness to the pressing needs of the nation; its contribution to the rebuilding of the human habitation; its willingness to help break down the social and economic barriers which still exclude large groups of Americans from full participation in the benefits of our economic system; and finally a corporation will have to display forbearance and self-discipline in evaluating the fruits of its own technology so that socially and physically harmful products are not manufactured simply because they can be manufactured.

From yet another dimension of our economic society we have a special kind of complaint against GAAP leveled by Otto Eck-

stein, Professor of Economics at Harvard. Under the caption
"The Astonishing Revision of Corporate Profits," datelined
July 21, 1971, we are told:

> A year ago, the Office of Business Economics [OBE] of the De-
> partment of Commerce lowered its estimate of corporate profits
> for 1969 from $93.8 to $91.2 billion. This week the OBE reduced
> this estimate to $84.2 billion, and also lowered its estimate for
> 1970 from $81.3 to $75.4 billion. These enormous revisions raise
> questions about the accounting practices of American business
> and the statistical measurement of profits by the Federal Govern-
> ment. Can the profits stated in the annual reports of corporations
> be in error by an average of 12%? Since the decisions of individ-
> ual and institutional investors are based on profit data, the
> quality of investment performance is hurt by reporting errors of
> the indicated magnitude.

After presenting a table showing the successive estimates
made by OBE, the Eckstein statement continues: "The OBE
bases its initial estimates of corporate profits on the public reports issued by companies. However, the conceptual basis of the
OBE profit series corresponds to the Internal Revenue Service
definitions of profits. Presumably the IRS concepts, with the
power of tax statutes behind them, have a greater stability than
the public reports which are affected by changing accounting
conventions and the management of earnings."

While some revision in the initial estimates must be expected
(as the tax data are accumulated), there has been a "recent ex-
plosion in the profit revisions," a phenomenon which Eckstein
attributes to the following causes (to the extent here relevant):

> Average accounting practice may have deteriorated dramatically
> in the last three years. If all of the differences in the figures were
> due to loosened reporting practices, it would imply that all of
> the profit increase between 1966 and 1969 was due to looser ac-
> counting, not to any improvement in real earnings. The stock
> market rose by over 30% during this period, and then lost all of
> this gain in the decline of 1969-70. Had earnings been as flat as
> they are now reported to have been, the stock market boom and

bust would have been milder and the economic boom would not have become so overheated.

What does the professor conclude from all this? "The revisions of the profit data and the apparent rapidly widening gap between publicly reported earnings and taxable earnings raise questions for the consumers of these data. These include financial analysts, economic policy makers, and the public, not to mention econometricians. Is business fooling itself?"

I will endeavor to answer the professor's rhetorical question— in fact, this entire work might well be deemed to be the affirmative response to his challenge.

Correspondingly critical and challenging views have been expressed in varying contexts by J. K. Galbraith, Wilbert E. Moore, Andrew Hacker, Eugene V. Rostow, Carl Kaysen, and, of course, A. A. Berle, Jr.

The Games Management Plays

In the light of all this criticism one might well have expected that the accounting profession would have recognized its special task to assure the fullest measure of visibility to the corporations and the greatest comprehension of the corporate enterprise for shareholders, government, customers, labor, competitors, *et al.*; a visibility and comprehension essential for assuring the viability of the corporate state. Instead, we find the condition described by the general counsel earlier in this chapter. We find the same theme expressed by Leonard M. Savoie, the Executive Vice President of the American Institute of Certified Public Accountants (AICPA), in an address entitled "Game Plans and Professional Standards." The phrase "game plan" implies a preconceived strategy for accomplishing certain objectives—and that is how Savoie sees managements acting, with a helpful assist from their independent auditors:

> In corporate financial reporting . . . the game plan is to show a steadily rising earnings-per-share, thus stimulating investor de-

mand for shares, with consequent rise in their price, and creating
a favorable atmosphere for the issuance of new securities in case
additional capital is needed.

Of course, the vast majority of businesses report their results,
whether favorable or unfavorable, as fairly as possible in accordance with applicable reporting requirements, but also in accordance with the game plan. This means that where there is a
choice of reporting methods (and we will soon be introduced to
the plethora of such choices), "a strong inclination arises to
choose the method which will produce the most favorable
results."

So it is that some companies (Savoie continues), "even when
their results are good, take advantage of any looseness in reporting standards to present a still better picture. When faced with
adversity, the temptation is even stronger to attain the game-
plan objectives by taking advantage of reporting standards."

While the name of the game is the same, the game is not
necessarily so, since:

> Game plans come in two kinds—offensive and defensive. The
> offense predominated during the late 1960s when the stock mar-
> ket was high, conglomerate mergers were commonplace and pros-
> perity reigned. Game plans then were designed with style and
> finesse, using "funny money," pooling of interests, deferral of re-
> search and development costs, stretched-out depreciation, front-
> end loading on instalment revenue of doubtful collectibility, and
> so on.

> As take-overs by the offense became commonplace, even the
> defensive-minded game planners were forced into liberal account-
> ing practices to make themselves a harder target. Witness the
> 1968 switch of the steel industry from declining-balance deprecia-
> tion to straight-line depreciation, thus increasing earnings per
> share and asset values.

Savoie adds some insights into the characters of the game
players:

> . . . Not everyone playing the game is a knight on a white horse,
> be he corporate manager or CPA. This fact becomes especially

significant when a company is, as you might say, "shopping" for the accounting principles which best suit its game plan. The company's present auditor may stand adamant against what the management wants to do, so management begins looking for an accounting firm that they hope will be more accommodating.

In a lecture before the Institute of Chartered Accountants in England and Wales, delivered in September, 1970, Leonard Spacek, a sometimes acerbic critic of the accounting profession, speaking from his special vantage point of principal partner of a major American accounting firm, responded as follows to his rhetorical question "What is Profit?":

> Our present dilemma in responding to the question "What is Profit?" arises from the fact that we have drifted into the practice of describing as being the fairly presented net profit, an undefinable balance resulting from accounting practices that are not designed to achieve the objectives of financial reporting to public investors. The word "fairly" in this context is misused and . . . results in a misrepresentation.
>
> Thus, profit as now reported is the consequence of observing a great number of accounting practices which we and the business community have been in the habit of following. And, this habit is the authority for their existence. These practices were not adopted because they were designed to arrive at some objective standard of measuring profit. They were adopted as patchwork compromises in bookkeeping to meet certain desired and often conflicting viewpoints at one time or another, and they have been continued regardless of changed conditions and the absence of basic objectivity. Their repetitive use is like copying last year's working papers in making this year's audit, a sure way to repeat all previous mistakes.

The Inner Contradiction

Here, then, is the inner contradiction in our present-day corporate society. We are at a critical moment in history, when corporate managements can increasingly be seen to have interests and objectives independent of, and frequently opposed to, those of the shareholders and our society generally; when the corporation itself is confronted with an identity crisis and a potential battle for survival as an essentially private institution; when our political and economic society is in urgent need of more meaningful interpretations of the objectives of corporations and their relationships with the entire environment in which they function. This combination of evolving forces imposes still greater burdens on the independent auditors. Despite the need for its acceptance of added responsibility, the accounting profession is in a serious state of disarray—involved in litigation of new seriousness and magnitude, with its principles seriously challenged ("What is Profit?") and its function confronting a credibility crisis.

The urgent demands of the times evoked a limp response from the profession. There is sharp contrast between the prevailing myth and the sad realities regarding the nature of the independent auditor's role and responsibility.

We are all familiar with the litany which the auditor appends to a corporation's audited financial statements; with some minor stylistic changes, the accountants' report or auditors' certificate reads essentially as follows:

First there is the so-called "scope paragraph":

> We have examined the accompanying balance sheet of X Industries, Inc., and the consolidated balance sheet of the Company and subsidiaries as of December 31, 1971, and the related statements of earnings, earnings retained in the business, additional paid-in capital and changes in financial position for the year then ended. Our examination was made in accordance with generally accepted auditing standards, and accordingly included such tests of the accounting records and such other auditing procedures as we considered necessary in the circumstances.

This is followed by the "opinion paragraph":

> In our opinion the financial statements referred to above present fairly the financial position of X Industries, Inc., and the consolidated financial position of the Company and subsidiaries at December 31, 1971, and the respective results of their operations

for the year then ended in conformity with generally accepted accounting principles applied on a consistent basis.

And then we see the full-blown signature of the attesting accountants and their assertion of credentials, "Certified Public Accountants." Now what do all these hallowed words mean?

We know of the myth which prevails among the masses of our society. They infer from the CPA's certification a *nihil obstat* and imprimatur; the masses assume that the auditors have pursued their tasks diligently and have ferreted out all aberrations with their gimlet eyes and red pencils; then, having discerned the good and true (even if not the beautiful), they proudly proclaim the fair presentation of the financial condition and operations of the corporation which they have thus scrutinized. These masses, with their trusting guilelessness, are confident that if the auditors failed to act consistent with this noble program and objective, then most assuredly the Securities and Exchange Commission, if not the American Institute of Certified Public Accountants, would manifest its wrath, and would move diligently to discipline the scoundrels, possibly even to deprive them of their professional prerogatives lest they do further damage to the body economic.

In fact, the realities are otherwise. No, in this context at least, God is not in His Heaven; sweetness and light do not prevail. This myth-reality dichotomy was dramatically demonstrated in a study undertaken by me a few years ago, and reported on extensively in *The Effectiveness of Accounting Communication.* This confusion is evident in the primary recommendation from a Select Committee created by the AICPA to study the Opinions of the Accounting Principles Board.

For the uninitiated the Accounting Principles Board (APB) was established by the Institute in 1959 as its prestigious principle promulgating group. The ultimate distillations of the Board's deliberations are enshrined in its formal Opinions; as of this writing twenty-one such opinions were promulgated— several others are in various stages of development.

This Select Committee was constituted under the chairmanship of the late William Werntz. Upon his death the chairmanship was assumed by J. S. Seidman. In their 1965 report to the Institute's Council, the committee asserted as its first recommendation that:

> At the earliest possible time the [Accounting Principles] Board should: (a) set forth its views as to the purposes and limitations of published financial statements and of the independent auditor's attest function, and (b) define such phrases in the auditor's report as present fairly and generally accepted accounting principles.

The committee expressed itself with a sense of urgency and intensity only infrequently found in AICPA committee reports:

> The focus of accounting principles is on their application to financial statements. . . . What purposes and limitations attach to financial statements and to the auditor's opinion? This question is of first importance to the public and the profession. Literature abounds on it, but the answer is cast in many different molds. Until the profession has an official utterance about it, there is no point in beginning.
>
> The Committee believes that such an utterance should be given top priority. It would be the subsoil on which subsequent pronouncements would be grounded and understood.

And to give the APB specific questions to which it might direct its deliberations, the report cited examples:

> . . . in the standard report of the auditor, he generally says that financial statements "present fairly" in conformity with generally accepted accounting principles—and so on. What does the auditor mean by the quoted words? Is he saying: (1) that the statements are fair *and* in accordance with [GAAP]; or (2) that they are fair *because* they are in accordance with [GAAP]; or (3) that they are fair only *to the extent* that [GAAP] are fair; or (4) that whatever [GAAP] may be, the *presentation* of them is fair? [Emphasis in original.]

What words could state the committee's concern more urgently? How did the AICPA's Accounting Principles Board respond to this question that the distinguished committee said was the "question of first importance," requiring an utterance that "should be given top priority"? Well, it's now only seven years after this *cri de coeur*—seven years of no response, or at least no publicly exposed response, from the APB.

Why hasn't the APB responded to this urgent plea? Because they are unable to face up to what they should say. The profession doesn't see the certification responsibility the way the vulgar masses do. But yet the profession prefers not to exorcise the myth, since the public's confidence in us (and our resultant affluence) are rooted in that illusion; there are, of course, times (especially, as we will see, in responding to litigation or in the remarks of the general counsel) when we are caught with the bald truth exposed. That truth is discernible in the literature of accountancy; it makes clear that the responsibility for the financial statements, and the selection of the GAAP on which the statements are predicated, rests with the entity's management. Thus, from the AICPA's Committee on Accounting Procedure:

> The Company and its Auditors:
>
> Underlying all committee opinions is the fact that the accounts of a company are primarily the responsibility of management. The responsibility of the auditor is to express his opinion concerning the financial statements and to state clearly such explanations, amplifications, disagreement, or disapproval, as he deems appropriate.

Myth vs. Reality

This myth-reality contradiction was implicit in a late November, 1971, *New York Times* article reporting on a "top-level Symposium on Ethics in Corporate Financial Reporting" sponsored by the AICPA, the Financial Analysts Federation, the Financial Executives Institute, and Robert Morris Associates. The participants in that Symposium (each of whom paid $300 for a weekend's retreat) upheld the "doctrine of 'fairness' in presenting financial statements." However, the article went on, "Certified public accountants shied away from having to say that a company's auditing was, in their judgment, fair as well as in accordance with 'generally accepted accounting principles.' "

This dichotomy was brought home to us especially poignantly in the tragic criminal proceedings against three CPAs associated with one of our leading accounting firms, in the Continental Vending Machine Corporation fiasco. In the course of its opinion on appeal, the United States Court of Appeals stated the principal issue as follows:

> Defendants [CPAs] asked for two instructions which, in substance, would have told the jury that a defendant could be found guilty only if, according to generally accepted accounting principles, the financial statements as a whole did not fairly present the financial condition of Continental at September 30, 1962, and then only if his departure from accepted standards was due to willful disregard of those standards with knowledge of the falsity of the statements and an intent to deceive. The judge declined to give these instructions. Dealing with the subject in the course of his charge, he said that the "critical test" was whether the financial statements as a whole "fairly" presented the financial position of Continental as of September 30, 1962, and whether it accurately reported the operations for fiscal 1962.

The trial court did assert that proof of compliance with generally accepted auditing standards was "evidence which may be very persuasive," yet it was not necessarily conclusive that the auditors acted in good faith "and that the facts as certified were not materially false or misleading." In their concurrence with the trial court the appellate court said:

> We think the judge was right in refusing to make the accountants' testimony so nearly a complete defense. . . . We do not think the jury was . . . required to accept the accountants' evaluation whether a given fact was material to overall fair presentation, at least not when the accountants' testimony was not based on specific rules or prohibitions to which they could point. . . .

Such evidence may be highly persuasive, but it is not conclusive, and so the trial judge correctly charged.

This critical conflict between the vulgar and elitist views of what "fairly presents" means was not lost on the defendants' counsel when they drafted their unsuccessful petition to the United States Supreme Court for certiorari; in their petition counsel took umbrage at the omission of the "critical standard 'according to generally accepted accounting principles,' " and then proceeded to make this crucial assertion: "This charge gave the lay jury license, acting with the benefit of hindsight, to judge practitioners' professional performance according to its own untutored and subjective judgment, based solely on some concept of what an investor would like to have disclosed." And in the same vein: "The charge thus permitted the jury to ignore the principle that the conduct of a professional man, as to any matter on which the standards of his profession might differ from those of a layman, must be tested against the standards of the profession."

This case clearly put into sharp perspective the contrast between the standards of the "town" and those of the "establishment," with a resounding confirmation of the judgment of the former regarding the meaning of the word "fair."

The implications of this case were put into especially clear perspective by A. A. Sommer, Jr., when addressing a 1970 meeting of the American Bar Association:

> More disturbing to the accounting profession . . . was the language in which Judge Henry J. Friendly, surely one of the most knowledgeable of federal judges in financial and accounting matters, wrapped the affirmance. He said in effect that the first law for accountants was not compliance with generally accepted accounting principles, but rather full and fair disclosure, fair presentation, and if the principles did not produce this brand of disclosure, accountants could not hide behind the principles but had to go beyond them and make whatever additional disclosures were necessary for full disclosure. In a word, "present fairly" was

a concept separate from "generally accepted accounting principles," and the latter did not necessarily result in the former.

Mr. Sommer then noted that this notion of Judge Friendly's was "not unprecedented." He cited a 1942 decision of the SEC in the Associated Gas & Electric Company proceeding, holding that:

> . . . Too much attention to the question whether the financial statement has formally complied with principles . . . accepted at that time should not be permitted to blind us to the basic question whether the financial statements performed their function of enlightenment, which is their only reason for existence.

These standards of fairness and enlightenment stand in sharp contrast with the observations by the general counsel for an accounting firm, cited at the outset of this chapter. While that counsel might have overlooked the wisdom of the SEC in 1942, how he could have so casually written off Continental Vending escapes me. But then, as Santayana informed us, we are destined to repeat the mistakes of history since we don't read it.

I have endeavored to describe the generally critical thrust of this work pertaining to the accountant's role and responsibility. I have first sought to describe those aspects of the corporate environment in which the auditor is constrained to function, setting forth some of the conflicting and frequently confusing operative forces. I then sketched the rather confused picture of the accounting profession: the ways it relates to management, and then to the world at large—those who have a right to be fairly informed regarding the functioning of the corporate society; I have referred to the cleavage between the prevailing myth and the realities of the independent auditor's role and function —a cleavage which is encouraged by my profession, except when we are confronted with a complaint from someone who has been taken in by these statements. Then my colleagues quite uniformly disclaim paternity.

Clearly, unless the accounting profession eliminates the contradictions implicit in its practices, and unless it recognizes its essential responsibility to make certain that its statements reflect fully, fairly, and truthfully the history of the corporate enterprise during a particular time span, it will have abdicated its role as historian and abandoned its claim to professional recognition.

The following chapter is intended to give something of an overview of generally accepted accounting principles, and some insights into the way in which they have evolved. Succeeding chapters demonstrate the ways in which this doctrine, our GAAP, has been seriously debased in practice. In short, Chapter 2 describes essentially good principles; Chapters 3 through 10 point up the all too many situations where independent auditors went astray.

Chapter 2

Alice in GAAP Land

AN appropriate way to introduce the accounting profession's "mystic bond of brotherhood"—generally accepted accounting principles—is to quote from an article in the May/June, 1971, *Financial Analysts Journal* by G. M. Loeb entitled "Peter and Leonard Attend an Annual Meeting." Loeb relates the following incident:

> Leonard motioned for the floor and stood up. "You commented previously that total sales increased. Will you comment on our apparent decrease in earnings?"
>
> "Perhaps I should have pointed out," replied President Jones, "that our figures from year to year reflect changes in accounting. For example, we have used LIFO and FIFO. Our depreciation policy is flexible. There is the question of reporting per share on the total amount of shares outstanding, the average amount, or the fully converted amount. Our figures also take into account pooling of interest of our latest acquisition. This is a company making a patented banana slicer suitable for any household. Thus it fits nicely into our banana sales. Let me also point out that our final bottom line figures are reduced by some writeoffs. In addition, we have written off some prepaid costs that we know we will incur in coming years. As a result, we had no taxable income this year. We were fortunate in being able to fund some of

our short-term borrowings but at an increased interest cost. These and other such adjustments are included in the footnotes to our annual report."

Of course, Loeb wrote the saga of Peter and Leonard tongue in cheek. It does, however, point up the double talk and double think which is all too pervasive in our game plan applications of GAAP. Let us then move from Loeb's fantasy land to the real world of debits and credits.

The opinion clause of the standard auditor's certificate concludes with this resounding note of certitude: "The statements are presented fairly in accordance with generally accepted accounting principles." Such certitude is, of course, all to the good—providing that the auditor and we know just what he means by the phrase "generally accepted," to say nothing of the "accounting principles" allusion. In the preceding chapter it was asserted that the auditor doesn't even know what "presents fairly" means—and that the accounting profession was seriously shaken when Judge Friendly asserted that statements are supposed to be fair! The investor should not be flim-flammed by the auditor's use of "in accordance with generally accepted accounting principles" as a hedge clause.

For the entire decade of the 1960s the accounting profession has had its Accounting Principles Board, a group of agonizing philosophers in pursuit of that elusive body of principles which should be the foundation of our calling; but the philosophers have been rebuffed on every side. Witness this "Just Grab the Nettle" editorial in a mid-1971 issue of *Forbes:*

> There are five major accounting firms which could, if they sat down together, in a couple of hours and with a handshake, give fair and meaningful meaning to the phrase, "according to generally accepted accounting procedures." If these five outfits announced agreement on what they'd certify and what they wouldn't certify without full and clear explanation, they could restore status to the profession and meaning to CPA certification.
>
> If they don't the Feds are soon going to do it, because the Government, in the form of the Internal Revenue Service, has

even more at stake in taking the flexibility out of present flexible bookkeeping than do stockholders.

If the Five would agree on the yeas and nays and announce publicly the standards they have agreed on, none of their major clients would dare flee the coop for a less rigid firm. And those with nothing to juggle or conceal and with no desire to mislead would flock to firms with the new standard, figuring that analysts, investors and the Government would regard as unsuspect—or at least less so—corporate reports certified by the Five and those pledged to the same practices.

The accounting profession is faced with no Gordian Knot. The noose their present flexibility is placing around their neck is easily slipped.

And it better be.

Unless they want Uncle to do it for them.

Which five firms *Forbes* may have had in mind is not clear, but the crucial point is that despite the Board's riding like Sir Galahad, they just can't seem to find the Holy Grail.

It may well be, as *Forbes* predicted, "Uncle" and the "Feds" are already in the act. Thus, the Revenue Act of 1971 provided (Sec. 101):

(c) Accounting for Investment Credit in Certain Financial Reports and Reports to Federal Agencies.—

(1) In General.—It was the intent of the Congress in enacting . . . the investment credit . . . to provide an incentive for modernization and growth of private industry. Accordingly, notwithstanding any other provision of law. . . .

(A) No taxpayer shall be required to use, for purposes of financial reports to the jurisdiction of any Federal agency or reports made to any Federal Agency [e.g., the SEC], any particular method of accounting for the [investment] credit, . . .

(B) a taxpayer shall disclose, in any such report, the method of accounting for such credit used by him, . . . and

(C) a taxpayer shall use the same method of accounting for such credit in all such reports made by him. . . .

The thrust of this provision is explained in the Report of the Senate Finance Committee as follows:

> The procedures employed in accounting for the investment credit in financial reports to shareholders, creditors, etc., can have a significant effect on reported net income and thus on economic recovery. The committee, as was the House, is concerned that the investment credit provided by the bill have as great a stimulative effect on the economy as possible. Therefore, from this standpoint it would appear undesirable to preclude the use of "flow through" in the financial reporting of net income.
>
> If the investment credit is thought of as decreasing the price of the equipment purchased, it can be argued that reflecting the benefit of the credit in income over the life of the asset is appropriate. However, the investment credit may also be thought of as a selective tax rate reduction applicable in those cases where the desired investments are being made. In this latter event, it is difficult to see why the current "flow through" should be prevented in the financial reporting of income.
>
> In view of these considerations the committee believes that it is unwise to require either type of financial reporting but believes that it is desirable that the companies generally indicate in their reports the method they follow in treating the investment credit for financial reporting purposes. Nothing in this discussion is intended to have any effect on the treatment of the credit for rate-making purposes in the case of regulated industries.

The reader should know that "flow through" is the term of art given to the method of accounting for the investment credit whereby the entire amount of the credit is injected in its entirety into the single year's income for the year when the credit is allowed. This is in contrast with the attenuated method of attribution which was contemplated by the Accounting Principles Board.

It may be that the Board was double-crossed in this process since it had circulated an "exposure draft" of an opinion, which would have precluded the "flow through" alternative, after a meeting between representatives of the Institute and the Chairman of the SEC. Presumably the APB moved only after obtaining assurances that the Administration would refrain from meddling in the accounting treatment to be accorded this proposed credit.

Is it any wonder, then, that the glamour issues reacted so excitedly on the New York Stock Exchange on the day the bill became law (December 10, 1971)? Through the stroke of the President's pen their numbers will be even more enthralling—and the auditors will not be able to stop them since "it's the law."

This cynic has an inspired suggestion to make to the Administration. Henceforth forbid any corporation to issue financial statements showing losses and ban the use of red ink by the auditors. By so doing, economic ebullience (or other term which would have the same smell) would be assured; in that way there would no longer be any Lockheed or Penn Central or brokerage firm crises to upset the nation's economic game plan. Of course, this proposal is hardly new since it has a long history of application in socialistic economies; but it is believed to be a revolutionary suggestion for our American Economic Republic.

To be fair, the APB is not the first august group which has set out on this Great Crusade—and, like the others, it probably is destined to return far short of its lofty objective.

State of Babel

It is, of course, essential that the current state of Babel be corrected; otherwise, there is no way in which those who prepare financial statements for corporations can communicate effectively with those who make meaningful decisions on the basis of those statements. It follows inexorably that the communication must be on a common wavelength—the special idiom used in the presentation of our statements must mean the same to those who initiate the message and those who receive it. It is essential to eliminate the "gap in GAAP"—at the very least to reduce its ambiguities.

This standard for effective communication is implicit in the report of a committee of the American Institute of Certified Public Accountants setting forth the long-range objectives of the profession. The following "Keys to Successful Data Communication" were provided by its report:

1. The issuer and user of economic data must have an understanding as to standards for measurement and summarization.
2. The issuer must have the requisite knowledge and skills to carry out the antecedent steps leading up to, and to prepare, the communication.
3. There must be absence of bias in the communication to a humanly feasible extent.
4. The communication must be intelligible to the user.

Common comprehension by the profession and the statement users as to these generally accepted principles of accounting was described by Andrew Barr, Chief Accountant for the SEC, as the most basic problem confronting the profession. Mr. Barr's concern was expressed in the course of an inquiry by Congress concerning investor protection. In the course of that inquiry Congressman Staggers, Chairman of the Subcommittee on Commerce and Finance of the Committee on Interstate and Foreign Commerce, put the following question to William L. Cary, then Chairman of the Securities and Exchange Commission:

> Can you file with this committee setting forth what you consider to be the areas of accounting where alternative practices could produce materially different results under generally accepted accounting principles? [And] if you would, with your conclusions as to the significance of each such area and with the reasons why you consider that investors who are considering and comparing various companies are adequately protected by your acceptance of these alternative practices.

The SEC's Chief Accountant, entered a demurrer to the second question above—he advised his chairman that while his staff could supply the committee with the examples, the cases, the situations, where there are divergencies, they would find it difficult to measure the impact of the divergence. Chairman Cary indicated that they would do their best but "cannot promise to do a very satisfactory job on that second phase." It might well be asked preliminarily that if the Chairman of the SEC and his Chief Accountant "cannot . . . do a very satisfactory job" in evaluating the significance of alternative accounting practices, who can, or should, do such an essential job satisfactorily?

Later, when speaking before the Financial Executives Institute, Chairman Cary counseled the accounting profession to move toward the narrowing of differences in alternative principles. He manifested an understanding of the dilemma which confronts the profession; nevertheless his words were unmistakably firm. He acknowledged that the question of uniformity in accounting principles was controversial; he went on to recognize that there were limitations on accounting, "that absolute certainty is chimera—impossible to achieve." Nevertheless, Cary observes (after first referring to the remarks by his predecessor, Judge Jerome Frank, on this question):

> Despite any difficulties, you and we should direct our efforts toward accelerating the move toward uniformity. At the same time, we should strive to make our disclosures more meaningful so that differences in accounting treatment are clearly brought out and better comparison of companies is possible.

These words of friendly counsel to the profession were preceded by the assertion that the government does have the power to set the rules of accounting. Then, offering the carrot, Cary tells the profession that it can help in "preventing the encroachment of government by participating directly in steps toward agreement upon accounting principles."

More recently (January 29, 1971) Congressman Wright Patman, Chairman of the House Banking and Currency Committee, when introducing articles from the *Wall Street Journal* and *Barron's* into the *Congressional Record,* addressed the House as follows:

> . . . the Banking and Currency Committee spurred a proposal to require the development of uniform accounting standards for

noncompetitive defense contracts. . . . During consideration of this proposal . . . persuasive testimony was taken from distinguished members of the accounting profession on the need for establishing uniform accounting standards so that the Government could determine more accurately the cost of its purchases. The lack of such standards has also been criticized in regard to the reporting of financial information of interest to the investing public.

Then, when referring to the *Barron's* article (about which I'll have more to say in a succeeding chapter), Congressman Patman continued:

[The] article dramatically illustrated the need for the accounting profession to reexamine its methods so that the public can obtain more precise and accurate information. It is hoped that the uniform accounting standards to be developed by a committee under the chairmanship of the Comptroller General of the United States . . . for defense contracts, can also be used as a guide for the accounting profession to adopt similiar standards in carrying out its vital function of accurately reflecting the financial condition of companies in which the public invests.

The Gap in GAAP

The existence of this "gap in GAAP" is readily discernible in the literature in accountancy; nor is the problem of recent vintage. In introducing his *The Search for Accounting Principles,* Reed Storey wove together extracts from "A Statement of Objectives of the American Accounting Association" (vintage 1936), and Maurice Stans' article "Accounting Weaknesses Which Inhibit Understanding of Free Enterprise" (1949), with Leonard Spacek's "Challenges to Public Accounting" (1948)— all of these extracts testifying to the fact that there is, in Spacek's words, "no general agreement as to the meaning of the phrase ['in accordance with generally accepted accounting principles'] or its applicability to the variety of situations in which it is used."

Had he chosen to do so, Storey could have included such classic comments as, "Accounting practices at present are based, in a large measure, upon the ethics and opinions of respectable accountants. . . . There is no unified body of opinion nor is there any official tribunal for the final determination of technical differences of opinion" (Sanders, Hatfield, and Moore, *A Statement of Accounting Principles*).

"The directors have another powerful weapon," said Berle and Means in *The Modern Corporation and Private Property*. "They have a large measure of control over the Company's income account. . . ." This weapon and control result from the fact that "accountants themselves have as yet failed to work out a series of standard rules."

Later we have the Arthur Andersen "postulate" asserting that: "The public cannot permit the responsibility for reliable financial accounting to rest upon the initiative of individual accountants or of individual accounting firms or upon any particular part of the profession operating independently of the rest."

And then we come to some more recent jeremiads, such as Prof. Robert Anthony's argument that accounting principles may end up eventually being prescribed by the SEC, which rests on two propositions:

1. If the American Institute of Certified Public Accountants fails in its present program for developing accounting principles, the Securities and Exchange Commission will act to develop these principles.
2. The AICPA effort is likely to fail.

Professor Anthony's concern is mirrored by Prof. David Hawkins' view that: "Once more, the possibility of further Government intervention in reporting matters is imminent, principally because of the accounting profession's inability to narrow the area of differences in accounting principles. . . ." Professor Hawkins concluded his analysis by asserting that, "In any case, the historical evolution of acceptable standards of financial disclosure among American industrial firms is far from complete."

Then there are the urgent questions of the Special Committee on Opinions of the Accounting Principles Board for the Board to consider: What is meant by the expression "generally accepted accounting principles"? How is "generally" measured? What are "accounting principles"? Where are they inscribed and by whom? The committee then underscored the crucial nature of its recommendation, thus: "Until the profession deals with all these matters satisfactorily, first for itself and then for understanding by the consumer of its product, there will continue to be an awkward failure to communicate in a field where clear communication is vital."

This, of course, takes us full circle to the "Just Grab the Nettle" blast from *Forbes*.

At this point I would not be surprised if the reader were to accuse me of luring him down the rabbit-hole, to "fall right *through* the earth . . . to come out among the people that walk with their heads downwards! The Antipathies, I think. . . ." I owe it to the lost reader to guide him through this never-never land, described (in a decision by a Maryland Appellate Court) as "an involuntary excursion into *terra incognita* known to accountants as GAAP. . . ." The Court continued: "As Judge Henry J. Friendly wisely observed . . . 'Accounting concepts are a foreign language to some lawyers in almost all cases, and to almost all lawyers in some cases. . . .' "

A Tour Through the Labyrinth

In this tour through the labyrinth I shall use the compass points suggested by the recent (October, 1970) Statement No. 4 of the Accounting Principles Board. This Statement (to be distinguished from an "Opinion" of the Board), entitled "Basic Concepts and Accounting Principles Underlying Financial Statements of Business Enterprises," is 219 numbered paragraphs (plus a greater number of unnumbered paragraphs). It represents the culmination of many man-years of deliberation by the leaders of the accounting profession—both in practice and in academic life. That not everyone is enthralled with the Statement is clearly evidenced by the following commentary by Leonard Spacek:

> This is a masterpiece in double talk on accounting. No document could be issued that would more aptly qualify for the recent title of a magazine article relating to the effort to improve accounting—"Words, Words, Words,—." This Statement is a 30,-000-word document that can be read only with difficulty and determination. It is full of meaningless statements, obvious elementary observations, or plain misleading statements.

I will use this Statement as my frame of reference without implying that I consider it the ultimate wisdom—far from it. But I do need a "firm spot on which to stand . . . [to] move the earth."

The Seven Cardinal Oughts

The Statement begins with a recital of the seven desirable characteristics of financial accounting: relevance, understandability, verifiability, neutrality, timeliness, comparability, and completeness. Clearly, each of these qualitative objectives is unimpeachable—if these terms were fully comprehended and effectively applied, financial statements would be far fairer than they are at present; certainly I would have far less complaint with the financial-accounting output of my profession. In fact, it may well be just because these qualitative objectives are not really comprehended that the accounting profession finds itself seriously enmeshed in controversy.

Let's start with *relevance,* which requires that "financial accounting information [bear] on the economic decisions for which it is used." The Statement goes on to assert that, "In judging relevance . . . attention is focused on the common needs of users and not on specific needs of particular users."

Earlier in the Statement the various user groups were identified: owners, creditors and suppliers (both present and potential), management, taxing authorities, employees—all of whom are said to have "direct interests"; and those with only indirect interests—lawyers, financial analysts, stock exchanges, regulatory agencies, the financial press, and labor unions. It is a tall order first to discern the information needs of this broad spectrum of users, and then to provide the information which they are presumed fairly to require for their decision making regarding both a particular corporate entity and, collectively, the "corporate state."

It is possible that the present financial-accounting product satisfies the standard of relevance for none of the user groups excepting, possibly, the casual investor—who is probably more interested in market quotations than financial statements; and the taxing authorities—who all but ignore GAAP and the resultant statements and, instead, decree their own field rules and information-gathering formats.

That the financial statements are not currently relevant to important users is implicit in the assertions by Congressman Patman alluded to previously; similarly, from the professional investor's viewpoint we have the friendly criticisms by Martin J. Whitman and Martin Shubik in the May, 1971, *Financial Executive* entitled "Corporate Reality and Accounting for Investors." The initial headnote gives the theme: "The SEC seems to want primary emphasis placed on financial statements even when the statements give few, if any, clues to business reality." Subsequently, that article challenges the statements' relevance, saying, "The basic misconceptions about accounting seem to stem from two sources: (1) a naïve, simplistic view of who the investors are, what their needs are, and how these needs should be satisfied, and (2) a stereotyped, old-fashioned view of how companies and their stocks should be analyzed."

Also detracting from the relevance of our accounting output is the fact that we are so intensely committed to the quantitative aspects of our existence that we block out the vital qualitative facets, the nonquantifiable "buzzing" which may be even more relevant than the numbers per se.

"Understandability" is, of course, the *sine qua non* of any effective communications process. The underlying thesis of this work on "unaccountable accounting" is that we are far from even approaching that laudable objective. The "confounding and confusion of tongues" has evoked strong criticism even from persons who are sophisticated in the accounting idiom.

If financial statements were "understandable," could Penn Central have disposed of its commercial paper to some of the most astute and prestigious banks, insurance companies, and other professional investors? Could there have been the psychedelic conglomerate craze of the 1960s? Would the land developers and leasing companies (as subsequent chapters will point out) have gotten away with it as long and as well as they did?

To cite a case in point, in early spring, 1971, numerous analysts all asked the same question: How could the Chrysler Corporation report a 1970 pre-tax loss of about $34 million and yet show on its balance sheet a current asset, "Refundable United States taxes on income," of precisely $80 million? It is of course incongruous at first blush since (using a 50 percent tax rate) $34 million in pre-tax loss should produce a $17 million refund. Looked at from the other end of the equation, $80 million of refund presupposes $160 million of losses.

If we tie together a number of disjointed items in the financial statements and their footnotes the tangled Chrysler web becomes discernible. It looks something like the tabulation on the following page; this collage produces a result sufficiently close to the $160 million for which we are searching.

If the reader has difficulty in comprehending this $40 million adjustment, it should be noted that while, for statement purposes, this amount got itself added to Chrysler's 1970 income (or more precisely, reduced its loss), under the tax laws the corporation was still on LIFO through 1970, thereby permitting the expanded-by-$40 million loss to stay on the Chrysler tax return.

Start with the pre-tax loss of.......................... $34 million

Since the "Taxes on Income" note indicates
that foreign taxes cost Chrysler $44.3 mil-
lion (the foreigners fared better than our
IRS) assume that the foreign income was
twice that amount, hence about..................... 89 million

For a subtotal of.................................. $123 million

Then, in another footnote, this one
entitled "Inventories-Accounting Changes" we
have what might be the rest of the jigsaw;
For the period January 1, 1957,
through December 31, 1961, the last in, first
out (LIFO) method of inventory valuation had
been used for approximately 60% of the consolidated inventory. Effective January 1,
1970, the FIFO (first in, first out) method of
inventory was adopted for inventories
previously valued using the LIFO method.
Inventory amounts December 31, 1969, and 1970
are stated higher by approximately $110 and
$150 million, respectively, than they would
have been had the LIFO method been continued.
The effect on 1970 income from this LIFO
switch was to reduce this statement loss vis-
à-vis tax-statement loss by the difference
between the $110 and $150 million, hence.............. 40 million

Total .... $163 million

But, there is yet a somewhat incomprehensible concluding
paragraph in that "Inventories-Accounting Change" footnote.
It reads: "For United States income tax purposes the adjustment to inventory amounts will be taken into taxable income
ratably over 20 years commencing January 1, 1971." Part of this
was readily comprehensible to me. Since Chrysler went off
LIFO, the $150 million of inventory values heretofore sup-
pressed, and now surfaced, requires an additional tax of about
$75 million to be paid (again, at the 50 percent rate).

By way of background, the IRS Commissioner, in early
March, 1969, announced (in Revenue Procedure No. 69–11)
that: "In those situations in which a taxpayer requests permission from the Service to discontinue the LIFO inventory

method, the taxpayer may, at the same time, request permission to allocate, over a period of 10 years, any positive adjustment resulting from the change."

Just what prompted the special dispensation to Chrysler permitting it to spread the tax effect over the next score of years, instead of only the next decade as provided by the 1969 dispensation, did not make sense to me even after a careful study of my tax charts. The effect, however, is to give to Chrysler the privilege of paying off the $75 million in accrued debt at the rate of $3,750,000 for the next 20 years instead of the usual $7,500,000 a year over a 10-year period. This means that the government is giving to Chrysler the equivalent of the free use of progressively increasing amounts over the next 10 years, to be repaid interest-free beginning with the eleventh year. I calculate this to be the equivalent of $37,500,000 loaned interest-free for 10 years (or $375,000,000 interest-free for one year). This not paltry special contribution to Chrysler is above and beyond the general 10-year amnesty granted in March, 1969. With an assumed 10 percent rate of interest, compounded annually, this *special* 20-year concession was worth about $14 million more than the benefit from the usual 10-year attenuation.

By way of expiation, Chrysler might fairly say they could have avoided the $75 million added tax merely by staying with their entirely legal LIFO inventory method. But Chrysler's 1970 pre-tax loss would have been $40 million more than what they did show—and that would have produced an even more disagreeable message to the shareholders than the attenuated tax. By going off LIFO, total assets were increased by $150 million in added inventories—giving the balance sheet a needed lift.

After giving the special nod to Chrysler leading to my misgivings regarding the 20-year dispensation, the Commissioner demonstrated that he too applies the law with "majestic equality" and applies it even-handedly to all who switch from LIFO to FIFO. They are all, henceforth, allowed to spread the deferred tax, interest free, for a score of years providing they were on the LIFO basis for a decade or more. (Revenue Procedure No. 71–16, promulgated May 24, 1971.) Clearly, no one can now accuse the tax collector of selling indulgences only to the rich.

For those who cannot distinguish LIFO from FIFO, the difference can be simply illustrated: Assume that a ton of metal is purchased for $1,000 in January of 1971 and consumed in production during the year; another ton is acquired for $1,500 in December of that year—and that one ton remains in inventory. Query: Which cost ($1,000 or $1,500) is presumed to have been consumed during 1971? Conversely, which cost ($1,000 or $1,500) should stay in inventory? First in, first out says the $1,000 went out in 1971 costs, leaving $1,500 in inventory. The last in, first outers say that it's the $1,500 of cost *deemed* consumed, leaving $1,000 in inventory. Clearly, in periods of rising prices LIFO shows higher costs of goods sold, lower profits; lower profits means lower taxes—that was the *summum bonum* during the Twiggy-statement days. But those days are now gone, so that the more revealing hot-pants attitude requires managements to be more daring, to expose more (sometimes getting nabbed for overexposure), even though this puts an added tax burden on the corporation and its shareholders.

Now that LIFO is clear, let's move on.

"Verifiability" is also a most laudable objective. This would direct that the accounting results "would be substantially duplicated by independent measurers using the same measurement methods." Unfortunately, this standard is generally put into practice pathologically. That is, after the patient (the corporation) has died, other accountants may move in for the postmortem—as in the case of Penn Central, Great Southwest, Commonwealth United, and some of the other situations to be discussed presently. Only after it is too late are we permitted to bear witness to the underlying factors which produced the accounting configuration. Granted, as the APB Statement em-

phasizes, the accounting process "must use human agents and human reasoning and therefore is not founded solely on an 'objective reality.'" But then the Statement should have gone further and asserted that nothing in our existence is founded solely on such an "objective reality." This sweeping assertion is confirmed by Prof. J. Robert Oppenheimer's statement of the "different notion of what we mean by objectivity" in the sciences, thus:

> All over the world . . . we check each other's experiments. In that sense it is a most objective part of our knowledge, and a most well-verified one. These comparisons are possible because we can tell each other how we have gone about an experiment and what we saw and what we found. Mistakes are made, but they are found very quickly. The objectivity which we see . . . is a characteristic of the way we can talk with others about it, of the lack of ambiguity and of the reproducibility and the verifiability of our communication with each other.

What is missing in the financial accounting process, at least as presently conceived and applied by the profession, is that we refuse to "tell each other how we have gone about an experiment and what we saw and what we found." On the contrary, we regularly beseech the legislatures and the courts to bestow upon us the "cloak of confidentiality," corresponding with that enjoyed by the medical and legal professions regarding their relations with patients and clients respectively. Our codes of professional ethics, to say nothing of the practicalities and economics of our client relationships, impose upon us a vow of silence or secrecy. Consequently, it is only in the rarest of situations, and even then, as noted, only pathologically, that the outside world is capable of discerning just how a particular management group, in concert with their auditors (sometimes even with the active participation of the SEC), went about a particular "experiment."

In his *Chance and Necessity* Nobel Laureate Jacques Monod points up yet another constraint on objectivity as the *conditio sine qua non*—this is because knowledge and ethics ("in essence *nonobjective"*) are "inevitably linked in and through action." Monod continues:

> Action brings knowledge and values *simultaneouly* into play, or into question. All action signifies a choice of values or pretends to. On the other hand, knowledge is essentially implied in all action, while reciprocally, action is one of the two necessary sources of knowledge.

If, then, values (i.e., nonobjective factors) are inexorable in the application of knowledge it follows that even if our accounting precepts per se are objective (an assumption which I deny) their application in practice would render them otherwise.

"Neutrality" is beyond my comprehension. I shall, therefore, begin by quoting the Statement in its entirety on this point:

> Neutral financial accounting information is directed toward the common needs of users and is independent of presumptions about particular needs and desires of specific users of the information.

Then, as its commentary on this profound objective, the Statement asserts:

> Measurements not based on presumptions about the particular needs of specific users enhance the relevance of the information to common needs of users. Preparers of financial accounting information should not try to increase the helpfulness of the information to a few users to the detriment of others who may have opposing needs.

The way in which the real substance of financial statements is buried in the footnotes gives the race to the agile—to those who, with some special insight, are capable of bringing together the half-truths (and thereby discerning the whole lie). If the APB expects all the users of financial statements to be treated equally, it should recognize (as I know that it has) that some are more so than others. Although the objective of neutrality is logical, it is preposterous in practice.

"Timeliness" is a most compelling objective in the financial-accounting process. Learning that a company is required to show precipitous losses through the writing off of huge sums of previously accrued income items is little comfort to those who bought shares or extended credit on the basis of prior euphoric statements.

A single issue of *The New York Times* (June 19, 1971) carried the following stories in the financial pages, each demonstrating the post-mortem proclivities of the accounting process.

CHIEF OF S.E.C. SAYS LOCKHEED ERRED IN SECRECY

William J. Casey, the chairman of the Securities and Exchange Commission, told Congress today that officials of the Lockheed Aircraft Corporation did the wrong thing, in 1967, when they failed to inform their shareholders and the public of the troubles they were encountering on the production of the C-5A military transport.

(Further consideration will be given to the Lockheed affair in a subsequent chapter. For the present the questions remain: Where were the auditors back in 1967? Where should they have been? Where was the presumed timeliness to which the Statement alludes?)

BOISE CASCADE WILL TAKE AN EXTRAORDINARY CHARGE

The Boise Cascade Corporation . . . engaged in land development, home-building, mobile and modular homes, . . . will take an extraordinary charge of $78 million, before taxes, in the second quarter this year.

(The details are not given by the article; apparently they were not supplied by the company in its press release. I will hazard a guess—the write-offs were a consequence of the earnings inflation perpetrated by land developers of the kind described in a succeeding chapter.)

GREAT SOUTHWEST CORP.

Consolidated net loss of the Great Southwest Corporation for 1970 aggregated $143,093,705, the audited report disclosed yesterday. . . . In 1969 the company had consolidated net earnings of $34,363,493. . . .

GSC noted that the 1970 financial statements are subject to several matters such as . . . certain investigations by Government Agencies, including a review by the Securities and Exchange Commission of the Company's 1968 and 1969 financial statements.

The Great Southwest Corporation is 95 per cent owned by . . . the bankrupt Penn Central Transportation Company.

(Great Southwest's financial statements have involved this author in serious controversy with the corporation's—and Penn Central's—auditors, as well as the AICPA. All this will be considered in some detail in a subsequent chapter. For the present I will rest with the question: Where was timeliness in the GSC context?)

The issue of timeliness will also be seen to be crucial in the Yale Express and National Student Marketing fiascos; both of these matters are considered in Chapter 11.

In another sense the objective of timeliness is especially compelling at present—and destined to become increasingly so as our communications and decision-making technologies become even more sophisticated and instantaneous than they are even now. The stock market now responds on almost an instantaneous basis to whatever comes along the Dow Jones "broad tape" or other news source. This was described a few years ago by David Babson in a *Financial Analysts Journal* article entitled "Performance—The Latest Name for Speculation?" We are told of the stages in the evolution in appraisal emphasis in stock investing: (1) Traditionally the emphasis had been on net worth, book value, physical assets; (2) then, the emphasis shifted to income return, dividends, and yield; (3) followed by earnings and earnings reliability and later by the long-run growth rate of earnings; (4) finally, at the time Babson wrote, the emphasis shifted to instant-earnings growth.

This new factor of instant-earnings growth demands that

meaningful and timely information be available to everyone involved in decision making regarding investment, or disinvestment. And providing data pertaining to the immediate future will have to become part of the financial-accounting process.

A new dimension of "timeliness" will probably soon become a part of the accounting scene. Possibly taking the lead from Homer Kripke, a professor of law, who has, for more than a decade, spoken out favoring current, fair value accounting, SEC Chairman Casey found himself asking the National Industrial Conference Board Conference on "New Challenges and New Directions for the Board of Directors" in mid-November, 1971, "What kind of information is the investing public entitled to?" His answer to this rhetorical question followed:

> I am going to try out on you some relatively new ideas which spring from my belief that the time has come to take a broader view of what is pertinent to investment values and the obligation to convey economic reality as management views it to stockholders and investors. I believe the time has come when we should re-examine the question of the inclusion of projections, forecasts and appraisals in our disclosure framework.

The Chairman then reviewed the past SEC position on these aspects of disclosure as well as the corresponding British experience; he next alluded to some recent decisions of the courts involving Leasco, American Metal Climax, and Gamble-Skogmo where the corporations were criticized for failing to divulge their *"estimates," "basis of evaluation,"* and *"appraisals,"* respectively. He concluded these ruminations by observing ". . . more work . . . in this area must be done before we reach definitive conclusions."

"Comparability" is especially vital in the financial-accounting process. This objective hopes that the "accounting information presents similarities and differences that arise from basic similarities and differences in the enterprise or enterprises and their transaction and not merely from differences in financial account-

ing treatments." If this standard prevailed in practice, there would be comparability within a single entity; and there would be comparability between enterprises.

For comparability to be achieved, it is necessary that the nature and terms of an entity's transactions be essentially constant from year to year; that these transactions correspond to those of similar entities; also, that the measurement standards be the same from year to year as well as entity to entity. That this standard is recognized as a mere platitude, or that comparability is essentially a shibboleth, has already been demonstrated by some of the sardonic comments regarding the previous objectives; the indictment will be spelled out in various specific contexts when discussing "unaccountable accountings" in subsequent chapters.

A major disintegration in this Ought of Comparability was described most dramatically in a *Wall Street Journal* article (February 16, 1972) entitled "Accountants Striking Dry Well in Attempts to Significantly Change Oil-Company Rules."

Under consideration by the Accounting Principles Board was a proposal to ban the so-called "full-cost method" of accounting by oil companies operating in the United States and Canada. This method, as the *Journal* put it, "gives a boost to current reported earnings . . . because it permits them to stretch over a period of years such current costs as unsuccessful exploration and drilling expenses."

The article goes on: "Most major oil companies shun the full-cost system and instead charge off these costs as they are incurred"; however, Occidental, Tenneco, and Texaco have opted for this more euphoric full costing.

The resultant dilemma confronting the investor is that the statements of two companies which are supposedly in the same industry are just not comparable—the two methods produce such disparate bottom lines for the income statements.

An adviser to the Board is quoted: "Actually, we don't have just two accounting methods right now, but more like 200, because each method is applied with many variations. . . ."

Implicit in these agonizing deliberations is the prevailing philosophy of the Board as I see it: "Comparability and fairness are our goals, providing that the application of these 'motherhood standards' do not generate important negative reactions from our clients."

Unquestionably, I thought, the Board will compromise—both the accounting issue as well as itself. By so doing, it will be making a mockery of the comparability precept to which it gave lip service in Statement 4—a conclusion consistent with the *Journal*'s final remarks: The Board is not compromising, it is "simply walking away from the problem."

Not unexpectedly, the Board did beat a valiant retreat. Thus, the March 24, 1972 *New York Times* reported: "Accounting Board Eases Rule Plans for Oil Units," saying: "Under heavy pressure from the oil industry, the Accounting Principles Board has softened considerably its proposed overhaul of the rules governing profit-and-loss reporting by petroleum producers."

This capitulation became evident to anyone who had the opportunity of witnessing the Board's agonizing deliberations on the question at its meeting earlier in March. It was almost embarrassing to hear the most highly regarded members of this most prestigious professional group making an invidious distinction between "voting their conscience" and "voting for what they believe will fly."

Summing up this comparability issue, it is likely that interentity comparability might ultimately be achieved through the workings of Gresham's Law. Thus, unless drastic change is effected the managements of all companies will be constrained to pursue the "cheap coin," the flexible-accounting options, used by "swinging" managements to create the psychedelic numbers which give them such flair. In order to survive, even staid managements will have to join the pack in their accountings.

The seventh objective, *"Completeness,"* merely tells us that complete financial accounting information "includes all financial accounting data that reasonably fulfill the requirements of the other qualitative objectives." This objective is, then, a mere tautology; nevertheless, one general and sweeping observation can now be fairly made: No financial statements for any publicly held enterprise ever reviewed by me is complete since none has "reasonably [fulfilled] the requirements of the other [six] qualitative objectives." And as was asserted in various previous contexts, this indictment of current practice will be amplified in the various cases described in the chapters which follow.

The Thirteen Features

Having thus set forth the APB's Seven Cardinal Oughts, or "Hopefullies," the Statement moves on to describe the Thirteen F's, or the basic *features* of financial accounting. These basic features many accounting texts consider the principles or standards of accounting.

Feature One postulates the "accounting entity" and states that accounting information pertains to a "circumscribed area of interest," namely, the business entity. This is important to bear in mind when predicating decisions on financial statements. Is the particular statement for the group of corporations comprising a unitary consolidation, or is it for the parent corporation alone, or is it merely for one of its subsidiaries? A failure to ask these timely questions has contributed to the confusion, and sometimes grief, of investors in the Penn Central complex.

Definition of the circumscribed area of interest is central to the pooling-of-interests controversy. The only justifiable rationale for pooling is that two separately circumscribed areas were destined from their conceptions ultimately to become a single circumscribed area of interest so that genetically they were one *ab initio*.

The presumption of a circumscribed entity nevertheless permits a business entity to ignore the social or other costs which it may impose on the community (for example, by pollution, or a reckless irresponsibility in its handling of human resources and environmental facilities).

This first feature caused the Board in March, 1971, to promote the so-called "equity method" for accounting for intercorporate investments by an investor owning a 20 percent or more interest in an "investee." It has been the prevalent practice that where a parent corporation owns more than 50 percent of a subsidiary corporation, consolidated financial statements would be prepared; this means that for all practical purposes the two separate entities would be treated as one. The profits or losses of the subsidiary would, with some adjustments, be merged into those of the parent. Correspondingly, the assets and liabilities would be integrated into a single consolidated balance sheet. As I will make clear in subsequent illustrations (in the case of Leasco for example), this combination of operations and assets and liabilities does not invariably lead to the most meaningful configuration.

In any event, the accounting profession was confronted with the problem of what to do where there is less than a consolidating interest (50 percent or less owned), so that a consolidation was not feasible, except in special cases (City Investing's almost 50 percent ownership of General Development, for example). Usually the holding company would pick up only the dividends from the underlying company, when the latter declares such dividends. As a consequence the underlying company might be accumulating huge amounts of profits without their being reflected in the parent's accounts from year to year (or losses might be festering in the underlying company, producing something of a time bomb for the parent).

Assume, however, the felicitous alternative of the underlying company accumulating profits (and assume that ownership gives the parent company some power), the parent could, in a year when its own operations have turned downward, induce a dividend out of the underlying company to paint a rosier picture for the parent's shareholders.

It is this kind of flexibility which the Board sought to strike down. Under this new Opinion 18, where company P owns at least 20 percent of T, P will be required to reflect from year to year, as a part of its operations, the proportionate share of T's profits or losses (again, with some adjustment). In the Opinion, P is referred to as the "investor," and T the "investee."

Theoretically this equity method is good—it will eliminate the "demand feeding" phenomenon, which could seriously distort the parent company's financial statements. But there are some very serious adverse contingencies. Thus, the reader of the parent's statements (say it is engaged in manufacture) undoubtedly already finds it difficult enough to comprehend the accounting field rules for the parent alone. Now, then, if the investee is engaged in some swinging real-estate operations or other kinds of accounting-gimmicked operations, how is the reader of the parent's statements going to comprehend the expanded statement? Especially where the reader will not, in all likelihood, be let in on the accounting field rules of the investee? Further, supposing the parent company is audited by a really responsible firm, but the investee's books are audited by a friend of the president's family? This essentially sank a giant Canadian company, Atlantic Acceptance, a few years back.

Feature Two postulates the "going concern." This is sometimes referred to as the "continuity concept" in accountancy. Thus, we assume that the enterprise has continuing existence, making it unnecessary to appraise its liquidation value. It permits us to defer the immediate write-off of research and development expenses, with the expectation that they will be offset by future revenues. Similarly, we follow the depreciation procedures whereby the cost of a building or a machine is allocated over various operating periods without any current concern.

Lockheed may have rationalized its ignoring of the C-5A

cost overruns and resultant loss contingency by reference to this going-concern concept—rooting its determination in the expectation that new contracts would somehow cut the festering losses. Of course, the controversy created by the exposé of the overruns and subsequent aborting of negotiations for additional lucrative contracts upset the going-concern game plan, with the resultant accounting flip-flops and loss write-offs.

Feature Three calls for "measurement of economic resources and obligations," and then makes clear that the financial-accounting process emphasizes *economic* activities that can be *quantified*. For that reason (and possibly also because of the entity concept) accounting does not deal directly with "subjective concepts of welfare or satisfactions; its focus is not sociological or psychological."

Feature Four, dealing with "time periods," is especially crucial to the present-day accounting process. This importance is implicit in the objective of timeliness alluded to earlier. Further, the prevailing price/earnings (P/E) syndrome, which relates the value of a share of stock to the corporation's earnings during a fiscal year, demands that the periodic earnings be determined with supposed circumspection. Thus, our accounting function might well be defined as the writing of the interpretative history of management's stewardship of the entity's resources *during a particular time period.*

Note how corporate managements search for ways of rationalizing losses as being extraordinary, or at least nonrecurring. (And thereby avoid their depressing effect on the critical bottom-line number, to wit, earnings per share). And as a corollary the same managements seek to attribute the pluses to the current operating cycle—thereby sweetening the message to shareholders.

The three features which follow are essentially mechanistic, calling for "measurement in terms of money," "accrual," "exchange price" (to make clear that we rely principally on transactions, supposedly at arm's length between unrelated parties, for our accounting recording).

The next four features appear to be platitudinous, informing us of the need for "approximation" and "judgment" and that the statements are "general purpose financial information" (apparently consistent with the objective of neutrality), and that the financial statements are "fundamentally related." All that this last bit of wisdom seems to imply is that the balance sheet and income statement are supposed to be part of a single mosaic.

Feature Twelve is, however, especially vital for the accounting process. In fact, if my colleagues really committed themselves to implementing this feature, this book would not have to be written; it emphasizes "substance over form." Here we are told: "Usually the economic substance of events to be accounted for agrees with the legal form. Sometimes, however, substance and form differ. Accountants emphasize the substance of events rather than their form so that the information provided better reflects the economic activities represented."

Again, had accountants reflected on these few, simple words, could they have countenanced the excesses of the accountings by the real-estate developers to be described subsequently? Or by Liberty Equities, Penn Central (re Great Southwest), Commonwealth United, Leasco, and the others, to be detailed presently? Or "cesspooling of interests" accounting?

In each of these situations, and others, transactions which were especially critical to the reported earnings were created out of whole cloth—and when exposed to the light, the fabric turned out to be as ephemeral as that woven by Andersen (Hans Christian) for the emperor's new clothes.

Feature Thirteen, the last of the basic features of financial accounting, sets forth the standard of materiality. As this standard is applied in practice, it might as well have been designated "Catch-22." Managements and auditors can evade all the other objectives and features by interposing the defense of lack of materiality.

As described in the Statement, "Financial reporting is only concerned with information that is significant enough to affect evaluations or decisions." (There is then a reference back to the paragraphs on the "Uses and Users of Financial Accounting Information.")

The Catch-22 implication stems from the fact that the APB has never defined materiality; it has never indicated when something is sufficiently substantive to be material. Is it 5 percent of gross income or 10 percent of net income which makes something material?

Is a penny a share material? If it increases the income from 10 cents to 11 cents a share, I suppose it is; but probably not if it moves the earnings from $5.00 to $5.01. But suppose 1970 earnings were $5.00, so that the 1971 penny makes the new earnings $5.01, maintaining the upward curve, however slight—is that material?

Let's take another. A company has been writing off research and development expenses as they go along; for 1971 they switch to the deferral of these expenses and the auditor, let us assume correctly, asserts the change was not material (only 1 cent a share, assuming that this penny doesn't seriously affect the trend line). But now, having made the nonmaterial change in 1971, the company effects a huge deferral for 1972 and subsequent years. Then does the 1971 switch become material?

This materiality dilemma was the theme of Charles Stabler's *Wall Street Journal* column of June 24, 1971. He began with the dictionary definition, "having real importance or great consequence . . . essential, relevant, pertinent." Stabler then quotes Thornton O'Glove, a financial analyst and keen observer of the accounting scene: "[Materiality] is the Achilles heel of the accounting profession, an escape hatch for corporate managements."

Then, after referring to the Occidental Petroleum and General Dynamics nondisclosures as being presumptively nonmaterial, O'Glove is quoted again: "The abuse of the concept is pervasive. . . . There are literally hundreds of public corporate audits taking place each year that contain important accounting transactions that aren't revealed, due to the 'Alice in Wonderland' judgment of materiality exercised by a large portion of the accounting fraternity."

Materiality was especially critical to the decision of the United States District Court, Southern District of New York, in the so-called Bar Chris case, involving the financial statements for a builder and supplier of bowling alleys. In its decision the court asserted, "It is a prerequisite to liability under Section 11 of the [Securities Act of 1933] that the fact which is falsely stated in a registration statement, or in the fact that is omitted when it should have been stated to avoid misleading, be 'material.' "

Turning then to the meaning of that elusive term "material," Judge McLean cited the SEC's regulations, informing us that: "The term . . . limits the information required to those matters as to which an average prudent investor ought reasonably to be informed before purchasing the security registered."

Proceeding next to the necessary empathizing with the "average prudent investor," the court determined that an overstatement of sales by about 7 percent and net income per share of about 15 percent were *not* material. However, Bar Chris's liabilities on the balance sheet were understated by $325,000 ($25,000 of this understatement being current liabilities), and its current assets were overstated by about $600,000. This had the effect of changing the company's current ratio (the ratio of current assets to its current liabilities) from 1.9 to 1 to 1.6 to 1. "Would it have made any difference if a prospective purchaser of [Bar Chris's] debentures had been advised of these facts?" asked the judge, rhetorically. "On all the evidence I find that these balance sheet errors were material within the meaning of Section 11," he ruled.

Now, one might argue that in the eyes of a generation brain-washed to believe in the supremacy of the income statement, the aberrations in that statement were more material than the swing in the current ratio.

Be that as it may, Bar Chris is now history and is frequently cited in current literature bearing on accountants' liability, since Judge McLean said: "I conclude that Peat, Marwick has not established its due diligence defense."

Let me demonstrate another facet of materiality, using the 1970 report of GAF Corporation—a company recently embroiled in a major proxy controversy. In note 1 to the consolidated financial statements the auditors inform us that: "Prior to 1970, the fiscal years of the Company's foreign subsidiaries generally ended on November 30. In 1970 the fiscal year-end of most of these subsidiaries was changed to December 31, and the 1970 consolidated financial statements include the results of their operations for the thirteen months [ended December 31, 1970]." Further, the "consolidated net income of such companies for the thirteenth month is not significant. . . ."

This is innocuous as far as it goes. Many companies require their foreign subsidiaries to close their books a month earlier to permit the relaying of the information, to permit currency conversions, and otherwise to expedite the eventual consolidation. But if GAF wanted a change, well, that's their prerogative. And it may well be that the inclusion of the thirteenth month may not have had a material effect on the consolidated net income— but then it might well have had such an effect. Let's continue with the facts. In note 2 we are informed that ". . . the Company's English subsidiary realized a net gain of $3,923,171 from the sale of its Stounton House headquarters in London after provision [for] income taxes. . . ." In the president's message we are told that the British headquarters building was sold "on November 27, 1970."

Now let's take those facts plus one other, not given by the report or the footnotes: The sale was not effective until seven days after the November 27 signing—during that time the GAF parent company had the right of rescission. (I will here even overlook the fact that the actual closing was not to occur until months later.)

With the foregoing facts before us let us develop a scenario. Supposing management realized (or is apprised by its auditors) that because of this right of rescission, the November 27 date will not permit the inclusion of this extraordinary gain in the British subsidiary's net income for its November 30 fiscal year. It should be noted that this gain was really material, amounting to over 25 percent of GAF's entire net income for the year.

Continuing with this hypothesis, supposing management tells its auditors that it very much wants the gain in its 1970 year, whereupon the fiscal-year switch is arranged. If, then, the lucky thirteenth month is December, 1970, rather than December, 1969, do we have a material effect on earnings resulting from the change?

As you can see, so much depends on how you set up the operation—not even her hairdresser knows—or the auditor.

It was because of a presumptive absence of materiality that the Penn Central auditors did not deem it necessary to spell out in the 1969 report the *single transaction* by Great Southwest which gave the parent company about six times the total ordinary net income for the year. Also because of a presumptive absence of materiality, items of extraordinary income are sometimes offset by certain operating losses—and the statement shows an essentially insignificant net sum, with the details of the pluses and minuses interred (unless, for some reason or other, the remains begin to stink).

These seven objectives and thirteen features might well be the warp and filler for the accounting canvas. The APB Statement then goes into the "nuts and bolts" aspects of the "Basic Concepts and Accounting Principles." Especially important for the development of much of the subsequent discussion in this work are those comments pertaining to the three R's in accountancy, that is Revenue, Recognition and Realization; and

those principles which specify the bases for recognizing the
expenses that are to be deducted from revenue in determining
the net income or loss of a period.

The "3 R's": Revenue, Recognition and Realization

The importance of two sets of operating precepts, those for
revenues and costs, respectively, cannot be overemphasized.
Since income for the period is, as pointed up above, the center
of gravity for modern accountancy, and income, in turn, is the
difference between the revenues and the costs attributed to the
period, it follows that we must have a reasonably clear understanding of these two countervailing forces.

The Statement describes the revenue process as follows:

> Revenue is conventionally recognized at a specific point in the
> process of a business enterprise, usually when assets are sold or
> services are rendered. This conventional recognition is the basis
> of the pervasive measurement principle known as realization.
>
> Realization. Revenue is generally recognized when both of the
> following conditions are met: (1) the earning process is complete
> or virtually complete, and (2) an exchange has taken place.
>
> The exchange required by the realization principle determines
> both the time at which to recognize revenue and the amount at
> which to record it. Revenue from sales of products is recognized
> under this principle at the date of sale, usually interpreted to
> mean the date of delivery to customers.
>
> The realization principle requires that revenue be earned be-
> fore it is recorded. This requirement usually causes no problems
> because the earning process is usually complete or nearly com-
> plete by the time of the required exchange. The requirement that
> revenue be earned becomes important, however, if money is re-
> ceived or amounts are billed in advance of the delivery of goods
> or rendering of services.

We will see how, in the cases of the land-office business and
the front-end loaders like Telex and the franchise operations,
the three-R precepts of the Statement did not seem to get themselves effectively applied in practice.

As to the attribution of expenses or costs to a particular time period, we are given a series of alternatives, to be applied as appropriate. Thus:

(1) Some costs are recognized as expenses on the basis of a presumed direct association with specific revenue.

This would most logically prevail for the cost of the goods given to a customer on the sale; it would clearly apply to a commission or brokerage paid *because* there was a sale, or to a royalty paid *based* on a particular volume of sales. This standard would also be applicable to any *ad valorem* taxes (for example, sales, gross receipts, and possibly even income).

It should be emphasized that even for these costs which are causally related to revenues or sales there may be some question regarding the *amount* of the cost to be attributed. Thus, for the cost of goods sold we have the old FIFO-LIFO duality. More recently we have been confronted with the question as to whether direct costing (only direct materials and direct labor should be charged to cost of the units) or full costing (overhead also is to be included) is the better measure of the cost of the units sold (or those remaining on hand, as inventory).

(2) In the absence of a direct means of associating cause and effect, some costs are associated with specific accounting periods as expenses on the basis of an attempt to allocate costs in a systematic and rational manner among the periods in which benefits are provided.

The Statement describes what the Board had in mind in promulgating this rule for cost attribution, thus:

If an asset provides benefits for several periods its cost is allocated to the periods in a systematic and rational manner in the absence of more direct basis for associating cause and effect. The cost of an asset that provides benefits for only one period is recognized as an expense of that period. This form of expense recognition always involves assumptions about the pattern of benefits and the relationship between costs and benefits because neither of these two factors can be conclusively demonstrated.

The allocation method used should appear reasonable to an un-biased observer and should be followed systematically. Examples of items that are recognized in a systematic and rational manner are depreciation of fixed assets, amortization of intangible assets, and allocation of rent and insurance.

That this relatively simple precept can produce much mischief is evidenced by the confusion regarding the amount of depre-ciation to be charged to a particular period (and we will see how critical this can be, in the case of the computer-leasing com-panies especially). Its complexity is discerned dramatically in the situations where research and development costs are being deferred—to be amortized on some logical (*sic!*) basis; similarly, much of the controversy regarding goodwill is rooted in this cost-attribution precept; the Lockheed affair is also illustrative.

In brief, all of these references to situations to be considered in the subsequent chapters demonstrate that while there may be a system or method, it is not necessarily "rational" in prac-tice. Thus, the Board's plea notwithstanding, the allocation method all too frequently does *not* "appear reasonable to an unbiased observer," even if it is being followed systematically.

With this crash course in accounting theory we are now ade-quately prepared to delve into the aberrations in its application in a number of important circumstances. And if the reader hasn't fully fathomed the traditional wisdom summarized in this chapter, it probably doesn't much matter since the account-ings we will be considering have taken leave of this very wisdom.

Chapter 3

Dirty Pooling and Polluted Purchase

THE decade of the 1960s may be remembered by future historians as the "Decade of the Twin Congs"—Viet Cong on the one hand, conglomerates on the other. The mention of either invariably generates intense emotion: also, the actions of the conglomerators are all too frequently analogized with those of the Viet Cong, what with their infiltration, facelessness, anonymity, the subversion and fear that they are capable of interjecting into the traditional corporate society, and so forth. Coincidentally, the antics of both, conglomerators and those involved in defending us against the Viet Cong, were proceeding in accordance with a scenario; and for both there was a sharp divergence between the public pose and the private truths, with extensive casualties while critical decisions were being predicated on fiction. As Walter Lippmann observed a half century ago, under certain conditions, men respond as powerfully to fiction as they do to realities, and in many cases, they help to create the very fictions to which they respond.

Fortunately for me, my responsibility and expertise are limited to the conglomerates, and even then only to the accounting roots and branches of this phenomenon of the sixties.

What follows may be principally of historical import, but the restatement here might give the reader insights into the managerial scenarios, or game plans, as well as a better basis for comprehending the changes wrought by the Accounting Principles Board in mid-1970 with regard to accounting for business combinations. As will be demonstrated, despite the prospective mitigation of the distortion potential of the old purchase-pooling rules, the changes house some serious booby traps. Unless we are aware of their existence, and how they developed, we may yet find the financial statements of the seventies to be as deceptive as those of the prior decade.

Consider then, the alternative methods of accounting for business combinations, known as "pooling of interests" and "purchase" accounting. Let me begin by defining these exotic terms. Here is the way the 1970 official pronouncement (Accounting Principles Board Opinion 16) describes the pooling of interests method:

> [This] method accounts for a business combination as the uniting of the ownership of two or more companies by exchange of equity securities. No acquisition is recognized because the combination is accomplished without disbursing resources of the constituents. Ownership interests continue and the former bases of accounting are retained. The recorded assets and liabilities of the constituents are carried forward to the combined corporation at their recorded amounts. Income of the combined corporation includes income of the constituents for the entire fiscal period in which the combination occurs. The reported income of the constituents for prior periods is combined and restated as income of the combined corporation.

On the other hand the purchase method (that opinion tells us):

> . . . accounts for a business combination as the acquisition of one company by another. The acquiring corporation records at its costs the acquired assets less liabilities assumed. A difference between the cost of an acquired company and the sum of the fair values of tangible and identifiable intangible assets less liabilties

is recorded as goodwill. The reported income of an acquiring corporation includes the operations of the acquired company after acquisition, based on the cost to the acquiring corporation.

For those who have not lost their innocence, let me illustrate the implications of the pooling-purchase dichotomy, thereby indicating why I have euphemistically referred to the two methods as "dirty pooling" and "polluted purchase," respectively.

Ajax and Tortoise in the Pool

Assume that Ajax Aero-Computer, a hot-shot company, is desirous of acquiring Tortoise Patents through an exchange of shares. Assume that Ajax's balance sheet shows Cash and Sundry Assets of $10,000; Capital Stock (1,000 shares at $1 par) $1,000, and Retained Earnings (Surplus) $9,000. Ajax earnings have been $4,000 annually ($4 a share), and its stock commands an exciting price/earnings ratio of 30, so that each share sells at $120 (30 × $4).

Tortoise's balance sheet shows under assets Patents $1,000 and Cash $8,000; its Stock (1,000 shares, $5 par) $5,000; Retained Earnings, $4,000. Tortoise also earned $4,000, or $4 a share—its P/E ratio is but 15, so that its stock is traded at $60 a share (15 × $4).

Ajax is anxious to get at Tortoise's patents, whereupon it offers to exchange 6/10 of an Ajax share (worth $72, that is, .6 × 120) for each Tortoise share. Tortoise shareholders would probably grab this opportunity before it gets away, since they're getting $72 on the exchange for each share which was selling for but $60 immediately prior to Ajax's tender offer. And now we're off to the races—let's see what happens if Ajax opts for the pooling alternative—or, I should say, structures the deal so that it is accounted for as a pooling of interests. The balance-sheet accounting would proceed as follows:

	Ajax Pre-Pool	Tortoise Acquisition	Combined
Cash and Sundry Assets	$10,000	$8,000	$18,000
Patents	0	1,000	1,000
Total Assets	$10,000	$9,000	$19,000
Capital Stock ($1 par)	$ 1,000	600*	$ 1,600
Paid-in Surplus	0	4,400*	4,400
Retained Earnings	9,000	4,000	13,000
Total Capital	$10,000	$9,000	$19,000

* 600 shares (6/10 × 1,000) were issued; they are recorded at Ajax's par value ($1 each)—the excess of Tortoise's $5,000 par value over this $600 ($4,400) is credited to Paid-in Surplus.

Notice that the debits meticulously equal the credits—the standards of modern-day accountancy have been accommodated. But here is where the excitement begins. Remember what the conventional wisdom tells us about post-pooling earnings: "Income of the combined corporation includes income of the constituents [Ajax and Tortoise] for the entire fiscal period in which the combination occurs."

As a consequence, Ajax's financial-relations representative promulgates a Dow-Jones broad-tape release—earnings are now $5 a share (the combined earnings of $8,000 divided by the 1,600 shares now outstanding produces an even, precise quotient of $5).

The tape watchers remember Ajax's P/E ratio of 30—Ajax shares get marked up to $150. Then possibly of even greater import—since Ajax's growth record indicates that it's up, up and away, the P/E ratio should be nudged upward somewhat, maybe to 36, say—so that Ajax shares will soon carry a market price of $180. Whereupon the stock is split 3 for 1, bringing the price down to only 60. But everyone remembers Ajax shares as priced at $120, whereupon the bargain hunters grab up its shares, boosting the price to 90.

To prove that it was really such a stellar performer, Ajax had to go out and earn even more than heretofore—and thereby justify the higher P/E ratio. At this juncture, after the 3 for 1 split it has 4,800 shares outstanding, and earnings of $8,000, or $1.67 per share. With a price of 90—my gosh, that's over 50 times earnings; clearly that won't do. Whereupon Ajax decides to sell the patents (which we know it had acquired in the Tortoise acquisition for $64,000, that is, the $72,000 market value of the 600 shares issued on the swap less the $8,000 in cash which Tortoise had in the till at the time of the takeover). Ajax sells the patents for $49,000—simple arithmetic tells you that Ajax lost $15,000; but you're wrong, dear Alice—you must put your simplistic arithmetic aside. Ajax *made* a $48,000 profit on the deal. You see, under the pooling wisdom Ajax was carrying these patents at only $1,000, so that a $49,000 selling price produced a huge profit injection of $48,000. This meant that Ajax profits are now reported at $52,000 (this $48,000 plus its traditional income of $4,000). Wall Street is jubilant—it guessed right, Ajax is a swinger, profits are now almost $11 a share, so that at $90 the stock is severely underpriced. What does Ajax now do for an encore? Well, we need not stop with Tortoise, there are many more creatures in the corporate forest.

This is, of course, a silly game, and its absurdity led to my "Dirty Pooling" story for *Barron's* in mid-July, 1968, when the pooling dynamics and conglomerate synergism were at their zenith. This is the way I unfolded the pooling ploy at that time.

*   *   *

In his lively and comprehensive article in *Barron's* (July 1), entitled "Pooling Must Go," my distinguished friend and colleague, J. S. Seidman, concluded: "I urge that we stop fooling with pooling. I think a pooling of interests can unwittingly result in a fooling of interests." In developing his indictment against the pooling-of-interests method of accounting for business combinations, Mr. Seidman used "some hypothetical and oversimplified situations." He avoided singling out "individual companies . . . (because) it would be unfair to single out individual companies doing what accounting says it is permissible to do."

While the Seidman article does make the point very fairly and dramatically, I believe that the moral can best be pointed up by reference to such individual companies, even though they are doing nothing different from "what accounting says it is permissible to do." In doing so I am undoubtedly indulging myself in the privilege of the academician to describe things as they are and to say why they should not be.

To begin with, I want to make it abundantly clear that I do comprehend the theoretical and historical justification for the pooling-of-interests method of accounting for business combinations. Unquestionably, Accounting Research Bulletin 48 (ARB 48), which last officially defined this accounting method, was rational and well intended; had its spirit been fairly implemented by the profession, or had our corporate society not manifested the urge to merge so frantically and frenetically, the pooling-of-interests method might well be permitted to remain in our arsenal of Generally Accepted Accounting Principles (GAAP) without arousing too much controversy.

Going further, if pooling were applied only to those cases involving a combination of two "major streams" which were destined from their very origins (however far apart they may have been) to converge at some time, and thereafter to become a mighty river, pooling would be congruous. So it is that I would not use the Pennsylvania Railroad–New York Central merger as a frame of reference for condemning pooling. But the Penn Centrals are not the typical situations with which we are confronted; * instead of "two mighty streams," we now find that we apply pooling of a metaphoric pond being emptied into another corporation's mainstream, and even to a bucket of water being poured (again speaking metaphorically) into a mighty river.

Further, I might fairly comprehend the application of pooling where, consistent with ARB 48, the shareholders and managements of both component entities effectively combine their resources and talents to form the more perfect union. Instead, we find in practice that even where the combination or union is patently tenuous the auditor will still follow management's pro-

* How could I have been so naïve in 1968? *Mea culpa!!*

pensity to pool, and permit the combination to be accounted for as a pooling rather than a purchase. As former SEC Chairman Manuel Cohen noted, this partiality toward pooling flows from its ability "to create an appearance of earnings and growth when they are not really present," and "to increase a company's reported sales and earnings without improving performance"; the easiest way to do this "is simply to add the sales and earnings of another company through merger or acquisition"—all this mythology is capable of being induced by the pooling device.

In short, it is not that the pooling-of-interests method, per se, is not rationalizable with accounting theory generally; it is just that the way in which it has been applied has motivated my desire to see this accounting practice discredited and disowned.

*   *   *

So it is that I move to the testing of the appropriateness of the accounting method or device through its application in practice. Those of us who fancy the philosophy of accountancy to be rooted in "pragmatism" or "operationalism" should recognize this as the procedure for determining the meaning of a word, or of a concept, in the context of action; that is, in the human context. Let us then see how the words of ARB 48 manifest themselves in the context of human action.

It was pooling-of-interests accounting which permitted Gulf & Western (G&W) to issue about $185,000,000 in securities during the year ended July 31, 1967, for a number of acquired companies (including Paramount Pictures and Desilu) and yet to quantify these securities at less than $100,000,000. It was this suppression of $85,000,000, permitted by pooling, which gave to Gulf & Western a submerged potential income pool, which, from all indications, it immediately and precipitously absorbed into current earnings.

Thus, during the few months intervening between the Paramount acquisition and July 31, 1967, G&W effected substantial and extensive television distribution contracts; these called for film rentals over an extended period, but were brought into current income in their entirety, even though the revenues were to be collected only over the extended period. Since the films acquired through the merger had been substantially amortized on Paramount's books prior to the acquisition, the distribution agreements had a most dramatic effect on 1967 earnings.

Briefly, G&W management was permitted to inject its 1967 earnings statement with the significant effect on earnings because the film properties which it bought (for stock, it is true, but bought nevertheless), and for which G&W paid a substantial price, were not recorded on the G&W statements at their actual cost. Instead, G&W was able to take the films over at merely the "substantially amortized" amounts shown on Paramount's books. This means that G&W was able to generate income almost on a demand basis without the full corresponding costs being reflected on the income statement—all because pooling-of-interests accounting permitted G&W to submerge most of the cost which it paid to acquire the Paramount library of films.

By way of describing this "Cartesian Diver" dynamics from another, and even possibly more spectacular, perspective, permit me to bring together for you a number of items regarding G&W earnings which appear in the 1967 report, in order to demonstrate the instant-earnings growth consequences of the process which we are here considering.

The Consolidated Statement of Earnings for the year ended July 31, 1966, as included in the 1967 report, tells us that the restated earnings for the 1966 year were $22,769,000—the restatement was, of course, necessary to include the earnings for that earlier year of entities pooled during the year ended July 31, 1967. By reference to the original 1966 statement, we know that 1966 earnings were then reported as $20,116,000. Simple subtraction tells us that the 1967-acquired entities must have enjoyed income of $2,653,000 during their separate 1966 years.

For 1967 the G&W Gestalt (which now includes the 1967-pooled entities) showed earnings of $46,199,000. In another context of the 1967 report, in order to demonstrate its "internal earnings growth," management pointed up that had G&W remained constant after July 31, 1966, and had it acquired no additional entities during the intervening year, its earnings for the year ended July 31, 1967, would have been $23,830,000. This leads to the logical conclusion that the 1967 acquisitions gave G&W $22,369,000 in 1967 earnings.

The gnawing question remains: What happened in 1967 to permit G&W to escalate the net earnings of the 1967-acquired entities from $2,653,000 to $22,369,000? In short, to what extent have earnings been expanded or "needled" by the distortions which are permitted, if not encouraged, by pooling-of-interests accounting?

A corresponding pattern of unwarranted and pretentious claims of growth appears in the 1967 annual report of Whittaker Corp. In a series of divisional sectors, the report sets forth action photographs for each such sector and then describes "the market challenge" and "Whittaker's thrust" regarding that sector. The "challenges" and "thrusts" thus emphasized by the sectoral presentation ran as follows:

Research and Development (p. 8): "Whittaker's Thrust. . . . Sales in 1967: $6,653,000, up 56.4% from $4,258,000 in 1966."

Materials and Structures (p. 14): "Whittaker's Thrust. . . . Sales in 1967: $67,519,000, up 138.9% from $28,256,000 in 1966."

Industrial and Commercial Metals (p. 20): "Whittaker's Thrust. . . . Sales in 1967: $60,209,000, up 306.8% from $14,-797,000 in 1966."

Architectural Products (p. 24): "Whittaker's Thrust. . . . Sales in 1967: $21,588,000, up 960.0% from $2,037,000 in 1966."

Technical Products (p. 26): "Whittaker's Thrust. . . . Sales in 1967: $47,634,000, up 91.6% from $24,859,000 in 1966."

Software and Services (p. 30): "Whittaker's Thrust. . . . Sales in 1967: $20,994,000, up 114.3% from $9,798,000 in 1966."

What did all this "thrusting" add up to? They were aggregated by Mr. William M. Duke, Whittaker's president, in his encyclical to the shareholders, thus: "In a year of rapid but solid growth our financial performance was noteworthy. Sales in 1967 reached the new high level of $224,597,000—a 167% increase over the $84,005,000 reported in fiscal 1966."

Thrust or Jibe?

Close inspection of these "thrusts" demonstrates that they are really jibes; they are rationalizable only through the irrational pooling concept. Thus, the sales in each instance are the sales of Whittaker as it stood on October 31, 1967; the 1966 amounts, on the other hand, were for Whittaker as it was constituted on October 31, 1966. During the intervening 12 months Whittaker had absorbed some 20 entities whose sales during the 1966 year exceeded $106,000,000. If the 1966 sales of the acquired entities were included in the 1966 standard from which the "thrusts" were measured, the overall increase would have been but 18% instead of the 167% proclaimed by President Duke. And it may well be that much, if not most, of this gain was experienced by the 1967-acquired entities prior to their moving into the Whittaker ambit—hence sales for which the Whittaker executives didn't really have to go into action (as portrayed by their photographs).

It is gratifying to observe that this pattern of reporting is now in official disfavor. Thus, in a June 18, 1968, policy statement, the Securities and Exchange Commission announced that in its opinion: ". . . it is misleading to make comparisons (which) invite or draw conclusions as to improvement in a company's operations by comparing pooled figures for a particular year with unpooled figures for the prior year. Comparisons in such cases should be made with financial data for the prior period restated on a combined (pooled) basis."

On this score, the *Wall Street Journal* for May 9, 1968, reported that: "LTV Ling Altec, Inc., a subsidiary of Ling-Temco-Vought, Inc., sent a letter to shareholders urging them to 'disregard' three major sections of its 1967 annual report in which its 1967 net income and per-share earnings were shown to be higher, rather than lower, than its 1966 earnings."

The rest of the article indicated that this might well be one of the cases of financial statement distortion resulting from the pooling-of-interests method of accounting for business combinations. Further probing into the LTV Ling Altec situation confirmed this hypothesis, and indicated even more serious perversions of the standards for pooling-of-interests accounting.

Thus, the letter (over the signature of the corporation's president, Lee D. Webster) to which the *Journal* article referred, contained the following critical paragraphs: "Your Company's 1967 Report to Shareholders was mailed to shareholders on April 2, 1968. The 1967 Report set forth on page 15 the consolidated statement of income of the Company and its subsidiaries for the years ended December 31, 1967, and December 31, 1966. The 1966 results were set forth as previously reported and also, as described more fully on page 19 in Note A to the financial statements, were retroactively restated on a 'pooling of interests' basis to include the accounts of Allied Radio Corp. and its subsidiaries which was acquired by the Company on October 29, 1967. A copy of page 15 of the 1967 Report is attached.

"The 'highlights' section on page 1 of the 1967 Report set forth the 1967 results on a 'pooling of interests' basis and compared these results with the 1966 results only as previously reported and not as retroactively restated on a 'pooling of interests' basis as was done on page 15. The third paragraph of the President's message to shareholders on page 2 and the charts on page 14 of the 1967 Report made the same comparisons. In each instance the 1967 earnings, as compared, were higher than the 1966 earnings, on a per share basis, rather than lower when compared with the 1966 results retroactively restated on a 'pooling of interests' basis.

"To avoid any possible confusion or misleading impression of the Company's earnings and growth resulting from the Highlights section, the President's message and the charts in the 1967 Report, shareholders are advised to disregard this material and rely solely upon the data set forth on page 15 of the Report. . . ."

What is it that the president's letter asked his fellow shareholders to ignore? He wants them to put out of mind statements like the following in the 1967 Report to Shareholders: "Sales increased 250% over 1966 with a 171% increase in net income. Net earnings per share increased from $0.33 to $0.65 on an adjusted basis—an increase of 97%. 1967 has been a particularly remarkable year, with its progress in all divisions. . . . Outlook (for 1968): Another excellent year of Sound Growth."

President Webster also asks his fellow shareholders to suppress a series of graphs included on page 14, which, under the caption "Sound Growth," shows charts comparing 1967 total assets, net sales, net income, and number of employes, with what are reputed to be the corresponding sums for 1966 and 1965. These, he now asserts, were misleading and confusing. They certainly were! Thus, the 1967 sales line measures about seven-and-a-half inches, whereas the 1966 bar is but two inches; the 1967 income bar spans three-and-three-quarter inches, in sharp contrast with one-and-a-half for the year preceding. Onward and Upward!

Of course, someone who has been practicing as a CPA for three decades, who is a Ph.D. and Professor of Accountancy, could have recognized immediately, even prior to the recantation, that the 1966 data were those reported previously in the 1966 financial statements, whereas the 1967 amounts included the operations of an important newly acquired entity, Allied Radio Corp. A person with the credentials described above would know that LTV Ling Altec was comparing unlike data (but expecting that the "medium will be the message," so that the "fellow shareholders" would get the message of "sound growth"). But neither decades of practice as a CPA nor a Ph.D. in Accountancy may be found among the prerequisites for acquiring shares in our great corporate society.

How then did this Ling-Temco-Vought subsidiary deviate from generally accepted standards of accountability? It didn't really; excepting that in early April 1968 it was constrained to file a prospectus with the Securities and Exchange Commission, which has apparently determined that Chairman Cohen's concern about unfair comparisons is now to be deemed the Commission's policy in its disciplining of any matters for which it has direct responsibility (e.g., in the review of prospectuses). Then, as indicated above, the SEC promulgated a definitive policy statement regarding this issue.

So it is that the *mea culpa* of LTV Ling Altec's president may well have been prompted by a reappraisal by the SEC of the standards of disclosure by corporations which had taken the "plunge into the pool" during the recent past (and, of course, conglomerates are those which are especially involved in this delightful pastime).

Consistent with the pleas to fellow academicians contained in my earlier "Dirty Pooling" article (*Accounting Review,* July 1967), I determined to pursue the LTV Ling Altec "happening" somewhat further. It is now my view, regardless of any justification for pooling-of-interests accounting generally, that the acquisition of Allied Radio by LTV Ling Altec should never have been accounted for as such a pooling. And, again in my view, the Securities and Exchange Commission and the corporation's auditors should not have indulged the corporation's management in its pooling proclivities to begin with.

What are the facts of this very important acquisition by LTV Ling Altec in October, 1967? We turn first to the proxy statement promulgated at the time of the acquisition. We there find that the acquisition was ultimately maneuvered (after other alternatives were considered, announced and then superseded) in such a way that it would not be tax-free to Allied shareholders; apparently the contaminant which prevented this from being a tax-free exchange under Section 368 of the Code was that in addition to the Allied shareholders receiving some $22,000,000 in Ling Altec shares, they also received all of $5,666.60 in cash. This amount of cash, then, made the acquisition something other than a tax-free swap for Allied's stockholders.

Everybody Wins

But this consequence was undoubtedly precisely what was intended—since the acquisition was structured (for tax purposes) as a purchase of Allied's assets (subject to its liabilities) after Allied had first resolved to dissolve under Section 337 of the Internal Revenue Code. Under Section 337, the general rule is that if within 12 months after adoption of a plan of complete liquidation all net assets of the corporation are distributed, no gain or loss is recognized *to the corporation* on the sale or exchange by it of its property. In brief, this means that Ling Altec bought the properties of Allied and did not acquire Allied, per se; through Section 337, Allied generally avoided a tax on the gain from the sale of its properties to Ling Altec; and the purchaser (Ling Altec) derived a tax basis by reference to the $22,000,000 paid in stock (and, of course, the $5,666.60 as well). Again, by this procedure Ling Altec enjoys a tax basis essentially independent of, and undoubtedly much higher than, that which prevailed for Allied.

Proceeding further, the 1967 proxy statement included provisions which clearly and unmistakably indicated that the Allied shareholders would be disposing of the Ling Altec shares with almost unseemly haste. Thus, as an incident to the acquisition, Ling-Temco-Vought (parent company of LTV Ling Altec) agreed that with respect to essentially 80% of the LTV Ling Altec shares acquired on their disposition of Allied: ". . . upon request of any of certain persons (those who have made such requests are referred to herein as the "Selling Stockholders"), made within four months of the Closing Date, under specified conditions, Ling Altec would, at its expense, file a registration statement under the Securities Act of 1933 covering shares of the Common Stock of Ling Altec proposed to be distributed by the Selling Stockholders and use its best efforts to arrange that underwriters make a public offering of such shares and purchase all such shares at a net price to the Selling Stockholders of not less than $22.22 per share.

"Ling-Temco-Vought, Inc. (also) agreed that, if the shares covered by the registration statement are purchased by underwriters at a net price of less than $22.22 per share to the Selling Stockholders, Ling-Temco-Vought, Inc., will pay to the Selling Stockholders in cash within five days after the shares are so purchased the difference between $22.22 per share and the net price per share received from the underwriters.

"Ling-Temco-Vought, Inc., also agreed that, at the time of the purchase by underwriters of the shares covered by the registration statement, it would make an offer to each of the persons (except the Selling Stockholders). . . . The terms of the Ling-Temco-Vought, Inc., offer will be to purchase, for $22.22 cash net to such persons, such shares of the Common Stock of Ling Altec which such persons desire to sell."

This right on the part of the erstwhile Allied shareholders to "put" 80% of their newly acquired Ling Altec stock was exercised by them in early April, 1968—just about the time when the 1967 financial statements were being mailed to the Ling Altec "fellow shareholders."

Clearly, the corporation (and its auditors) knew, at the time the statements were being mailed to shareholders, that there would be no continuity of Allied's ownership—a standard required for accounting for the combination as a pooling of interests.

Furthermore, the undertaking by the company to indemnify the erstwhile Allied shareholders for the difference between the proceeds from the sale of 80% of their shares and $22.22 proved to be most substantive—the shares were sold when the market price for Ling Altec was under $16 per share.

That Ling Altec (with the concurrence of its auditors) apparently determined to be oblivious to the standards for the purchase-pooling dichotomy set forth by ARB 48 is evidenced by their ignoring the Bulletin's clear assertions that: "3. For accounting purposes, a purchase may be described as a business combination of two or more corporations in which an important part of the ownership interests in the acquired corporation or corporations is eliminated . . . 5 . . . a plan or firm intention

and understanding to retire a substantial part of the capital
stock issued to the owners of one or more of the constituent corporations or substantial changes in ownership . . . planned to
occur shortly after the combination, tends to indicate that the
combination is a purchase."

What is it that really happened in this important transaction?
Putting aside all rhetoric, Ling Altec acquired for about $22,-
000,000 (a sum which was essentially guaranteed by its parent
corporation) the following (at the book values shown by Allied's
Balance Sheet as of July 28, 1967):

Assets:

Cash	$ 2,136,500
Receivables	18,166,800
Inventories	14,752,800
Prepaid Expenses	551,000
Miscellaneous Receivables and Investments	404,900
Land and Leasehold Improvements	1,417,400
Machinery and Equipment (Net of Depreciation)	646,500
Total Assets	$38,075,900

Liabilities:

Notes Payable Banks	$10,500,000
Accounts Payable	4,697,500
Accrued Expenses	1,597,300
Federal Income Taxes	3,057,700
Long-term Debt	6,000,000
Total Liabilities	$25,852,500
Net Assets (at Allied Book Values)	$12,223,400

(Of the $12.2 million in net assets, $3.6 million was paid-in
capital; the remaining $8.6 million represented the earnings re-
tained in the business.)

Basket of Assets

For this basket of assets, Ling Altec paid out over $22,000,000
in stock (at values essentially guaranteed by its parent), plus, of
course, $5,666.60 in cash. For what was this $10,000,000 excess

paid? I cannot tell—but Ling Altec and its auditors know, since in this instance (unlike tax-free exchange transactions generally) they were *required* by the Internal Revenue Code to allocate this $22,000,000 among the various assets and properties acquired (net of liabilities). So it is that the argument frequently heard from pooling proponents that one cannot determine where the excess belongs (which I consider to be a specious argument in all cases) is unqualifiedly inapplicable here.

Nor are we here insisting on the acquiring corporations reflecting a cost on its books (e.g., for the full value of inventories, equipment, copyrights, leaseholds and the like) which would not be correspondingly deductible for tax purposes. To the contrary, the tax consequences here were precisely those resulting from a purchase; in fact, by the pooling device, Ling Altec will be able to report the appearance of up to $10,000,000 in income to shareholders without any tax being paid thereon.

What we have here then is a case of management's desire to run with the hare and hunt with the hounds—*vis-à-vis* the tax collector, the acquisition was accounted for as an outright purchase (thereby significantly reducing taxable income); on the other hand, for presenting "fairly . . . in conformity with generally accepted accounting principles" (from the auditor's certificate signed on Lincoln's Birthday, 1968), the pooling option was exercised, thereby significantly increasing reported earnings.

To return to where we began with our deliberations regarding this *cause célèbre,* one might well be grateful to the SEC for its valiant endeavors to discourage specious comparisons; in this instance, at least, they might well have frustrated the very pooling decision *ab initio,* when they had jurisdiction for the October, 1967, proxy material.

It should be emphasized that I am not so obsessed with the pooling-of-interests problem as to believe that if this device were discredited and disowned, sweetness and light would thereupon prevail in our profession. To the contrary, I see it as being merely symptomatic of the myth-reality dichotomy which is all too prevalent in our professional pursuit.

Litton's Very Stained-Glass Windows

Another prominent pooler in its halcyon days was Litton Industries. When they really should have known better, Litton's management created some dazzling illusions in their 1967 financial statements. Their financial report for the year was a most beautiful document; the esthetic theme was rooted in stained-glass windows; and especially in point is the frontispiece, which carried the legend:

> This stained glass window symbolizes the ethics of 15th century commercial life at Tournai, Belgium. The citizen in the purple robe has volunteered to authenticate weights and measures. A shopman is moving a cask onto the scale while a clerk records the weight in circles and crosses.

We were then led to the annual report itself, which symbolized the ethics of twentieth-century commercial life in the New Industrial State. Presumably it is the CPA who is now wearing the purple robe; corporate management is undoubtedly the twentieth-century shopman as well as the clerk's employer. And we were still using circles and crosses—at least when it came to the presentation of financial data subsequent to a pooling of interests.

Thus, Litton's chairman of the board and the president introduced their letter "to our shareholders" on the following felicitous note:

> In a world economy marked by burgeoning opportunity, multinational Litton Industries continues to advance steadily. For the fiscal year ended July 31, 1967, Litton's sales rose to $1,561,510,000, a 33% increase over the fiscal 1966 figure of $1,172,233,000. At the same time, earnings rose to $70,070,000, a 26% increase from the $55,614,000 reported during the comparable period last year.

It is regrettable that the president and the chairman did not reflect on the stained-glass windows a little while longer before they determined upon these particular "circles and crosses." They might then have recognized that the 1967 sales and income amounts included the sales revenues and earnings of entities acquired during the 1967 year, whereas the preceding year's data did not reflect these later injections. Had they looked at the smaller-print footnotes of the report, they would have found that the more logical, and more truthful, comparisons would have been to report increases of but 15 percent and 16 percent instead of the 33 percent and 26 percent, respectively, asserted in the letter. Similarly distorted was the series of graphs most beautifully portrayed in the colorful brochure. It is true that the perceptive eye will catch a legend in type so tiny as to defy description that the charts were based on the data "as reported in the company's annual reports"—but even then the curves which the eye is invited to make were optical illusions, capable of inducing inappropriate investment decisions.

Leasco Pools Reliance

Then we have the Leasco-Reliance accountings. In late summer of 1968, Leasco paid out about $400 million in cash, preferred stock, and warrants for the Reliance Insurance Company; but, according to its books, this acquisition was assigned a cost of only $171 million (again, following pooling-fooling). Through this process Leasco's consolidated statements picked up the Reliance common-stock investment portfolio at its century-and-a-half accumulated basis of about $111 million despite the fact that the value of the portfolio was about $215 million at the time that Leasco moved in; Leasco was undoubtedly made to pay at least that much for the portfolio as a part of the $400 million total it paid on the Reliance acquisition. In any event, Leasco was able to acquire a potential for instant earnings of over $100 million by carrying over the Reliance securities portfolio at its historical cost to Reliance, not its market value on the date that Leasco absorbed Reliance.

Leasco had a most effective use for this latent pool: It injected more than $24 million of that suppression into its 1969 fiscal-year income statements as "realized gains on investments of property and casualty companies"—an injection equal to almost 60 percent of its entire net income for the year. This would have been a most phenomenal performance—if only it were true. But it was not true excepting to the extent that truth is made to lie in GAAP. My view, of course, diverges from the way in which Leasco's auditors saw it: They certified their client's performance records without exception or qualification.

In my view, instead of this $24 million profit, Leasco's statements for 1969 should have actually shown an adverse consequence from their portfolio management during the year of almost $58 million. I make this assertion because as noted Reliance started its 1969 year (just about the time Leasco took over) with an unrealized appreciation of $111 million, and by the end of that year the appreciation had shriveled to $29 million—for a deterioration of some $82 million. Subtract from this $82 million the $24 million of booked profits and you have what I consider to be a truer, fairer picture of the portfolio management for that year, namely, a loss of $58 million.

What, it might be asked, had Leasco done that the traditional Reliance Insurance managers would not have done? My answer is "plenty." First, the traditional managers would not have churned the portfolios just to create realized gains for improving the earnings statement. It is only very recently that they have even permitted such gains to go into income. Second, if the traditional management had reflected these gains, they might at least have said that it was *their* investment acumen which created the gains in the first place; they made the investment decision to buy the securities when they did, and at their original cost. Leasco management on the other hand took over the portfolio (paying the full late-1968 market prices therefor), but then was permitted to pretend that these gains were its gains—only because it pooled Reliance's accounts. Third, Leasco had a vested interest in creating these not really realized gains since it thereby forced Reliance to pay it, as the parent company, the hypothetical tax that would have been paid had Reliance stood all by itself. Because of Leasco's available write-offs it did not actually have to pay these taxes to our government. These gains, then, produced an adverse cash flow for Reliance, but one which was salutary for Leasco. Fourth, the traditional insurance-company management would have husbanded its resources, since it was bitterly aware of the implications of adverse market trends on vital reserves. It would not go about declaring extraordinary dividends like the $39 million that Leasco induced Reliance to pay out during 1969.

All of these differences (mirrored in drainages by National General from Great American and by other conglomerates which acquired insurance companies) add up to a shrinkage in the insurance capacity of American underwriters at a time when inflationary trends and the complexity of our technological society require even greater reserves.

As a historical digression, despite these and previous barbs at Leasco's accounting practices (and more, subsequently), I sincerely believe that our economic society owes Leasco its gratitude. The financial community, and legislators generally, first became acutely aware of the potential conglomerate menace when Leasco, flushed with victory after its Reliance coup, moved toward a takeover of one of the major New York banks. It then became clear to all that the conglomerates were not satisfied merely to ride herd on tired old industrial managements, nor were they confined to knocking off small traditional entrepreneurs. When Leasco crossed the financial Rubicon the threat became abundantly clear. We are, by now, aware of the significant legislation in the tax realm that followed Leasco's bold move; and to an important degree this legislation significantly slowed down the takeover wave in general (at least for a while).

Ajax and Tortoise Pool with Purchase

All right—enough of this "pooling-fooling" syndrome—surely, purchase accounting will produce the keys to the Kingdom. Well, let's see, going back to the Ajax-Tortoise magic.

Of course, if it's being booked as a purchase Ajax would have

to show the acquisition at $72,000 (again, that was the market
value of the 600 shares given up for the Tortoise shares). Following the traditional pattern of accounting (and Opinion 16 notwithstanding, I don't expect sweetness and light to come forth in
future reportings), we would have a work sheet which would
look like this:

	Ajax Pre-Purchase	Tortoise Acquisition	Total
Cash and Sundry Assets	$10,000	$ 8,000	$18,000
Patents	0	1,000	1,000
Excess of cost over book value of acquired companies (hereinafter referred to as "Goodwill")	0	63,000	63,000
Total Assets	$10,000	$72,000	$82,000
Capital Stock ($1 par)	$ 1,000	$ 600	$ 1,600
Paid-In Surplus	0	71,400	71,400
Retained Earnings	9,000	0	9,000
Total Capital	$10,000	$72,000	$82,000

Obviously this was a revolving-door phenomenon since the
end result, at least insofar as the cost assigned to the patents was
concerned, was the same tired old $1,000 we saw in the dirty-
pooling process. In fact, there may have been something even
more pernicious about this purchase antic than with pooling
since here the statement readers might have expected that Ajax
was really telling it like it is, and eschewing the cheap pooling
coin. And so, in "Much Abused Goodwill" (*Barron's,* April 28,
1969), I reviewed a number of the polluted-purchase cases, the
simplest of which involved an acquisition by a giant conglomerate, National General Corporation:

How National General Did It

One of the simplest situations demonstrating how purchase
accounting may be miniskirted is found in the accounting by
National General Corp. In the notes to its 1969 financial statements we are told that: "In March 1968 . . . the company pur-

chased, for cash, approximately 75% of the outstanding capital stock of Grosset & Dunlap, Inc. Subsequently, the additional 25% was acquired. The total cost was approximately $49,215,-000 . . . which was $33,048,694 in excess of the consolidated net tangible assets at date of acquisition."

National General accounted for this transaction as a purchase. Logically, that $49 million should have been allocated to the balances of cash and receivables (net of payables) with the surplus attributed to the pools of inventories, land, building, other fixed assets and the like, based on their March, 1968, values. Then, one might have expected an analysis would have been made of Grosset's copyrights relating to its 2,400 titles currently in print, to determine the fair values thereof, as well as of the Bantam operations, which Grosset owns. Similarly, the publisher's contracts with Book-of-the-Month and others should have been appraised, and part of the purchase price attributed to it.

It was for all this, and then some, that National General parted with $49 million. Did it, then, in good faith move to the "telling of it like it is?" Of course not. That would have necessitated National General's charging the $49 million to future operations, consistent with cost-revenue matching procedures so fundamental to the accounting process.

Instead, National General merely carried over Grosset's old balance sheet (reflecting only $16 million net assets) into the consolidation, and added the remainder ($33 million) into an "excess of cost" account (read this as a euphemism for "goodwill"). There it will stay until management decides otherwise.

In short, excepting the fact National General has effected an additional credit to its capital account, and a compensatory added debit to its goodwill account, it has done very little, if anything, that is different from what would have happened using dirty-pooling accounting.

Yet another remarkable purchase ploy involved the acquisition by the conglomerate City Investing of the stock of Home Insurance. In a 1968 prospectus published on the occasion of the exchange offer, as well as by assertions in its 1969 annual report,

City Investing categorically and unequivocally rejected pooling accounting and, instead, opted for nice, clean purchase accounting.

City Investing's Game Plan

This gave rise to a hosanna—for the ultimate integrity, utter disdain for the cheap coin of the poolers (such as Leasco, and International Telephone & Telegraph when it took over the Hartford Insurance group); a rejection of the temptation to claim as gains suppressed appreciation existing at the time of the acquisition. So faith in mankind suffered an especially agonizing blow when a December, 1969, City Investing prospectus revealed that the voice of Jacob disguised the hand of Esau:

> City accounted for its acquisitions of The Home Insurance Company on August 31, 1968, as a "purchase of assets" rather than as a "pooling of interests." As a result, City was required, in accordance with generally accepted accounting principles, to establish a new cost basis of Home's net assets at the date of acquisition based upon the fair values of Home's assets and liabilities in the light of conditions then prevailing. In arriving at such fair values . . . (ii) in determining the estimated realizable value of Home's investment portfolio as of the date of acquisition, it was considered appropriate, in the opinion of City's investment bankers, to recognize a discount from quoted market of $65,709,000 in the case of equity securities and $14,074,000 in the case of bonds and other evidence of indebtedness so as to reflect liquidation factors such as block transaction discounts, type of market, trading volume and similar factors. . . . As a result of the foregoing adjustment . . . (iii) the aggregate amount of gains ultimately recognized in City's income from the sale of all portfolio securities held by Home at the date of acquisition (when and if all such securities are sold) will exceed by $79,783,000 the amount that would have been recognized if such adjustments had not been made.

Now this revelation raised the following urgent question: How were the City Investing auditors able to satisfy the standards presumed for purchase accounting and yet give to management a flying head start of about $80 million for the acquired securities portfolio? City Investing was thus able to inject its 1969 statements (as well as subsequent statements) with gains which it assured us in its 1968 prospectus it was disavowing, and which its 1969 report implied it had actually rejected. This kind of earnings injection is precisely what we had a right to presume purchase accounting proscribed. As it turned out, the proscription was a myth.

We could go on from here to describe the somewhat different purchase ploy executed by National General when it acquired the Great American Insurance Company—but since the story is too long to retell, I'll just refer the curious reader to my article in the Summer 1970 issue of the *Notre Dame Lawyer*.

Hermaphroditic Accounting

Having thus examined the pooling-purchase dichotomy, we must consider an extraordinary mutation (heretofore disowned by theoreticians and even the most sophisticated practitioners), namely, the part-purchase, part-pooling hybrid. To exemplify this aberration I turn to the accounting patterns pursued by that most fabulous of conglomerators, James J. Ling, especially on the acquisition by his Ling-Temco-Vought empire (LTV) of Wilson & Co.

Here LTV bought 53 percent of Wilson for cash, and subsequently acquired the remaining interest through a "statutory merger." It accounted for the cash portion as a purchase; the remainder was "put into the pool." Again, there is no logical or theoretical justification for the maneuver—they just did it. But it probably matters little since the end result was the carrying over to LTV of nothing but Wilson's vestigial book values. This result prevailed because (1) on the purchase portion, the $23 million in cash that LTV paid in excess over 53 percent of the old book values was stashed away in LTV's goodwill account, and (2) the $65 million excess actually paid as goodwill on the stock swap was completely and forever lost from sight (consistent with the suppression permitted by pooling). As a consequence, $88 million paid by LTV to get at Wilson's operating assets would not wend its way into LTV's operating costs.

Then, to make things more interesting, when LTV stepped down old Wilson's assets into three new little Wilsons—Wilson & Co., Wilson Pharmaceutical, and Wilson Sporting (referred to by Wall Street pundits as the "three balls"—"meat," "goof," and "golf," respectively)—the carrying values assigned after the disgorging were carved out of old Wilson's balance sheet so that even the $23 million in goodwill established as a cost under purchase accounting stayed in LTV's sack. Then, later, when Meat Wilson was "subdeployed" into four new tiny Wilsons, the carrying values were correspondingly carved out of the vestigial costs—out of the unrealistically depressed bookkeeping costs going back for over a century.

Again, this process of suppressing the carrying values of the operating assets permitted LTV as the acquiring entity to show substantially lesser costs for its subsequent operating cycles. Perhaps an even more dramatic result is that the acquiring company was then permitted to dispose of segments of these newly acquired assets, and to compute and report appreciable gains by reference to the depressed carrying values permitted by GAAP—although these gains would evaporate if the proceeds were compared with the amounts actually paid on the acquisition. Once again, these inordinate and artificial gains contributed importantly to the much-heralded synergism—the elixir of the conglomerate movement whereby 2 plus 2 was supposed to generate 5.

Nunc pro Tunc Pooling

There is yet another accounting maneuver that our conglomerators found to be especially effective in their earnings-injection endeavors. I refer to the retrospective, or *nunc pro tunc,* pooling process, which was so crucial to the Westec scenario. In this ploy, the corporation completed its year with inadequate earnings; and its management was sent scurrying for new corporate acquisitions—it mattered little where they were located or what businesses they were involved in, just so long as they had earnings during the conglomerate's already-closed fiscal year. In the meantime the conglomerate's statements were held in abeyance, frequently for an inordinate period of time.

Then, after the dragnet was successfully completed and the managerial option to pool duly noted by the auditors, the earnings of the newly acquired companies were merged into those of their new parent. The result sought and achieved was, of course, that once again management's prophecy of increased year-to-year earnings had been fulfilled.

By way of an intimate glimpse into this retroactive pooling dynamics, I turn to a complaint filed in 1968 by Westec's Trustee in Reorganization against the officers of the ill-fated corporation and its auditors.

Included in that 161-paragraph document are the following allegations (culled, and sometimes paraphrased, from paragraphs 78 through 112) which are especially relevant here:

From the outset of their Westec audit engagement, Ernst & Ernst and Clarence T. Isensee, one of its partners, "were made aware of the ambitious goals of the [Westec] control group to establish quickly a consistent history of reporting dramatic increases in earnings from each reporting period to the next."

In the fall of 1964 James W. Williams, a principal Westec executive, "announced that the company was estimating consolidated net earnings . . . for the year ending December 31, 1964 to be at least forty cents (40) per share. This was more than three times the twelve cents (12) per share previously reported . . . for the prior year. Isensee was continuously aware of the predetermined goal to reach this and other projected figures. . . ."

Then, by mid-February 1965, "it became obvious to the . . . insiders, including Ernst & Ernst, that the company books would not support the earnings figure previously projected for 1964."

Undaunted, the company entered into a series of "highly unusual and misleading transactions," including, from paragraph
80(c) of the complaint:

> Pooling acquisitions: In early March, 1965, Hall [another prin-
> cipal Westec executive] discussed various methods to improve the
> 1964 earnings picture with Isensee. Hall was told by Isensee that
> he would permit the earnings of any company acquired in a pool-
> ing of interest transaction between the year end and the release of
> the audit report to be carried back and included in 1964. This
> advice resulted in a scramble to acquire, within the space of a few
> days, three companies with favorable earnings for the period in
> question. . . .

The complaint then goes on to allege that: "In addition to
being generally objectionable from the standpoint of retroactive inclusion none of the three (3) acquisitions met the established criteria for pooling-of-interest treatment. . . ."

So Westec, as the Trustee asserts, created the fiction of 1964
earnings by a mad 1965 race to acquire companies whose earnings could be insinuated retroactively—and we now know what
happened to Westec. The curious reader might well be informed that this litigation, begun in 1968, is still pending—and
has not, to my knowledge, yet come to trial. Will it ever?

One might have expected that in the wake of the Westec fiasco
this particular finesse would have been banned absolutely and
peremptorily. Expectations notwithstanding, manifestations of
this procedure are found in subsequent financial statements, and
they still carried the auditor's imprimatur.

For example, National Student Marketing was able to wheel
a huge Trojan horse into their August 31, 1969, report, duly certified at the end of November of that year. The report was
certified as being in accordance with "generally accepted accounting principles applied on a basis consistent with that of the
preceding year in all material respects." This "consistent" report
came down with a net of more than $3 million for the year—a
profit for which NSM's management sought the shareholders'

approbation. "This year," the president's letter told us, "has been one of dramatic development, progress and growth for us. . . ." More specifically: "In short, the past year has been one of bringing together new sources of strength and creativity—people, organizations, clients. . . . One immediate indication of how synergy or interaction has worked is found in . . . this year's sales and profit figures."

What the president didn't say (but which one of the auditor's footnotes did reveal) was that when he said "this year" and the "past year" he wasn't necessarily referring to the year covered by the report (that is, the one ended August 31, 1969). And when the auditors were attesting to the financial statements for *that* year neither were they necessarily alluding to NSM's year ended August 31, 1969, since (from their footnotes) no fewer than eight major acquisitions were effected after August 31, 1969; and of these eight, five were not even agreed to in principle until after that date—and yet they were wheeled into the statements for that 1969 fiscal year, bag and baggage, income statements and balance sheets, all as though NSM had dominion over these entities during the year being accounted for—all in accordance with GAAP. These *ex post facto* acquisitions, accounted for *nunc pro tunc,* were no flyspecks. The effect on NSM earnings was especially spectacular. Thus, these Johnny-come-lately acquisitions contributed $3,754,103 to NSM's reported profits for the year—a mighty contribution especially when we see that *inclusive* of these injected earnings the net before extraordinary items was $3,195,-127. Absent these acquisitions, the 1969 operations would have shown a loss rather than the substantial profits revealed by the statements.

We take our leave of National Student Marketing—but not for very long. We will see that their creative accounting did not stop with the use and abuse of pooling; we will meet up with it in different contexts in Chapters 5 and 11.

Chapter 4

The APB and the "P" in the Pool

THE criticism of the business combinations accounting mayhem intensified in 1968 and 1969; it reached its crescendo in late summer, 1969, when Leonard M. Savoie, the AICPA's Executive Vice President, addressed a Graduate Accounting Conference at Penn State University:

> The [Accounting Principles] Board was born in crisis and has been continually beset by crises. In my view, the prospects for Board progress in the 1970s will be greatly influenced by its response to a current crisis. This one involves accounting for business combinations and goodwill.
>
> Abuses in this area have become so prevalent that prompt, corrective action will be taken—whether by the profession itself or by government.

Mr. Savoie then proceeded to reject pooling of interests accounting for business combinations, referring to it as "discredited," possessed of "excesses [which] have been widely publicized," and bereft of any sound conceptual basis. He then informed his audience that the Board was going to meet within two days to deliberate further on this subject. And from these deliberations Savoie expected "that substantial agreement will be reached" and that a recommendation abolishing pooling would be promulgated. He then continued:

This draft will call for purchase accounting for business combinations, with recognition for fair values of purchased assets,
including goodwill—and the mandatory amortization of that goodwill against future income of the combined business. Anything
less than this solution will mean simply a "repositioning" of the
abuses which have become so rampant in recent years.

A forthright solution to this issue is a premise upon which my
other forecasts are based. If this solution is not reached, then I
predict little progress for the profession in the development of
accounting principles in the 1970s.

As it turned out this eulogy for pooling of interests accounting
was premature. Shortly after Mr. Savoie's prophecy there was
much talk about the situations where this mode of accounting
should be perpetuated. We heard of size tests (for example: 1
to 1, 2 to 1, 9 to 1, etc., until it began to sound like a betting
parlor rather than deliberations by the APB), and other enclaves
where poolings were still to be permitted. Finally, in August,
1970, two separate Opinions were promulgated simultaneously.
(This Solomonic maneuver was necessary since one of the major
firms was willing to vote for the Business Combinations Opinion, per se, but refused to accede to the Intangible Assets, or
Goodwill, phase—and they needed that firm's vote to get the required twelve affirmative votes—thus, the Board crawled into a
box and sawed itself in two.)

In any event, Opinion No. 16, entitled "Business Combinations," containing 99 separately numbered paragraphs, and No.
17, "Intangible Assets," with but 35, are now enshrined as
GAAP. Many learned treatises have been written analyzing these
134 paragraphs tittle by tittle; this is neither the time nor place
for yet another such analysis. However, a brief overview might
be helpful for the general reader.

Since we're now intimately familiar with the pooling-purchase duality, there is no need for recapitulating the nature or
background of the problem; nor do we have to define the various
terms of art implicit in the discourse (thereby skipping the first
41 numbered paragraphs of Opinion 16).

We can move on to the trinity of conditions precedent to the new look for pooling accounting (paragraphs 45 through 48):

1. Attributes of the "combining companies":
   a. Each must be autonomous and not have been a subsidiary or a division of another corporation within the two years preceding the initiation of the plan of combination. (A new company organized during this two-year period meets this autonomy test.)
   b. Each of the combining companies is independent of the other (that is, no more than a 10 percent incestuous relationship is permitted).
2. Mode of "combining of interests":
   a. The combination must be effected in a single transaction or be completed within one year pursuant to a specific plan.
   b. The acquiring corporation offers and issues only common stock with rights identical to those of the majority of its outstanding voting common stock. However, the acquiring corporation may purchase up to 10 percent of the acquired company's shares (for example, of dissenting shareholders).
   c. Extraordinary distributions anticipatory to the combination are prohibited.
   d. Treasury stock may not be unduly accumulated by the acquiring company anticipatory to the plan of combination.
   e. The "ratio of interest" of an individual common stockholder is to be preserved *vis-à-vis* other stockholders.
   f. The voting rights of the newly issued shares are exercizable by the shareholders immediately (so that voting trusts are out).
   g. The combination must be resolved at the date the plan is consummated—hence, no contingent or escrowed shares are to be left dangling.
3. Absence of certain "planned transactions":
   a. The combined corporation may not agree to retire or reacquire any of the newly issued shares.
   b. The combined corporation does not enter into a "financial arrangement" in favor of any of the shareholders of the

acquired company (for example, to give them a "guaranteed take out" or a "put" option).

c. The combined corporation does not intend or plan to dispose of a significant part of the assets of the combining companies within two years after the combination other than disposals in the ordinary course of business of the formerly separate companies and to eliminate duplicate facilities or excess capacity.

The actual pooling accountings would then be carried on as heretofore, that is, the old book values would be perpetuated, regardless of the value of the shares issued on the exchange. However, by reason of paragraph 61, *"nunc pro tunc"* pooling (the kind perpetrated by, for example, Westec and National Student Marketing) would be out. Thus, if the combination is effected after the date of the financial statements (but before they are actually issued), the acquired-company operations would *not* be integrated into the statements per se, but would, instead, be disclosed as supplemental information.

Opinion 16 then moves to the purchase-accounting alternative which is applicable whenever all the pooling standards are not met. (It should be noted, in passing, that management could most expeditiously avoid pooling accounting if it chose to do so, where its accounting objectives could be better attained through purchase accounting. All it need do is to issue a few preferred shares or warrants, or offer a contingent share "sweetener," or give some few of the old holders a put option—or a combination of these pool pollutants.)

Where purchase accounting is required, Opinion 16 sets forth a catechism for first quantifying the total consideration paid on the acquisition but then, even more extensively, the way in which such an aggregate cost is to be sprinkled among the various assets (subject to the liabilities) acquired on the swap.

The "general guides for assigning amounts to the individual assets acquired and liabilities assumed except goodwill" relate to:

a. Marketable securities
b. Receivables

    c. Inventories of various kinds
    d. Plant and equipment
    e. Identifiable intangible assets (for example, contracts, patents, franchises)
    f. Other assets (land, natural resources)
    g. Payables of various kinds
    h. Liabilities and accruals (for example, pension cost, warranties, vacation pay)
    i. "Other liabilities and commitments including unfavorable leases, contracts, and commitments and plant closing expense incident to the acquisition"

Should the reader fancy that a dollar's worth of assets will henceforth be appraised and recorded under purchasing accounting at a dollar, he may be sorely disillusioned to read paragraph 89:

> The market or appraisal values of specific assets and liabilities . . . may differ from the income tax bases of these items. Estimated future tax effects of differences between the tax basis and amounts otherwise appropriate to assign to an asset or a liability are one of the variables in estimating fair value. Amounts assigned to identifiable assets . . . should, for example, recognize that the fair value of an asset to an acquirer is less than its market or appraisal value if all or a portion of the market or appraisal value is not deductible for income taxes.

Finally, after a judicious allocation of the consideration parted with on an acquisition has been made to all the identifiable assets acquired less liabilities assumed, any overplus is recorded as goodwill. This moves us to Opinion 17.

Seventeen Follows Sixteen

After an exhaustive consideration of the accounting dilemma stemming from intangible assets (especially goodwill), the "Accounting Pragmatics Board" determined to promulgate "a practical solution," that is, "to set minimum and maximum amortization periods." The crux of this practical solution is found in paragraphs 27 to 29, "Amortization of Intangible Assets," namely:

The Board believes that the value of intangible assets at any one date eventually disappears and that the recorded costs of intangible assets should be amortized by systematic charges to income over the periods estimated to be benefited. Factors which should be considered in estimating the useful lives of intangible assets include:

a. Legal, regulatory, or contractual provisions may limit the maximum useful life.

b. Provisions for renewal or extension may alter a specified limit on useful life.

c. Effects of obsolescence, demand, competition, and other economic factors may reduce a useful life.

d. A useful life may parallel the service life expectancies of individuals or groups of employees.

e. Expected actions of competitors and others may restrict present competitive advantages.

f. An apparently unlimited useful life may in fact be indefinite and benefits cannot be reasonably projected.

g. An intangible asset may be a composite of many individual factors with varying effective lives.

The period of amortization of intangible assets should be determined from the pertinent factors.

The cost of each type of intangible asset should be amortized on the basis of the estimated life of that specific asset and should not be written off in the period of acquisition. Analysis of all factors should result in a reasonable estimate of the useful life of most intangible assets. A reasonable estimate of the useful life may often be based on upper and lower limits even though a fixed existence is not determinable.

The period of amortization should not, however, exceed forty years. Analysis at the time of acquisition may indicate that the indeterminate lives of some intangible assets are likely to exceed forty years and the cost of those assets should be amortized over the maximum period of forty years, not an arbitrary shorter period.

What, then, hath the Accounting Principles Board wrought

with these 134 separately numbered paragraphs? Have they effectively foreclosed dirty pooling or polluted purchase accounting? If these prescriptions (or recipes) had been given a decade
ago, would they have prevented the obloquy of the accounting
profession for condoning patent abuses of standards of fairness
determined fairly (rather than in accordance with GAAP)?

To a degree. For example, it would have avoided the situation
referred to in a late-1967 *Wall Street Journal* article reporting
that the SEC had raised some questions regarding Occidental
Petroleum's "market-skimming" practices which were, a corporate officer said, "for use in certain acquisitions we were making." Specifically, it would have aborted American Tobacco
Company's operation reported in its 1966 report, as follows:

> In May 1966, the company delivered 3,349,737 of its shares in
> exchange for all the stock of a newly formed corporation which
> had acquired the assets and assumed the liabilities of Sunshine
> Biscuits, Inc. Of the shares used in this exchange 2,056,165 were
> newly issued and 1,293,572 were treasury stock, including 828,800
> shares purchased during 1966.
>
> For accounting purposes this exchange was treated as "pooling-
> of-interest." . . . Retained earnings was charged with $27,824,000
> in 1966 representing the excess of cost over par value of the
> treasury shares reissued in this exchange less $2,203,000 applied
> against paid-in surplus.

This means that almost 40 percent of the Sunshine acquisition
was accomplished by a cash payment, at one remove, but that a
pooling of interest was nevertheless determined upon. And specifically some $30 million of cash actually paid by American
Tobacco to acquire (again, at one remove) the properties and
business of Sunshine Biscuits was submerged and suppressed—
the $30 million was charged to the corporation's surplus account
and a cost incurred by American's management will never flow
through its income account. For the sake of completeness, it
should be emphasized that the revenues corresponding to this
submerged cost will pass through the income account, but, as
was seen, without being offset by any of the cost submerged.

It most certainly would have banned the LTV Ling Altec pooling with Allied Radio (the transaction featured in the *Barron's* "Dirty Pooling" article). Similarly, the very special privilege extended to an important group of institutional investors by Leasco when it acquired Reliance would have been prevented. Because this last deal has ramifications beyond the mere accounting aspects, reflecting adversely on the maneuvers by our most highly regarded institutional investors and corporate trustees, I will digress briefly to describe the operation in some detail.

Leasco Somersaults into the Pool

It should be noted that Leasco found that to achieve its optimum pooling result it would have to acquire 95 percent of Reliance Insurance Company. There were important holdouts (owning over 15 percent of Reliance) among the Reliance shareholders—these holdouts were not especially intrigued by the idea of becoming liege servants in the Saul Steinberg empire. Whereupon, as described retrospectively in a Leasco April 9, 1971, prospectus captioned "arrangements with certain security holders"—it was not in the prospectus published originally for the Reliance takeover, but was inserted only later by an amendment:

> In connection with the Company's acquisition of Reliance, certain Reliance stockholders exchanged 164,430 shares of Reliance common stock and 63,462 shares of Reliance Class A common stock for 799,050 shares of Series B preferred stock and 1978 warrants . . . and concurrently sold such Series B preferred stock and 1978 warrants to a group of twenty buyers. In connection with such sale, the Company entered into an agreement with the buyers which provided that prior to September 19, 1969 . . . the Company would arrange for the resale of such securities pursuant to an underwritten public offering, or otherwise, and would guarantee that such buyers would receive a net price for such securities of not less than the purchase price thereof (being $72 for each Unit . . .) plus $.75 per Unit for each month or portion thereof that such Unit is owned by a buyer. . . .

As of July 24, 1969, fourteen buyers ("Consenting Buyers"), owning approximately 74.6% of the Units, entered into an amendment to the agreement which extended the termination date to October 1, 1970. . . . In addition, on October 1, 1969, the Consenting Buyers received a payment of $9 per Unit held, an aggregate of $5,372,568.

On September 10, 1969, those buyers ("Non-Consenting Buyers") who had not entered into such amendment sold their securities for $72 per Unit to a group of fourteen new buyers with whom the Company entered into an agreement on substantially the same terms as the agreement, as amended, between the Consenting Buyers and the Company. In connection with such transaction, the Company paid the Non-Consenting Buyers $9 per Unit sold, an aggregate of $1,818,882. Pursuant to such agreements, the Company, on June 29, 1970, purchased 399,525 of such Units for an aggregate purchase price of $31,900,000 and, on October 1, 1970, pursuant to the Company's notice letter dated September 9, 1970, purchased the remaining 399,525 of such Units for an aggregate purchase price of $32,800,000. Additional payments of $7,272,000 (including commissions and legal fees) arising from this transaction were charged to additional paid-in capital. Continental Illinois, in various fiduciary capacities, was one of such buyers and had owned 106,946 Units.

(Note: The reference to Continental Illinois's 106,946 units held as fiduciary is unintentionally ambiguous. It represented the number of such units held by that bank *after* the June, 1970, reacquisition; actually, Continental originally held over 222,000 of such units; a 1970 prospectus referred to 213,891 Continental-owned units.)

As is evident from the foregoing, Leasco's shares dropped precipitously by the time the critical September 19, 1969, date approached so that Leasco was constrained to renegotiate the 1968 put option given to the 14 institutional "warehousemen"; this they did, and as the 1969 financial statements disclosed (consistent with the 1971 prospectus assertions) Leasco paid the accumulated "warehousing" charge of $9 annually on the approximately 800,-

000 Leasco units, or $7,272,000. This accommodation or inter-
mediary fee was charged in the 1969 financial statements to
Additional Paid-in Capital (that is, Capital Surplus) account
rather than to operating expenses.

Subsequently, during the 1970 Year of the Bear, Leasco's
shares disintegrated further—apparently causing some very anxious moments on the part of these institutional investors, whereupon Leasco (as reported by the notes to its 1970 financial statements and reiterated in the 1971 prospectus) was constrained to
reacquire the units originally acquired by the institutional investors to accommodate Leasco's takeover of Reliance.

It now appears clear that Leasco and the favored-few institutional investors* entered into a symbiotic relationship to accommodate the then-prevalent pooling standards. The banks among
these favored few found it necessary to liquidate their Leasco
securities, which they held in a fiduciary capacity (possibly to
avoid a surcharge). Whereupon Leasco's bankers, especially
Continental Illinois, joined in a loan to Leasco to permit
the put option bail-out, thereby transferring the risk from the
trust departments to the banking windows. Then, to hedge their
risks the banks (as lenders, now) insisted on collateral for these
new advances. As reported in the 1971 prospectus under "Recent
Transactions":

> On September 25, 1970, the Company, pursuant to a term loan
> agreement dated as of September 22, 1970, borrowed from a group
> of seven banks, including Continental Illinois National Bank and
> Trust Company of Chicago ("Continental Illinois") and The
> Fidelity Bank of Philadelphia, an aggregate of $20,000,000 and
> issued its promissory notes due on October 31, 1972, in the ag-
> gregate principal amount of $20,000,000. . . . In connection with
> such loans, the Company pledged with Continental Illinois, as

---

* The prinicipal institutions thus involved were, as indicated previously, Continental Illinois National Bank and Trust Company of Chicago, in various fiduciary
capacities, 222,224 units, or 28 percent of the "warehoused" units; Chase Manhattan Bank, as Trustee 208,334 units, 26 percent; Commonwealth Capital Fund,
69,446 units; Technology Fund and Yale University, 41,668 units each.

Agent, 2,010,000 shares of Common Stock of Reliance Insurance
Company.*

On September 25, 1970, the Company, pursuant to a credit
agreement dated as of September 23, 1970, borrowed from a group
of seven banks, including Continental Illinois and The Fidelity
Bank of Philadelphia, an aggregate $20,000,000 and issued its
promissory notes due on October 31, 1972, in the aggregate principal amount of $20,000,000. . . . In connection with such loans,
the Company pledged with Continental Illinois, as Agent, 1,407,-
000 shares of Common Stock of Reliance Insurance Company.*

Under the old pooling standards, should Leasco's auditors
have permitted the pooling under these apparently gerrymandered circumstances? But I'm beating a dead horse—it cannot
happen again—at least not in this precise fashion.

Let's look at this chain of transactions (from the institutional
investors becoming a part of the takeover program until the
eventual liquidation of their investment at a huge cost to
Leasco) from yet another perspective.

As noted, the 1969 "warehousing costs" were charged to
Leasco's Capital Surplus; the 1970 charges were added to the $72
per unit put-option price, so that the entire amount of $64,775,-
000 paid to the institutions is laid to rest in Leasco's balance
sheet in an item labeled "Treasury Securities at cost—$64,775,-
000." Of this sum about $7 million is attributable to the 75 cents
per unit per month "carrying charge"—the equivalent of the
amount paid the previous year. In addition, as the 1971 prospectus informed us, still another $7,272,000 of costs incidental to the
accommodation was charged to Capital Surplus. It follows that a
total of about $22 million in costs and carrying charges incurred
during the two years while the accommodation was in process
were charged to one capital account or another and that no
portion of these costs found their way into the income account
as a charge to operations. Should the Leasco management be able
to exculpate itself so expeditiously? Should not their wrong judg-

---

* It is of some significance to note that the 3,417,000 Reliance shares thus
pledged amount to 62 percent of Leasco's ownership of the insurance company.

ment be charged to operations so that all can measure the
acumen of Saul Steinberg and his colleagues on this money-
management team?

What makes this especially intriguing to me is a complaint
filed in March, 1971, in the United States District Court against
the institutional investors involved in the accommodation deal,
asserting that they engaged in an illegal *lending* transaction;
thus, when Leasco needed the moneys to acquire the shares of
certain nonacquiescent Reliance shareholders, the Reliance
holdouts, Leasco "turned to . . . White Weld and Lehman for
help. They arranged for the Lenders [the institutions] to extend
credit to Leasco to buy the Leasco Package [of 799,050 units].
. . ." These loans, the complaint asserts, "violated Section 7 of
the Exchange Act and Regulations G, T and U. . . ."

Whether the allegations are true or not, the complaint does
raise a most interesting collateral challenge to the Leasco accountings. If the transaction was, in fact, a loan, then, in addition to aborting the pooling, at least *pro tanto,* the $22 million
in carrying charges and loan costs must be deemed to be interest,
and accordingly chargeable to 1969 and 1970 operations (and not
to Capital Surplus and/or Treasury Stock).

Let's leave Leasco for the moment, with apologies for that digression. As noted heretofore, the National Student Marketing
(and Westec) *nunc pro tunc* pooling is out—managements will
now have to plan a week or two ahead of time if they want to
beef up their current reports. And, of course, the hermaphroditic
phenomenon of part-pooling, part-purchase is officially in the
discard (even though it was never really sanctioned).

The "Catch-22's" in 16 and 17

But now let's think positively. What are some of the "Catch-
22's" discernible in this 16–17 tandem?

Well, for one, read what Samuel P. Gunther wrote in the
January, 1971, *New York Certified Public Accountant*:

> . . . virtually any purchase can now be turned into a "manda-
> tory" pooling. For example, assume that A Corporation wants to

combine with B Corporation but only on a pooling basis. B's shareholders, however, consider A's shares a poor investment and demand cash. Solution: A issues its voting common stock to B's shareholders in a merger. The shares are registered and immediately sold in a secondary offering. Results: (1) A gets its pooling. (2) B shareholders receive cash. (3) Because the combination is not a reorganization for tax purposes (failing the taxation continuity of interest test), if the tax basis of assets received by A exceed the book bases carried over in the pooling, a permanent difference results. To the extent that the excess is attributable to depreciable property, continuing tax benefits arise and are reflected in the financial statements by way of reduced tax provisions. Crediting the tax benefits to capital surplus is no longer appropriate (as it would have been under the old rules) because Opinion 16 explicitly states that a pooling is not a capital transaction. This scheme would have failed as a pooling under the old rules.

Thus, it appears that the APB's aim to limit pooling usage can easily be bypassed. Unfortunately, a detailed "legislative" approach which eliminates judgment places a premium on deft maneuvering.

Now while I may not necessarily agree with Mr. Gunther's tax analysis, it is clear that Opinion 16 eliminates the last vestige of any theoretical justification for pooling accounting. Thus, it was heretofore presumed that pooling was rationalizable on the ground that two mighty streams have converged and they now go their collective ways collectively. If we abandon the presumption of a continuity of interests on the part of the shareholders (which probably necessitated the Ling Altec and Leasco détentes), we have abandoned any pretense for pooling justification—excepting on purely pragmatic grounds.

Let us take a recent and simple situation to demonstrate how this ultimate defense of pooling has been corroded in post-APBO 16 practice.

On March 31, 1971, according to a listing application filed by V.F. Corporation (once proudly named Vanity Fair, the lingerie line it manufactured and sold under that name) the corporation registered with the New York Stock Exchange 611,830 additional shares of common stock issued in connection with its acquisition of Kay Windsor, Inc.

At the time of filing the application the shares had a market value of over $30 million; however, when the acquisition deal was being negotiated the 611,830 shares were worth about $20 million. This acquistion, the application informed us, "will be accounted for as a 'pooling of interests.' Such accounting treatment has been reviewed and approved by Ernst & Ernst, V.F.'s independent public accountants."

And so, consistent with the pooling sleight of hand, the $20 or $30 million paid by V.F. will be accounted for at but $6,861,325. You should by now know why—that's all that the Kay Windsor balance sheet showed for the worth of that little business. Thereafter, it should be duly noted, the V.F. management gets the use of anywhere from $13 to $23 million worth of Kay's assets without ever having to account for them to anyone, at any time.

But that's now an old story for us; what then is new as a consequence of Opinion 16? Well, on June 15, 1971, Merrill Lynch issued a prospectus for the sale of 384,838 of V.F.'s shares. As it turns out, 184,838 of these shares were being offered by the former principals in Kay Windsor's operations. Thus, they were selling off about half of the shares they had received on the swap.

In the old pre-APBO 16 days, V.F.'s independent public accountants would have gagged on allowing a pooling since there was such a serious breach in the necessary continuity. They might have had to proceed with a roundaboutedness (as in the LTV Ling Altec–Allied deal). It's nice to know we don't have to sneak around corners any longer the disposition, as Samuel Gunther said, could be effected openly and peremptorily. But then how do we rationalize the persistence of pooling on any basis other than Pope's pragmatism, "Whatever is, is right"?

Conceivably because pooling accounting is still under a cloud, the real game plans may, in the foreseeable future, be in the purchase-accounting ball park.

Let's step back a bit and consider the accountings by AMK

(now United Brands) when it acquired, by purchase, about 80 percent of United Fruit Company in early 1969. In so doing, AMK gave up some cash, but mostly bonds and stock—a total of over $630 million. Of this amount, it charged $286 million to the net assets deemed taken over from United and charged the remainder, over a third of a billion dollars, to the goodwill account. Now, AMK knew this was not right because in a July, 1969, prospectus, it told us: "A study will be undertaken to determine whether any portion of the excess cost [the goodwill] of the United investment will be allocated to specific assets acquired or liabilities assumed. Such an allocation if made to depreciable assets, may materially reduce . . . net income." In all of its interim statements for 1969 and 1970 (as well as in the audited 1969 annual report), earnings were reported without any recognition being given to the promised allocation—the study or appraisal was still in process. By how much the United periodic earnings would have been reduced by reference to this allocation is not now determinable. [And even with a "restated 1969" income statement included in United Brands Company's (née AMK) income statement, one cannot really tell what might have been the effect of the reallocation.] In any event, spring, 1971, did bring forth the appraiser's wisdom, to wit:

> The Company, with the assistance of independent appraisers, undertook a study in 1969 to determine the fair value of the United Fruit assets acquired and liabilities assumed and whether any portion of the excess cost of this investment [$344,446,000] should be allocated to specific assets acquired or liabilities assumed. This study was completed in March, 1971, and the assets acquired and liabilities assumed were recorded retroactively as of January 1, 1969, at their fair values. Where appropriate these values take into account the effect of differences between appraised values and income tax bases and the present value of future benefits and costs. As a result of this study, $91,520,000 of the excess cost was allocated to the net assets acquired. . . .

And lest you presume that even this $91 million will be flowing through the property accounts (and thereby producing a cost for depreciation), about half of that sum was charged to "Trademarks and leaseholds," so that the effect on property, plant, and equipment is further minimized. And then, as a clincher, the auditor's notes inform us that while the leaseholds are being amortized at the rate of $103,000 annually, "It is the opinion of the Company that the benefits to be derived from trademarks acquired from United Fruit . . . will be of indefinite duration. Accordingly, the cost of such trademarks and the excess of cost over fair value [goodwill] . . . is not being amortized."

Of course, the Opinion 17 rules will no longer permit the approximately $300 million to stay in goodwill and patents as a dead lump—it will have to be amortized over 40 years.

But whether pre- or post-17, $300 million for United Fruit's goodwill (and trademarks) is preposterous. If goodwill means anything, it's supposed to imply excess earning capacity. AMK paid out $630 million for about 80 percent, which means an $800 million value for the whole works, of which about $500 million would represent the net asset value (by the determinations made by the appraisers for AMK). Since United Fruit's historical earnings pattern would indicate net income of no more than $30 million annually—hence about 6 percent on the net asset value—I fail to see where AMK's management could rationalize a goodwill (supposedly *excess* earnings) value of about a third of a billion dollars. Maybe they thought they were recording bananas, not dollars.

With or without Opinions 16 and 17, managements are going to be able to continue the old carrying values without any really significant impact on the reported results—unless their independent auditors insist upon an independent appraisal of the residuum called "excess of cost over fair value of net assets acquired" (or call that rose by any other name) to satisfy themselves that there is a logical basis for that residual blob.

Another potential booby trap in the purchase-accounting field rules relates to the concession granted management to set up reserves for absorbing future costs resulting from the combination of operations, elimination of duplicate facilities, etc. We

now know of the questions raised regarding the ways in which
Penn Central used a similar reserve after their amalgamation.
Any current cost which management was able to rationalize as a
charge to this pot, they charged against it—thereby avoiding a
corresponding charge to current income. We have thereby created a great temptation for management to inflate liabilities
assumed on the takeover (thereby loading the cost on the scape-
goats—the old managements and their independent auditors)—
producing a corresponding cushion or layer of fat to be absorbed during the succeeding operating periods.

And, of course, there is nothing which would prevent the successor managements in a post-pooling operation from changing
the manner in which the assets taken over on the pooling are
thereafter to be utilized "in the ordinary course of operations."
Would the Gulf & Western–Paramount Pictures maneuver be
prevented? Would a real-estate operator be prevented from disposing of acquired rental properties at huge profits, and then
say with a straight face "the profits arose in the ordinary course
of my business, as a real-estate operator."

By way of another retrospective glance, the halcyon days of
pooling accounting have produced something which I call the
"nerve-gas syndrome." We all understood why we produced the
stuff—and Opinions 16 and 17 sort of discouraged the production
of any more of it. But the old lethal gas is still about—like spores
waiting to burst into action. Just study the huge profits realized
by Ling-Temco-Vought on their disposition of Wilson Sporting,
Wilson Pharmaceutical, Allied Radio—profits which were feasible only because the old pooling game produced those substantially suppressed costs.

So the consumers of statements for the foreseeable future
should be on the alert for manifestations of these "nerve-gas"
leaks. We didn't even move to put the old stuff into coffins, leaking or otherwise. And as we saw with AMK, since they purchased
United Fruit pre-Opinion 17, they can get away without amor-
tizing that third of a billion dollars of "bananas." Similarly, In-

ternational Telephone & Telegraph will be able to pursue its "demand-feeding process" by weaving into its earnings whatever portion of the quarter of a billion dollars of security-value suppression it was able to achieve after it took over the Hartford Insurance Group.

This continuing dilemma of interpreting the financial statements of companies with intensive acquisitions programs (both pre- and post-Opinions 16 and 17) will be considered in some detail in Chapter 9.

Is there any wonder that I cannot see these new Opinions as a panacea? What might be a positive response to this still critical dilemma? It matters little whether the acquiring entity opts for the pooling or purchase alternative—the one can be as dirty as the other is polluted. The independent auditor, honestly and truly independent and not platitudinously so, must probe the operating data of the entity *continuously* so as to exclude from currently reported earnings (both interim and annual) so much thereof as he can see is attributable to values discernible as existing at the time of the combination (whether it occured pre- or post-16 and 17). This exclusion might take the form of increasing the depreciation charge and/or excluding profits on disposition of acquired inventories or other assets taken over on the combination.

Insofar as goodwill is concerned, I would be willing to ignore any charge therefore, providing that I were assured that no values discernible at the time of the takeover were leaked into the current earnings stream, permitting the successor or surviving managements to pretend to be bigger and better than they really are.

An Ironic Postscript

An ironic postscript to these chapters on accounting for business combinations was provided by the keynote speaker at the August, 1971, meeting of the American Accounting Association.

Addressing himself to the question "Why Aren't We Solving Our Problems?" Richard T. Baker, the Managing Partner of Ernst & Ernst, had the following to say:

> From the early to the mid-Sixties, actual practice had so eroded the concepts of the 1957 pronouncement [on Business Combinations] that almost all of the so-called criteria for a pooling of interest were disregarded. As a result of this complete deterioration, almost any combination could be a pooling unless cash or its equivalent was used as the medium of exchange. Even when cash was used there came into being a creature known as a part-pooling, part-purchase which amounted to a half-man, half-woman approach. As far as I am concerned this has to rank as our all-time low point in debasing accounting principles.
>
> The business combination issue in the Sixties thus contributed significantly to the serious credibility gap that exists in financial reporting today. Since the APB had repeatedly endorsed the accounting philosophies to be used for business combinations, the logical question is "Why weren't they followed?" This failure, I believe, represents the most significant problem we have in accounting today. . . .
>
> The criteria for poolings were eroded gradually—case by case. First the relative size test went out the window. Next continuity of management was ignored. Then continuity of business was considered to be unimportant. Then came the creative packages of convertible securities of literally all types and varieties; and finally, warrants and even more imaginative schemes to effect poolings. This continued until we no longer had a logical basis to be followed in accounting for business combinations. Each time financial statements containing a further breach of the pooling principles were made public and went unchallenged, they became the new low-water mark for everyone to try to lower even further.

Considering that Mr. Baker is managing partner of the firm that gave us so much "Dirty Pooling" (LTV–Ling Altec as well as Gulf & Western–Paramount) and Westec, as well as the part-purchase, part-pooling hermaphrodite (to use his inspired metaphor) of the LTV–Wilson "Funny-Money Game," one might

well have presumed that Mr. Baker would have pleaded for forgiveness in behalf of his partners for having contributed so seriously to the gradual erosion of the criteria for poolings "case by
case." He might well be asking for forgiveness for this erosion,
first in the relative size test, then continuity of management and
business, followed by the convertible securities ploy, climaxed
by the part-purchase, part-pooling perversion. He might also be
asking that his firm be pardoned for its leadership role in this
case by case erosion.

But does he thus come to the temples of the academicians
(that is, the American Accounting Association) prostrating himself and asking for absolution? Not so that you would recognize
it. You see, Baker has found the villain in the piece, namely,
the SEC. This is how he fixed the blame:

> During the mid-Sixties, a senior staff member of the Securities
> and Exchange Commission stated in a paper prepared for a pro
> fessional development course that ARB No. 48 had ". . . been in
> terpreted with increasing liberality over the years, so that many
> transactions previously considered to be a purchase may now be
> treated as a pooling or a part-purchase, part-pooling." He went
> on to state that "The general principle has been that any com
> bination may properly be treated as a purchase, but that a pool
> ing is permissive only and not mandatory."

Were the auditors and the APB at fault, even partially? Let's
hear it from Mr. Baker:

> Is there any wonder that the APB, after reiterating the prin
> ciples to be followed on business combinations, would become
> discouraged with the manner in which these principles were
> ignored in actual practice, with the full acquiescence of a stat
> utory authority?

So instead of a hosanna for a fallen angel who cometh to repent, I react to Baker's lament the way I reacted to Bernard
Cornfeld's castigation of the same Commission as the principal
culprit in the IOS devastation—it is unmitigated hubris.

Chapter 5

A Look at Some Inflated Bosoms and Big Busts

H AVING considered the ways in which the accounting principles governing business combinations were confounded, let us see how some of the other principles were capable of being perverted, or at least eroded and corroded, in practice.

The sagas of recent financial fiascos which follow are remindful of the young lady in the limerick:

> There was a young lady from Kent
> Who said that she knew what it meant
> When men asked her to dine,
> Gave her cocktails and wine.
> She knew what it meant but she went.

Thus, like that young lady, I am of the view that the auditors in each of these instances knew, or as responsible professionals should have known, that the particular statements were not telling the story really fairly; they knew, or should have known, why and how the relevant accounting principles were being distorted or stretched—they must have known what it meant—but yet they went. Let us explore a few of these *causes célèbres*.

On this *via dolorosa* I turn first to one of the real high flying industries of the late 1960s, franchising operations. The companies in this industry (Performance Systems, Career Academies,

Four Seasons Nursing Homes, *et al.*) are, we know, now in the doghouse—the only surprise in all this is that so many supposedly astute investors were caught flat-footed with huge bundles of these securities. How could astute "money managers" have been found holding the bag at year-end with a loss on a single franchisor of the magnitude of over $23 million? National General had to take a mark-down of that magnitude on its ground-floor investment in Minnie Pearl (subsequently renamed Performance Systems, Inc.).

Unless National General was just playing the greater sucker game, whereby it knew the shares weren't worth what it was paying for them, but was confident it could find a bigger sucker who would overpay even more, one would have been certain that National General, and the various institutional fund managers who were also caught with Minnie Pearl, knew that the franchisor's accountings were canards. During the summer of 1969 the AICPA's Committee on Cooperation with the SEC and Stock Exchanges was advised that the SEC staff was concerned that the income claimed by franchisors was not justified. It was demonstrated that the prevailing accounting practices allowed initial franchise fees to be recognized as revenue prior to their being earned, and that there was insufficient provision for losses which might occur on the booked revenues. It was generally known that these practices permitted the current recognition of specious revenues, despite the fact that substantial portions were in the form of paper (only some of which was interest-bearing), issued by "shell corporations" formed with negligible capital contributions by franchisees who had little or no experience in business affairs.

But it wasn't until almost Thanksgiving, 1969, that the Institute sounded the alarm. And even then, they did it by indirection in a "News from the AICPA" release reporting on a talk given by its Executive Vice President, Leonard M. Savoie, before a group of Atlanta businessmen. In his address Savoie went even further than what was summarized in the release; included in his talk was the following:

Franchise failure rates are high. . . . Often, too, the franchisees lack experience and capital. . . . Thus, franchisors who seek to improve their earnings consistently through increased sales of fran chises can end up with serious discrepancies between reported profits and actual revenues. To counter this, some have branched out into new fields of franchising simply to maintain an earnings record, thus compounding the distortion.

If, then, this unduly liberal accounting contribution to the evil machinations of the get-rich-quick specialists was so evident the preceding summer (and the SEC and the independent auditors knew it long before that), one is led to wondering, along the lines of the query put by Sir Henry to Doctor Livingston: "What took them so long?" Ironically, the Accounting Principles Board has not yet (spring, 1972) spoken on this problem.

Scrutinizing Minnie Pearl

For a detailed look at the accounting principles and practices of these franchise operators, let's probe the 1968 annual report of Performance Systems, Inc. (née Minnie Pearl's Chicken System, Inc.), the company which enthralled National General. The financial statement of that report is preceded by the "Auditor's Report" which comprises a "clean certificate," a term of art meaning that the auditors have diligently pursued their appointed tasks, and finding no exceptions to these statements, assert that in their opinion they "present fairly the consolidated financial position [of the corporation] and the results of [its] operations for the year, in conformity with generally accepted accounting principles. . . ." As it turned out the certificate can be characterized as "clean" only because the generally accepted accounting principles on which it was predicated were "dirty."

Thus, it came to pass that in a February 13, 1970, "Dear Stockholder" epistle setting forth the "unaudited 1969 Semiannual Report which the Company filed last week, covering the results of its operations for the 28-week period ending July 13, 1969," we read of some very serious contaminating factors which existed at least as far back as the end of 1968 (when, as I noted, the auditors completed their appointed rounds and found that God was in His heaven and all was right in Minnie's world).

In Note 2 to the 1969 statements we are informed that they are now picking up income only on a when-collected basis; in addition, they are providing a "reserve in the amount of $5,424,-888 . . . with respect to notes . . . which were received in connection with pre-1969 [1968 and earlier] sales of franchises." They explain this reserve, and their about-face in accounting methods, by referring to competition, stock market declines and the like—rooting all of this perversity in troubles outside of Minnie Pearl, or at least beyond its control.

But as it turns out, their whole franchising business was permeated by incest. Thus, all of the revenues accounted for during the 1969 period "were derived from sales to six franchisees in which Company officers and directors and their immediate families had ownership interests at the dates of the respective franchise sales." In addition, we were there told, again most explicitly, that of the total franchise notes receivable as of July 13, 1969, stemming from franchise sales made through December, 1968 (the "clean certificate" date) over 60 percent were "due from franchisees in which the Company believes its officers and directors (including their immediate families) and the underwriter of the original public offering had an ownership interest. . . ."

Going further in the footnotes to this February, 1970, *mea culpa* report, we are told that "the Company was contingently liable as a guarantor of long-term leases for property and equipment of franchisees with aggregate minimum rentals of approximately $11,100,000."

How closely do the foregoing confessions contained in the February, 1970, statement match those in the footnotes to the auditor's clean-certificated report? Well, if you're trying to find the "Catch-22's," you'll find that the footnotes do refer to the same underlying phenomena—but note the words and the context in which they're uttered.

Note 2—Revenues and notes receivable:
Revenues to December 29, 1968, arose principally from the
sale of franchises reported as income for financial purposes upon
receipt of each down payment and the execution of notes and
franchise agreement by the franchisees. . . . Such revenues and
related notes receivable include amounts collectible from franchisees in which Company officials have a minority ownership
interest. . . .

Note 7—Commitments and contingent liabilities:
Commitments for property and equipment used in the Company's operations and other services covered by various long-
term leases and an agreement at December 29, 1968, aggregated
$7,590,000. . . .

There are, as we can see, a number of critical differences between the two sets of expository notes. First, of course, is the size
of the type. Those accompanying the auditor's clean certificate
are set forth in the ultrafine print we now find all too commonly
in financial statements. Heretofore, this kind of print was restricted to bills of lading, baggage receipts, airline and railroad
company disclaimers, and the like; the 1970 pronouncements
are, if anything, in a type size larger than that used for the statements per se.

Second, remembering the McLuhan thesis regarding the medium being the message, note how the original message was pure
"soft sell" and benign, set forth pretty much in passing, probably putting the reader under sedation; compare it with the
shrieking, detailed urgency of the 1970 assertions.

Third, the reference to the revenues and receivables including
"amounts collectible from franchisees in which Company officials have a minority ownership interest" diverges so markedly,
so as to be far more than a mere difference in degree from the
statement of facts (with accompanying tabulations) included
with the 1970 epistle. And as a postscript to this last revelation,
we see that during 1968 Messrs. John Jay Hooker and Henry W.
Hooker (who were Chairman and Vice Chairman of the Board)

had guaranteed loans whereby "two individuals purchased 16 percent and 9 percent of the stock of [a] franchisee" in which the Company's officers, *et al.,* owned a 15 percent ownership interest.

What am I criticizing through this repeated reference to the incestuous transactions between Minnie Pearl and various corporations in which "her" officers and directors and underwriters and their families had an interest and whose obligation Minnie guaranteed? Essentially, I am indicting the company's (and their auditor's) failure to consider the *substance* of the franchising agreements and instead swallowed the form. Thus, as it turned out, these officers, *et al.,* participated importantly in forming a corporation, with only a minor capital contribution and with only limited capital resources. These corporations then entered into franchising agreements with Performance Systems whereby (and this presumes the typical franchising arrangement):

(1) The newly formed franchisee is obligated to pay an initial franchise fee—mostly payable in notes (with or without interest).

(2) For this fee the franchisee receives the right to use the franchisor's name, patents, etc., for an indefinite period (frequently, however with a right on the part of the franchisor to cancel under certain circumstances); the franchisee was also entitled to assistance in site selection, lease negotiation, equipping the premises, advertising, and in selecting personnel.

(3) The franchisee was also obligated to pay a royalty based on sales; and was frequently required to purchase inventory and supplies from the franchisor.

Where then was there an abuse of logic and reality, to say nothing of fairness, in the application of GAAP? Briefly, despite the limited capitalization of the franchisees, the franchisor (Minnie Pearl, for example) would pick up as income at the time of the initial franchise agreement the entire amount of the fee—even though, as we have seen, so much of it is in the form of paper generated by the undercapitalized franchisee—with little or no provision for collection and cancellation losses.

All that the principals in the franchisor operations had to do was to form a corporation with a minimal capital, use some ink and paper to sign up with themselves acting in behalf of the franchisor, and Presto!! Merlin reports income for the franchisor.

We must be living in the Age of Deception, rather than that of Aquarius. How else could we permit ourselves to be taken in by this sort of a shell game? That supposedly sophisticated auditors, money managers, the stock exchanges, and the SEC, among others, could be thus cuckolded, and for so long, is entirely incomprehensible to me.

I don't know whether the AICPA has "opened a file" on any of these clean-certificated audits which related to dirty franchising accounting. My guess is that if it did open such files, nothing will come of it because there would be at least one such file for each of the major firms comprising the AICPA's power structure; who could be found to cast the first stone?

I leave it for the readers to determine whether any set of clean accounting principles, applied with any logical standards of fairness and disclosure to those entitled to know, could conceivably have supported the recognition of revenues from such "self dealings." The auditors must have discerned the huge pools of injected income in the 1968 reports. It should not have required any deliberations on any exalted plane, by the SEC or the APB, for example, to tell the Hookers to quit this psychedelic process.

And it wasn't merely the widows and orphans nor the ingenuous plunger who were thus hooked. As I pointed out, so astute a money manager as National General Corporation, a conglomerate of such omniscience and omnipotence that it felt itself capable of handling the huge resources of the highly esteemed Great American Insurance Company, among others, was mesmerized, and fell into the Minnie Pearl trap—and parted with $23 million in the process. National General probably had too much money anyway, being flush with the $174 million it drained out of the Great American Insurance reserves. Besides, they were sure they were getting a basement bargain, since they bought Minnie's Pearls in a private placement.

Learning from National Student Marketing

And then we have the National Student Marketing Corporation (NSM) report for its fiscal year ended August 31, 1969 (it is of some interest to note that this report wasn't finally certified by their auditors until that November 21), complete with its footnote 4, informing us of contracts in progress:

> (a) Fixed-Fee Type Contracts—$1,826,962: One aspect of the company's business involves fixed-fee type arrangements whereby employees of the company develop overall marketing and/or advertising programs for clients. The major portion of the work done by the company involves determination of the client's requirements and proposal of the company of an overall program. . . . Owing to the nature of this activity, income is matched against costs directly connected with the production of this income by recording the estimated gross profit based on the percentage of time incurred by the employees in development of the over-all program for the clients.
>
> (b) Market Research Studies—$973,226: During the year the company acquired W. R. Simmons and Associates Research, Inc., . . . The principal source of revenue of these companies is from contracted sales market research studies. Profits on contracts are recognized on the basis of the company's estimate of the percentage of completion of a study, commencing when the program reaches a point where experience is sufficient to estimate final results with reasonable accuracy. That portion of the total price of the contracts is accrued which is allocable on the basis of the company's estimates of the percentage of completion to study-expenditures incurred and work performed. . . .
>
> For tax purposes the company considers income on the above described contracts to be earned when billed. . . .

So NSM opted for the flexible accrual-of-revenues methods deemed to be appropriate for so-called cost-plus-fixed-fee contracts. Under this special accounting convention revenues are recognizable on the basis of partial performance, provided that "the circumstances are such that this profit can be estimated with reasonable accuracy and ultimate realization is reasonably assured." This wording of the American Institute's pronouncement supporting this procedure (Accounting Research Bulletin No. 43, Chapter 11) is captioned "government contracts," and at various points the phraseology makes explicit that it was such contracts which were envisaged by the Committee on Accounting Procedure (the predecessor to the Accounting Principles Board). Conceivably, NSM's practice was rooted, instead, in Bulletin No. 45—but that 1955 pronouncement was explicitly restricted "to construction-type contracts in the case of commercial organizations engaged . . . in the contracting business." But these exceptional and highly restricted accounting methods ostensibly served to support the NSM accrual of revenues.

As of but five days following the auditors' certification (and this brief period even included the 1969 Thanksgiving weekend), the phenomenal NSM coach turned into a pumpkin. Thus, its November 30, 1969, quarterly report dolefully informed the reader: "As the result of significant changes in the method of operations with respect to fixed-fee contracts, the company has changed its basis of accounting for this segment of the business from the " 'percentage-of-completion' basis to the 'completed contract' basis." The quarterly report also advises that the "company has determined that it does not have the capability to fulfill certain aspects of its on-campus programs. As a result, the receivables relating to certain of these programs have been reduced at November 30, 1969, resulting in a charge against earnings of approximately $510,000." These revelations, as well as those regarding the company's pooling practices, pricked the NSM bubble, and it exploded in some prominent faces for, as the *Wall Street Journal* told it:

> Probably not since Atlantic Acceptance Co. foundered in the mid-1960s, leaving many large pension funds and university endowments adrift, have so many institutional investors been affected. Late last year, National Student Marketing identified some of its stockholders as the University of Chicago and the en-

dowment funds of Harvard University and Cornell University as well as Morgan Guaranty Trust Co. of New York, U.S. Trust Co. and Continental Illinois National Bank of Chicago. Some of these institutions undoubtedly are out of the stock by now, but several large mutual funds concede they're still holding NSM shares, vastly depleted in value from the original purchase price.

The losses of these prominent investors must be of mammoth proportions, considering that as of late 1969 the shares were selling at $71.50, the year's high; the shares are currently (late spring, 1972) being quoted over the counter at about $1 a share. Again, the only source of amazement is that these investors, and their undoubtedly astute and highly regarded investment advisors, could have been had so badly. It may be the "greater sucker theory" working again; or were they assuming that the auditors' affirmation meant that the statements were really fair? Also surprising to me was that the bubble's bursting followed so soon after it was let out of the pipe—with the auditors' certification, it goes without saying.

According to a February 3, 1972, complaint by the Securities and Exchange Commission, NSM had engaged in income exaggeration by use of this percentage of completion "fudginess." Among the allegations in that complaint, which will be considered even more pointedly in Chapter 11, are the following (paragraph numbers are those in the complaint):

28(b). The consolidated statement of earnings for the fiscal year ended August 31, 1968 materially overstated sales by approximately $1,700,000, . . . and earnings before income taxes and extraordinary items by $695,689 (out of a total of such earnings reported of $699,116) as a result of the improper recording of sales and related costs from purported contracts in progress.

28(d). Footnote 3 [to the August 31, 1968 report] does not disclose that a material amount of the purported contracts in progress which were accounted for on the basis of their being contracts at August 31, 1968 were not, in fact, contracts, never existed as client commitments, were entered into after August 31, 1968 or contained guarantees which precluded their being recorded as income.

31(a). The [February 28, 1969] Consolidated Statement of Income materially overstates sales by approximately $1,400,000 . . . as a result of the improper recording of contracts in progress.

31(c). The report failed to disclose that unbilled accounts receivable totalling approximately $1,000,000 previously reported for the fiscal year ended August 31, 1968, and for the three months ended November 30, 1968, were reversed as of or prior to February 28, 1969, in recognition of the fact that these unbilled receivables never existed or were bad for other reaons. The report failed to disclose the reasons for such reversals and the amount of the reduction in net income and retained earnings resulting from such reversals. Of the approximately $1,000,000 in unbilled accounts receivable written off, approximately $750,000 were applied retroactive to August 31, 1968. Said report failed to disclose the effect on sales, costs of sales, and earnings of such retroactive reversals.

33(a). Defendant NSMC's Consolidated Balance Sheet as of May 31, 1969 materially overstates assets by approximately $2,100,000 as a result of the improper recording of $1,900,000 in unbilled receivables . . . and the overstatement by approximately $200,000 in deferred costs relating to prepared sales program and promotional items.

33(g). Footnote 3 to the Consolidated Financial Statements of defendant NSMC "Contracts in Progress" fails to disclose that a material amount of contracts in progress, which were accounted for on the basis of obtaining client commitments, were never in fact client commitments, were not in fact contracts, were entered into after May 31, 1969 or contained guarantees which precluded their being recorded as income.

33(k). Defendant NSMC failed to disclose adequately in the proxy statement that unbilled receivables and accrued costs and estimated earnings on contracts in progress of approximately $750,000 reflected as assets in NSMC's annual report to shareholders for fiscal year ended August 31, 1968 . . . were written off during the nine-month period ended May 31, 1969 and applied retroactive to defendant NSMC's fiscal year ended August 31, 1968.

33(l). Defendant NSMC failed to disclose adequately in the proxy statement that the write-off referred to in subparagraph (k), above, had the effect of materially reducing sales by approximately

$750,000 and earnings before taxes and extraordinary items by approximately $210,000 and of materially reducing net earnings in the Consolidate Statement of Earnings for the fiscal year ended August 31, 1968.

It should, by now, be abundantly clear that the percentage of completion method of accounting for profits affords to management an extraordinary measure of flexibility and subjectivity; my experiences, direct and vicarious, tell me that the auditor is almost powerless to discipline the data. Remember, the auditor is not especially well versed in sleuthing or appraising—as a consequence, management is given essentially unfettered license, for good or evil.

Yet another skeleton in my profession's closet resulting from the aberrations feasible under the percentage of completion method of income accounting is discernible in the report of R. Hoe & Co., Inc., for 1968, its last full year of operations. Its balance sheet included among the assets:

Unbilled receivables related to printing equipment contracts in process:	
Current portion	$ 11,764,377
Noncurrent portion	3,294,003
Total	$ 15,058,380

This was a hefty sum, comprising about 70 percent of R. Hoe's total capital. Subsequent developments indicated that much, if not most, of the supposed actual costs incurred in the development of these "unbilled receivables" were not worth the paper on which the numbers were written—to say nothing about the as yet unrealized profits which were tacked on to the asset values, with the resultant addition to net income.

How do I know R. Hoe "cranked in" these unrealized profits on this entirely conjectural basis of counting chickens before they're hatched? Well, for one thing, the auditor's certified footnote 3 relating to deferred income taxes tells us that they pertain principally to: "The additional income recognized in the accounts on the percentage-of-completion basis on contracts for the manufacture of printing equipment over taxable income computed on the completed contract method. . . ."

So it is that while I am willing to accept the percentage of completion method in extraordinary circumstances (i.e., those for which this method was originally intended) I have a visceral distrust of the method in practice. This distrust was fully justified in the NSM-Hoe situations; it helps explain my disenchantment with the homebuilders' statements (considered in Chapters 9 and 10) that are showing an increasing propensity to apply this method of income accounting.

The Tale of Telex

The Telex Corporation's revenue injection was somewhat more innovative and remarkable—they availed themselves of the provisions of Accounting Principles Board Opinion No. 7, whereby a manufacturer is permitted to mark up its manufactured product to the prevailing selling price at the time the product is turned over for leasing. Thereafter, the accounting cycle switches to the so-called "financing lease" method, so that the marked-up amount becomes the new cost basis, and the spread between that hypothetical cost and the anticipated aggregate lease revenues (as well as the salvage value at the termination of the lease) is allocated on some attenuated basis to subsequent operating periods.

Regrettably, the Board has never yet gotten around to doing what it promised to do a half dozen years ago, when it promulgated its Opinion—that is to conform this opinion governing the accountings by lessors with those of lessees, on which the Board pontificated in its Opinion 5. As a consequence, one can only surmise the circumstances which the Board had in mind in giving this special dispensation to manufacturers turned lessors. It may be that it realized that in some cases the putative lessee is really the buyer who preferred the lease route because it helped give a better face to his balance sheet. Or it may be that they analogized this leasing ploy with that of selling on the instalment basis. Whatever the reasons, Opinion 7 permitted this transmutative phenomenon for manufacturers.

But then the Board, in its wisdom, provided that for this process to become operative in a particular case, the lessor would first have to consider the usual financing-lease standards, thus:

1. The nature of the lessor's business—generally this method of accounting is appropriate for banks, pension funds, and money lenders who use the leasing device to secure their loans.

2. The usual incidents of ownership and risk are presumed to have passed to the lessee—because the leases are supposed to be "full-payout" leases.

In addition, where a manufacturer seeks to avail himself of this accounting method, so that it may immediately pick up as manufacturing revenues the "amounts which would have been obtained in a regular sale or the discounted amount of future rentals whichever is lower," it must meet *all* of these added conditions: "(*a*) credit risks are reasonably predictable, (*b*) the lessor does not retain sizable risks of ownership . . . and (*c*) there are no uncertainties surrounding the amount of costs yet to be incurred or revenues yet to be earned under the lease."

For emphasis the Board added: "If any of these conditions is not met manufacturing profit should be recognized . . . only as realized in the form of rental over the term of the lease. . . ."

After ferreting out the facts (only a few glimpses were given in Telex's 1969 financial statements—most of the facts had to be obtain from filings with the New York Stock Exchange and prospectuses published by Hudson Leasing Corp., Telex's financier), we saw how Telex picked up the bundles of manufacturing revenues despite the fact that the leases were, for the most part, for but one year; the burdens of re-leasing or selling upon the lease termination remained with Telex; the risks of obsolescence, idle capacity, and the like stayed with Telex; there will be expenses of obtaining the new lease, and the like.

All this notwithstanding, Telex's financial statements (at least through its 1970 fiscal year) were permitted to wax fat with unrealized revenues, blessed as they were with the auditor's *nihil obstat*—and the financial community ate it up, making Telex the 1969 *wunderkind*.

But it may be that in this instance even the auditors could not anticipate what it would ultimately mean when (like the young lady from Kent) "they went." Thus, the 1970 fiscal-year report revealed that more than $7 million, over 25 percent, of its revenues recorded that year was from equipment of which the company continued as lessor at year's end. (The major portion of these lease interests, we were told, were *expected to be sold* to a financial institution.) What I interpret this to mean is that Telex was using a method of accounting for income presumed to be all right for lessors, when, in fact, it didn't really contemplate being such a lessor at all. Instead, the company was engaged in the manufacture of equipment which it fully *expected* to sell, but hadn't yet sold as of the March 31, 1970, balance sheet date. The wording of this item indicated that it wasn't even sold almost three months after the close of the statement period, and (it is my understanding) wasn't even sold for many months after such period. Could the auditors really have envisaged this kind of income anticipation when first they went?

If the auditors really approve this kind of income anticipation, then they must certainly permit a builder who can't sell a house but can lease it for a year to pick up currently the full sales price of the house. Why? Because he contemplates the sale thereof *mañana*. Corresponding illustrations could be cited *ad absurdum*.

In any event, how did Telex's management and its auditors square their deeds with the relevant factors set forth in the APB's Statement 4, especially those relating to the significance of time periods for proper income measurement, the pervasive principles regarding revenue recognition and realization, and the related cost attribution concepts?

Memorex Figures Its Earnings

The controversy regarding the Telex accountings is paralleled in some important respects by the confusion surrounding the booking of income by another manufacturer of computer peripheral equipment, Memorex Corporation. In mid-December, 1970, a letter from its president to shareholders asked that they ignore the previously reported nine months' earnings of $6.1 million, or $1.64 a share, and substitute, instead, $3.6 million, or 97 cents a share. As a consequence, instead of these interim earnings being about 25 percent *ahead* of the corresponding 1969 period, they were really 25 percent *behind*.

What caused this 180° reversal? Let's read what Memorex's president said: The previously reported interim earnings "included sales to Independent Leasing Corporation (ILC), a new corporation organized to purchase peripheral equipment which Memorex manufactures and which ILC purchases and then leases to computer users." The permanent financing of ILC had not yet been consummated by September 30, whereupon "because of comment by members of the accounting profession that the accounting was inappropriate . . . [Memorex] desires to again report the operating results . . . using accounting methods which do not report any of the company's shipments of peripheral equipment to ILC's lessees as sales." This exclusion of the not-yet-really-sold equipment produced the precipitous reversal in direction of Memorex's earnings.

I fully concur in what must have been the critical inquiries and "comment by members of the accounting profession"; but yet I just cannot understand why the same inquiries and comments were not forthcoming with regard to Telex's inclusion of not-yet-really-sold equipment (and their resultant inclusion in that entity's income) in their 1970 certified statements. In fact, Memorex could at least say it sold the equipment to ILC, whereas all that Telex was able to assert was that a sale was contemplated. Conceivably, it takes a threat of an epidemic to alert my colleagues to initiate "inquiries and comment."

Inevitably, this revised accounting configuration had a correspondingly adverse impact on the Memorex year-end report —the income for 1970 was less than half that for the year preceding, 83 cents a share contrasted with $1.85. The year-end accountings made explicitly clear that its contract with ILC provided, among other things, that Memorex will (1) provide maintenance service for ILC's equipment on lease with its lessees, for which Memorex receives a portion of the maintenance revenue, and (2) re-lease ILC-owned equipment on a best efforts basis. For these anticipated contingencies Memorex has set up a reserve in the amount of over $4 million. Again, by way of an invidious distinction, even though Telex's contracts with at least one of its major equipment purchasers carried provisions corresponding to those recited above, Telex, until 1970, did not see the need for any provision out of its operations for the year when the revenues were being booked to accommodate these anticipatory costs.

Memorex's difficulties did not end there. Thus, on June 24, 1971, the SEC filed a complaint in a federal district court charging Memorex with violations of federal securities laws. This action was terminated the following month by the entry of a consent decree against the company, *et al.*

The allegations as reported by the *Wall Street Journal* are not significantly at variance from the facts summarized above (based on the December, 1970, letter to shareholders and the 1970 annual report). Apparently, the SEC took umbrage at the fact that Memorex did not make explicitly clear that their front-end loading of income on the aborted sales to ILC was challenged by its auditors. Instead, the letter was couched in some face-saving rhetoric.

Again, Memorex may have been grievously at fault in injecting its 1970 interim reports with income from not-really-sold computer peripheral equipment. But then I add the SEC and the accounting profession are *in pari delicto*.

Remember, neither of these institutions raised their voices to criticize Telex for picking up substantial income amounts from as yet unsold equipment manufactured by it. Telex did this through stepping up the carrying value of its equipment by the use of the financing lease option (an unfair use of that option as I saw it). Further, and going beyond even this income-injection ploy, their 1970 fiscal-year statements show that they had stepped up to market values substantial amounts of equipment just because it *expected to sell* this equipment and lease interests to a financial institution.

Nor could the accounting profession and the SEC fairly say they didn't know about this. As a consequence of my *Barron's* article criticizing Telex's accounting practices, several of its shareholders instituted lawsuits (all soon abandoned) aggregating $165 million. And yet there was not a single critical commentary, to my knowledge, from the SEC or the APB.

I carry no brief for Memorex—but certainly they had a right to presuppose that what was good for one Ex should be good for another. There may, of course, be undercurrents and crosscurrents with which I am not presently familiar; I cannot see why Memorex's accountings were thus singled out for special obloquy instead of imposing a ban on all corresponding kinds of front-end loading by the use of the financing lease method by manufacturers who do not squarely meet the standards of Opinion 7 of the Accounting Principles Board.

As might have been expected, especially in the light of these Memorex revelations, Telex's 1971 accountings manifest a determination to come clean—or almost so. Thus, we have a long Note 2 to these recent statements informing us, among other things, that:

> In . . . 1970, for transactions in which 50% interests were sold to a leasing company the total amount was treated as a sale. No such transaction existed in . . . 1971.
>
> In other cases the placement of equipment under lease has been accounted for as owned equipment under the operating method in which rental income is recognized as earned and the equipment cost is depreciated over its estimated useful life on the straight-line method for financial statement purposes.

During 1971 the Company has retained ownership of a much greater portion of the equipment rather than selling it to third party leasing companies and accordingly the ultimate recognition of a greater portion of the total revenues to be derived from the equipment has been deferred over the estimated useful life.

During 1971 all equipment that had been placed under lease and had not been sold at March 31, 1971, to an end-user or a leasing company has been accounted for under the operating method.

So let's send up a hosanna for a redeemed soul; no longer are we fed some $25 million as sales (and resultant income) from equipment retained on financing leases (or portions thereof where half interests were sold). No longer do we find such cryptic references like the one referring to $7,352,000 in the 1970 assets, for "Units of equipment as to which the Company continues as lessor at March 31, 1970. (The major portion of these lease interests is expected to be sold to a financial institution.)"

Without detracting from the felicity of the victory of the angels over the dragon, I must confess to a few questions raised by my study of this most recent report.

Again using some simple relationships, I'm wondering whether Telex has collected anything on account of the financing leases established on its books through 1970 (they assured us there was no corresponding contaminant in their 1971 fiscal year). Here are the significant numbers which I've brought together:

	For 1970	For 1971
Contracts receivable for equipment rentals under financing leases due within one year	$ 3,290,000	$ 2,860,000
Remaining unrecovered portion of the "selling price" value of the financing lease equipment before deducting "allowance for return of equipment"	13,962,000	7,337,000
Total	$17,252,000	$10,197,000

Now, then, if they did nothing more than what they promised in their 1970 report, namely, that they were going to sell $7,352,000 of the financing lease stuff then on their balance sheet, the $17,252,000 would have been brought down to a nice round $9,900,000. Maybe they didn't sell all, maybe their arrangements with the purchasers of the old financing leases necessitated a slowdown in Telex's recoveries of its investments. But all I can see is an essential moratorium in Telex's old financing-lease cycle. I may be missing something in the statements (proving that CPAs may have to consult other CPAs to interpret the statements), but it certainly appears as though their old financing leases are not producing any current liquidity for Telex. But transcending the preceding inquiries, I just cannot see how Telex's prestigious independent accountants were able to conclude their attestation saying: "In our opinion, the financial statements . . . present fairly the consolidated financial position of The Telex Corporation . . . at March 31, 1970 and 1971, the consolidated results of their operations for the five years ended March 31, 1971, in conformity with generally accepted accounting principles applied on a consistent basis during the periods." Would that I knew just what they meant by "on a consistent basis" in the light of the dramatic flip-flops in Telex's operations referred to in their Note 2, and excerpted above. It may well be that the auditors have been imbued with the wisdom of Lewis Carroll: " 'When I use a word,' Humpty Dumpty said in a rather scornful tone, 'it means just what I choose it to mean,—neither more nor less.' " Poor Alice! Poor us!

How much of a difference did this income injection via the financing lease maneuver have for Telex's 1970 statements? I'm not really sure—I wish I could be confident that Telex really knew, and if it did know, that it was really telling. Thus, on February 9, 1970, Telex reported that for the nine-month period ended December 31, 1969, the difference between their method and the appropriate (as I saw it) method would "have been less than five percent."

Now in their September 30, 1971, interim report we see something very much different from "less than five percent." We are told that the *restated* data for the six months ended September 30, 1970, were: "Sales $33.1 million; Income $3.2 million or 30 cents a share." Going back to the *original* data for the same six-month period we find that they were: "Sales $40.4 million; Income $5.2 million or 50 cents a share."

Now, then, while I don't have any computer equipment (peripheral or otherwise), I do have a slide rule and I get a reduction of 18 percent in sales, 38 percent in income, and 40 percent in earnings per share. It may, of course, be that the operations of the nine months to which Telex alluded were so drastically at variance from those during the six months involved in their reported accounting flip-flop that they are not comparable. Whatever the circumstances, there is something patently incongruous in all this—leaving yet another enigma in this Tale of Telex.

Mill Factors Through the Mill

I move on to the Mill Factors flop; the climax of this fiasco was reported in a *New York Times* story in September, 1970, headlined "Lybrand Sets Large Settlement on Role in Mill Factors Failure." The story begins:

> Lybrand, Ross Brothers & Montgomery, one of the nation's largest public accounting firms, has tentatively agreed to settle for $4.95 million the claims arising from its role in the collapse of the Mill Factors Corporation almost two years ago.
>
> Mill Factors, which today is insolvent was once considered to be a "Tiffany" among commercial finance companies.

The full story of this fall from grace has not yet been told—at least not publicly, though there are extensive and voluminous documents in the SEC archives in Washington. However, the curtain was lifted slightly in a late-1969 *New York Times* article regarding the report by the pathologists (special auditors called in by the trustees in bankruptcy), headlined "Accountants Find Mill Factors Corp. Was Insolvent in '65."

The article refers to a "confidential report [it's in the SEC files] by the accounting firm of S. D. Leidesdorf & Co." commissioned at the insistence of Mill Factors creditors, and states: "According to the report . . . as of December 31, 1965, Mill Factors should have set aside loss reserves ranging between $13.4 million and $18.5 million to cover possible losses on its then-existing commercial loan portfolio of $33.6 million."

Some of the more intimate details regarding the Mill Factors fall were provided by F. J. McDiarmid, Senior Vice President of a large life insurance company which extended substantial credit to Mill Factors. In a front-page *Barron's* article (understandably angry in tone, entitled "Blow to Confidence"), McDiarmid informs us (paraphrased in part):

1. As in the case of Atlantic Acceptance (which, I might add, was a huge Canadian "bust") the main trouble in Mill Factors lay in the area of large commercial loans. Out of approximately $56 million of such loans, as much as $35 million is expected to be lost, a sum roughly equal to three times the company's total equity capital.
2. Like with Atlantic, Mill Factors showed a concentration of lending which made no sense as related either to its size or underlying net worth. One group of loans totaled nearly $11 million, an amount greater than Mill's common stock equity.
3. Another group of loans, totaling over $8 million, was made to a group of four interrelated companies . . . located mainly in Florida. They manufactured steel doors, enameled paneling and auto locks. Of the $7 million advanced by Mill Factors to these companies, allegedly against receivables, about $5 million turned out to be advanced against unfilled sales orders.
4. There were a number of other loans, or related groups of loans, in the $2 million to $4 million range which had one thing in common—they were very bad loans. One company in the yarn business, founded in 1965 with a net worth of $35,000, was

financed by Mill Factors ever since in spite of showing losses in most years. The total sum advanced to this company was nearly $4 million; losses may run to 75%.

5. Mill Factors had other things in common with Atlantic Acceptance: "Its management didn't believe in telling lenders and investors very much. Its audit reports were flimsy pamphlets containing little more than an income account and balance sheet, lacking such back-up material as schedules showing its large loan concentrations and the record of payments thereon, which, in the circumstances, would have made very interesting reading." Its last published annual report (1967) was equally innocuous, describing its business in general, but in rather glowing terms and pointing with pride to the length of service and qualifications of its chief officers. When asked for more detailed information, it was the Mill Factors management's custom to protest at the cost of making this available, and to suggest that what was good enough for major New York banks ought to satisfy anybody.

6. The management of Mill Factors apparently suffered from the same twin deficiencies as plagued Atlantic Acceptance, the cult of secrecy and the cult of personality. In both instances, they brought disaster on a huge scale.

7. The cult of secrecy in the finance business appears to be quite wide-spread. When big trouble occurs, investors often are slow to find out about it and only learn the facts as a result of laboriously prying and digging, with scant help from auditors.

All the foregoing is but prologue to McDiarmid's attribution of fault to those responsible for the attest function, thus:

Whose Fault?

As in the case of Atlantic Acceptance, Mill Factors provided just one more instance where auditors provided no advance warning that trouble was brewing. An investigation by a creditors' committee after things turned sour indicated that several large debtors had been ailing for years and were in poor financial shape prior to 1968. . . . In the early weeks of 1969, it took representatives of the creditors only a few days to appraise the general shape of the mess. . . . Owing to the experience with Atlantic Acceptance and other bankrupt finance companies, the process through which such a horrendous situation can arise is increasingly understood. What generally happens is this. A loan officer makes a substantial loan that goes sour. Instead of admitting his mistake, passing on the information to the company's investors and creditors, and possibly risking his reputation and job, he decides to cover up. If the mistake were large enough and were made public, a shadow would be cast over the credit rating of the company. The covering-up process is done by advancing more money to the ailing client to enable it to pay interest and principal on the loan, and often to advance more besides. If the client went broke, the cat, of course, would be out of the bag.

There then follows yet another lament, "should not the auditors have been required to smoke out the concentration of loans referred to above," a process which would have required "the services of a real financial sleuth"? The despairing response:

The kind of auditing required to do this is no doubt both laborious and expensive and requires highly skilled people. It may not be forthcoming until finance company auditors feel that their primary responsibility is to investors and not to company management. One may doubt whether this will be fully achieved until auditors are retained and paid by the investors themselves.

McDiarmid closes with the following dismal prophecy:

Lenders relied on the auditors; if the latter failed to do their job, institutional lenders should take warning. If the lenders are to be faulted in the case of Mill Factors, it is in not demanding more information than they got. . . . However, in view of the way things turned out, such lenders may be forgiven for wondering whether, even if more data had been furnished in the audit or otherwise pried out, they could have told the correct story.

If finance companies hope to survive, they had better do something about the cult of secrecy and the cult of personality which apparently had much to do with the troubles of Atlantic Acceptance four years ago and now of Mill Factors. They also had better do something about improving the credibility of their audit reports. In the old days the auditing profession in this country was largely recruited from Scotland. It looks as though it could use a fresh shipment of gimlet-eyed talent.

So the Mill Factors creditors are up the creek; the auditors and/or their insurors—and the auditors' colleagues in the accounting profession, whose liability insurance premiums increase geometrically from year to year—are out $5 million. What has the American Institute of CPAs done in all this? I must assume there is another open file yawning somewhere waiting for God knows what. It may be of interest that the principal partner of Mill Factors' auditors is, as of this writing, the chairman of the Accounting Principles Board, responsible for decreeing the good doctrine. Our colleagues, may they always be right, are our esteemed colleagues right or wrong.

Corresponding breakdowns in the effectiveness of the auditing process are discernible in the Yale Express crack-up as well as the Back-Office Mess in Wall Street. These will be considered in Chapter 11 when studying the conflicts of interest which confront auditors whose firms are also engaged in performing the broad spectrum of services known as management consulting.

Chapter 6

Some More "Flap in GAAP"

A REMARKABLE phenomenon of the 1960s was the mushrooming of the computer-leasing industry—firms who purchased computer hardware from the manufacturer (IBM, Control Data, Honeywell, etc.) and leased it to customers who, for economic reasons, or because their financial statements took on a prettier face that way, preferred to lease rather than buy. For a while it appeared that there could be no end to their phenomenal accomplishments—at least when judged by the way in which Wall Street looked upon one of the more important computer lessors, Leasco Data Processing Equipment Corporation, and especially its then-under-thirty president and guiding genius, Saul Steinberg.

There was good reason for Wall Street's implicit faith in Steinberg. It was he who, sheepskin in hand fom Wharton, took over his family's most modest business, involved it in some leasing activities, under the rubric Ideal Leasing, and soon had this mom and pop business transmuted (by exponential extrapolation) into Leasco. How proud his father must have been to see Saul Steinberg's stellar performance, whereby a humble business begun in 1961 as a "predecessor partnership" (as the prospectuses told us) within seven years zoomed into a major firm listed on the New York Stock Exchange, acquired almost all of the shares of a respectable 150-year-old insurance company (Reliance), and threatened the almighties in the banking world by moving to take over a keystone of the Establishment, the Chemical Bank New York Trust.

Leasco Again: Profit or Loss?

How sad it is, then to read in an early-1971 *Forbes* article about how fate has turned, and how the mighty mountains have tumbled. Here's the way the article described the decline, if not the fall:

> Late last month Steinberg announced the long-anticipated bad news: Leasco had lost $30.8 million in fiscal 1970 (ended Sept. 30).
>
> But what the highly publicized problems of Pergamon overshadowed were many other setbacks; Leasco discontinued several consulting and software operations; $5.7 million of unused computer time-sharing equipment was written down; carrying value of land was reduced by $1.9 million; $2.6 million of investment in two foreign data processing companies was written off. All told, Leasco's noninsurance businesses (mostly computer) reported extraordinary losses of $20.2 million plus operating losses of another $4 million.
>
> In other words, excluding the $24 million Pergamon write-off and $17.5 million in profits from Reliance Insurance, acquired in 1968, Leasco lost $24 million last year in the noninsurance ventures, mostly the computer business. This exceeds the $17.2 million Leasco claimed it made from its noninsurance operations from 1962 to 1969. Conclusion: In its nine-year history, insurance profits aside, Leasco has lost $7 million, mainly in the computer business.

The Pergamon loss to which *Forbes* alluded was on a 38 percent investment in the shares of Pergamon Press Ltd., an international technical and scientific publishing company based in Oxford, England. Leasco bought those shares in June, 1969, for $24 million and was offering to acquire the other 62 percent at the same price of $4.44 per share (which would have involved another $38 million or so).

In any event, after committing itself, Leasco did some checking of Pergamon's books, whereupon, in August, 1969, it withdrew its offer. As a consequence trading in Pergamon's shares was suspended on the London Stock Exchange; a major controversy brewed in England as to the reliability of Pergamon's audit reports (causing the halos of the English chartered accountants to tarnish a bit); then, a reaudit by Price Waterhouse & Co. disclosed that Pergamon sustained losses for 1968 and 1969.

Because of these subsequent disclosures Leasco aborted any further negotiations and wrote this $24 million investment all the way down to $1.

We haven't heard the end of this saga. Robert Maxwell, Pergamon's guiding genius, is suing Leasco and "certain of its directors and officers"; to round out the Donnybrook, Leasco is suing Maxwell—and no one knows how that will end.

But it will leave me with a certain sense of regret. I cannot help but feel that both English and American financial circles would have been much enlivened had Steinberg and Maxwell been permitted to develop a working relationship.

The *Forbes* article continued: "After all that was written about 'boy-genius' Steinberg . . . it is almost comic to realize that Leasco has never made a nickel except for Reliance Insurance. . . ." In the light of my late-1968 *Barron's* article describing the accounting practices of this "industry," I'm amazed *Forbes* is amazed. As I saw it then (and as Leasco and *Forbes* now confirm) the industry was essentially floating on the flabbiness in GAAP.

Because it may be of more than mere historical interest, here's the article from the December 2, 1968, issue of *Barron's*, entitled "All a Fandangle? Computer Leasing Accountancy, Says an Expert, Is Dazzling and Unreal."

*   *   *

The dictionary defines a fandangle as a "fantastic ornament" or "tomfoolery." Yet the term perhaps best is described by the kind of glorious, spectacular entertainment found in the Texas hill country—an entertainment that's bound to impress even the most sophisticated Easterner. From Wall Street's vantage point "fandangle" aptly describes the accounting practices used by that recent phenomenon on the economic horizon—the computer leasing company.

More specifically, we find ourselves bedazzled by the accounting by this fledgling industry for depreciation, income taxes, corporate acquisitions and the issuance of equity securities. Our belief is that these practices and procedures have been lifted from Generally Accepted Accounting Principles ("GAAP") with one primary objective—to create an air of excitement regarding performance, to give an unreal appearance of accomplishments and to offer the promise of even greater attainments tomorrow. In short, it's all a fandangle.

Ex the Tomfoolery

The industry's economics, stripped of its ornamentation and tomfoolery, is relatively simple to understand. By way of illustration, say that a computer leasing company finds a customer in need of an IBM 360-40 system, which can be either bought for $900,000 or leased from IBM for $19,550 per month. The leasing company will arrange to buy the computer from IBM and rent it to the client at a substantial discount from IBM's charge, provided the user enters into a long-term lease.

Now, let's make a few other assumptions. One is that the initial lease is for four years at a rental of $16,000 a month (about 82% of IBM's charge). Another is that the leasing company succeeds immediately in renting the 360 for another four years at $14,000 a month (about 87% of the initial rental) and that it can place the system during the ninth and tenth years at $12,000 a month (about 85% of the previous rate). We further assume that at the end of this 10-year period the system has a $135,000 salvage value (15% of the $900,000 original cost).

Apart from anything else, it should be evident that the assumptions figure on a most optimistic decade of utilization for the 360, since they anticipated no gaps in the leasing stream and a 15% residual value at the end of 10 years.

So far as income taxes are concerned, in our example, the leasing company obtains the immediate benefit from the 7% investment credit and need pay no tax until it has recouped the entire amount of its outlay (to which we add a nominal cost of $8,000 for procuring the lease). At first blush, this cost recovery for tax purposes might appear unrealistically generous. Nonetheless, the use of the declining-balance depreciation methods provided by the Internal Revenue Code, and the relatively short life expectancies used by these companies for tax purposes, permits us to make this assumption without seriously distorting the computations in favor of the leasing company. Putting all these factors into better perspective, we have Table I.

TABLE I

Period	Description	Amount	Total
Immediately	Purchase of Computer	ᵃ $(900,000)	
	Investment Credit	63,000	
	Procurement Expense	(8,000)	(845,000)
First 48 months	Monthly Rentals	16,000 × 48	768,000
Next 10 months	Monthly Rentals	14,000 × 10	140,000
Next 38 months	Monthly Rentals	14,000	
	Tax at 50%	(7,000)	
	Net Rentals	7,000 × 38	266,000
Next 24 months	Monthly Rentals	12,000	
	Tax at 50%	(6,000)	
	Net Rentals	6,000 × 24	144,000
End of 10 years	Residual Value	135,000	
	Tax at 50%	67,500	67,500
Net Cash Inflow Over the 10-Year Period			$540,500

ᵃ Amounts in brackets represent cash outflows; all other sums are inflows.

When we apply the common capital budgeting technique of determining the rate of return on this computer leasing company's investment we find that this investment is producing a gross yield of only about 13% per annum (slightly over 1% per month). This relatively speaking modest return for a high risk is without any deduction for administrative costs, losses from uncollectible rentals, and again, after making all of the favorable assumptions described above.

Now, we turn to the ways in which the accounting profession may have contributed to the confusion which prevails over earnings of computer leasing companies. Opinion No. 7 of the American Institute of CPA's Accounting Principles Board, entitled "Accounting for Leases in Financial Statements of Lessors," establishes two means of accounting for revenues and costs—the "financing" and "operating" methods. The financing method is generally appropriate for basically financial institutions where the lease is designed "to pass all or most of the usual ownership risks or rewards to the lessee, and to assure the lessor of, and generally limit him to, a full recovery of his investment plus a reasonable return on the use of the funds invested, subject only to the credit risks generally associated with secured loans."

Risks or Rewards

In various published investment analyses, Leasco Data Processing has been singled out to exemplify lessors that indulge in this kind of lease, since it is presumed to write almost exclusively "non-cancellable full payout leases." As one analyst stated: "This lease . . . is non-cancellable during the initial term, thereby assuring that Leasco will recoup its entire investment. By removing the risk that equipment will be returned before its full investment is recovered, Leasco can offer this type of lease at a saving of 20% and more over the manufacturers' lease rentals."

By contrast, the "operating" method comes into play where a lessor retains "the usual risks or rewards of ownership in connection with their leasing activity." Also, the lessor may be expected to maintain the leased property or furnish related services which involve future costs. Here, rental revenues "are designed to cover the costs of these services; depreciation and obsolescence, and to provide an adequate profit for assuming the risks involved." While they don't exactly render related services (usually the lessee is expected to enter into a maintenance contract with the manufacturer), Levin-Townsend and most others in the business follow this "operating" method.

The two methods produce significantly different results. Thus, the financial method (which we'll call the "Leasco method," for the moment) would take the excess of the gross inflow (gross rentals expected over the 10-year-life plus the ultimate residual value) over the cost, and spread the difference over the 10-year period of the lease. The excess in our example would be determined about as follows:

Inflows:		
First 48 months at 16,000	$768,000	
Next 48 months at 14,000	672,000	
Next 24 months at 12,000	288,000	
Residual Value	135,000	
Total Inflows		$1,863,000
Outflows:		
Cost of Computer	$900,000	
Procurement Cost	8,000	
Total Outflows		908,000
Excess of Inflows Over Outflows		$ 955,000

(The foregoing deliberately ignores income taxes; they will, however, be considered subsequently.)

To allocate profits over the lease period, the lessor would use the sum-of-the-year's-digits method so that the $955,000 excess would be allocated over 10 years in the ratio of 10/55ths for the first year and on down to 1/55th for the final year. (The denominator 55 represents the sum-of-the-years' digits for the years 1 through 10; the numerator 10 is the weight assigned to the first year, and the 1 for the last; the second year's allocation would be 9/55, and the eighth year 3/55, etc.) Under the financing method, the first year would receive a credit for lease income of $174,000 (10/55 × 995,000).

Under the "operating" alternative, the lessor would show first year's income from operations (again on a pre-tax basis) of $107,500, determined as follows:

Rental Income	$192,000
Less Depreciation	
(Most companies are using a 10-year life with a residual value of 15% and report the depreciation on a straight line basis for financial statement purposes, hence: 10% × 85% × 900,000)	76,500
Income Net of Depreciation	$115,500
Less Procurement Cost	
(Here some companies will write off the entire sum in a single year, others will defer the cost over the life of the lease—we'll assume an immediate write-off for the sake of conservative accounting)	8,000
First Year's Income Before Taxes	$107,500

What income taxes come due under either method? Actually, very little. In fact, for tax purposes both would report income collected of $192,000 and deduct the full acquisition cost of $8,000, leaving $184,000 as the net revenues for the first year.

Furthermore, both would claim double-declining balance depreciation, using an eight-year life (to get the full measure of the investment credit). Depreciation for the first year would be $225,000 (2 × 12½% × $900,000). Hence, an actual operating loss is being reflected on the tax returns, and there is an "extra shot in the locker"—the $63,000 investment credit available whenever a lessor needs to generate some extraordinary income.

Of course, financial statements now are required to give at least a curtsy to the income tax law; under present rules corporations are permitted (even if not encouraged) by the AICPA to "flow through" the investment credit, but must "normalize" the tax with reference to the depreciation charge (so that the liability is shown on the income statement as if depreciation claimed on the tax return was identical with the far lesser sums claimed in shareholder reports).

Using a rate of 50%, the "financing method" lessor would show a tax cost on its financial statements of $24,000 (50% of the income of $174,000, or $87,000, minus the $63,000 investment credit). Again, none of this is currently payable—it all goes into the deferred tax account. The "operating method" lessor, in turn, would probably show no tax for the initial year, even for financial statement purposes; the 50% tax on $107,500 —$53,750—would be more than offset by the investment credit.

This critical distinction between the "financial method" and the "operating method" was especially well formulated by Saul P. Steinberg, Leasco's chairman. In a letter to *Barron's* in the fall of 1966, responding to a criticism of Leasco's accounting methods, Steinberg asserted that, if anything, his company's commitment to the full payout lease, and its use of the financing method, produces a much lower amount of reported income than the operating method of lease income accounting—the one used by almost all other computer lessors.

Here's How

Because of his special expertise, and because it demonstrates that when you change the ingredients for the fandangle you get a diametrically opposite reaction from the accounting mix, we set forth Mr. Steinberg's illustrative comparison.

Mr. Steinberg used as the basis for his comparison a five-year lease of equipment costing $10,000, for a total rental over the five-year period of $13,000. His comparison is set forth in Table II.

Mr. Steinberg emphasized that companies using the Levin-Townsend method in this example would earn $8,500 after depreciation, while Leasco would net $3,500. In addition, while at the end of the five-year period Leasco would be left with a residual book value or estimated additional amount of $500, companies "using" the operating method would carry on their books equipment valued at $5,500.

TABLE II

Leasco Method:

Gross Rental	$13,000
Estimated Salvage Value (5% of cost)	500
Total Inflow	$13,500
Less Cost of Equipment	10,000
Total Profit To Be Reported	$ 3,500

	Years					
	1	2	3	4	5	Total
Portion of Total Profit (Based on Sum-of-Years'-Digits Method)	5/15	4/15	3/15	2/15	1/15	15/15
Profit Reported	1155	910	700	455	280	3500
Interest and Credit Insurance	(819)	(637)	(455)	(273)	(91)	(2275)
Income Before Operating Expenses and Taxes	336	273	245	182	189	1225

Levin-Townsend, et al., Method:

	Years					
	1	2	3	4	5	Total
Rental Income	2600	2600	2600	2600	2600	13000
Depreciation 10% of Cost After Deducting a 10% Salvage Value	(900)	(900)	(900)	(900)	(900)	4500
Income After Depreciation	1700	1700	1700	1700	1700	8500
Interest and Assumed Credit Insurance	(819)	(637)	(455)	(273)	(91)	(2275)
Income Before Operating Expenses and Taxes	881	1063	1245	1427	1809	8225

By way of extending this invidious distinction, Leasco (as reported in one brokerage house analysis) estimated that its "reported pre-tax profit of $679,000 for the fiscal year ended September 30, 1966, would have been $1.988 million had the revenue method of accounting employed by Management Assistance, Levin-Townsend, etc. been used." Incidentally, this study added: "It may be noted that no other leasing company has credit insurance, nor will its equipment be fully amortized until at least five years after Leasco's."

We are not questioning Mr. Steinberg's arithmetic—he is, as noted, chairman of Leasco and is particularly knowledgeable with regard to the accounting for computer leasing companies. The young executive succinctly and effectively demonstrates the serious gap in reported income capable of being generated by the two principal accounting alternatives—both of which carry the full approval of the AICPA and the legitimacy of GAAP.

But that is not the entire moral pointed up by the Steinberg denigration of the Levin-Townsend type of accounting. His letter made the following additional points:

1. His company writes only leases that bring back the full cost of the equipment.

2. It amortizes the cost of the equipment over the original term of the lease and is left with a salvage or estimated residual value of only approximately 5%.

3. It insures every lease against default for any reason whatsoever. This coverage is for 85% of the receivable.

Thus spoke Leasco in late 1966—and again in 1967. More recent security analyses have perpetuated this Steinberg gospel regarding Leasco's special brand of accounting virtue. And so it came as something of a surprise to see, neatly tucked away (literally, because of the unique foldover in the report), the following footnote 2 (b) to the 1967 report:

"For leases where the company will not recover its cost during the initial term, the accompanying financial statements reflect rentals as income and the equipment is being depreciated over its estimated useful life (8 to 10 years) computed on a straight line basis after allowing for a salvage value of 10%."

And lest the reader assume that Leasco has been contaminated only ever so slightly, a proxy statement issued in June, 1968, showed the following comparative data regarding revenues derived during the six-month periods ended in 1967 and 1968:

	1967	1968
Earned income on lease contracts (i.e., from the much-heralded Leasco full-payout lease)	$1,916,054	$3,086,703
Computer rental income (the vulgar kind realized by Levin-Townsend, *et al.*)	zero	$4,068,827

Obviously, the accounting method which Mr. Steinberg criticized as producing a major overstatement *vis-à-vis* the Leasco method has now become the dominant method at his company during the current fiscal year. One can only surmise regarding the reasons why, but we cannot help but be reminded of Will Rogers' counsel: "Beware when you wear a halo—when it slips, it becomes a noose."

Further, we would have been far happier regarding the implications of the auditor's certificate for 1967 if it had set forth loud and clear that while the accounting principles may have been consistent from year to year, the business practices and policies had changed so drastically as to make the 1967 statements inconsistent with those for the year preceding. Instead, the certificate concludes with the traditional *nihil obstat*: "In our opinion, the financial statements . . . (are) in conformity with generally accepted accounting principles applied on a basis consistent with that of the preceding year."

In truth: Are they really?

In the very last subparagraph of the "Notes to Financial Statements" in the June, 1968, proxy, we are told: "Until January 1, 1968, the company carried credit insurance at which time the policy was not renewed. The company's management believes that the cost of credit insurance is not now justified in the light of its credit experience and the size and diversification of its lease receivables. Accordingly, the company intends to be a self-insurer in this respect in the future, and to the extent necessary, has established reserves of approximately $20,000 in respect of anticipated losses. The company has filed an action against the insurance carrier for refusal to pay certain claims asserted by the company under the credit insurance policy. For additional information see 'litigation' in the prospectus."

The "litigation" section essentially restates the foregoing facts, adding: "It is the opinion of . . . counsel for Leasco, that Leasco should prevail with respect to all claims filed prior to the date provided for in the policy." But from Leasco's amended complaint filed in Nassau County Supreme Court last May, we culled a few other significant details regarding the litigation. Apparently, it was the Insurance Co. of North America (INA) which "refused to renew" the policy, not Leasco. Moreover, while Leasco, in the view of counsel, should be expected to prevail, and $20,000 might be the appropriate reserve for doubtful accounts, the complaint demands almost $8.6 million (with interest thereon, together with the costs and disbursements) as the amount owing by INA by reference to amounts then in default on Leasco's leases.

Clearly, then, Mr. Steinberg's protestations, however valid they may have been when he asserted them in 1966, are now merely vestigial. Paralleling his numbered assertions, and in their stead, we submit:

1. Leasco no longer writes only leases that bring back the full cost of the equipment. In fact, such leases are becoming a minor portion of its leasing activities.

2. Leasco no longer amortizes the cost of the equipment over the original term of the lease.

3. Leasco's accounting no longer leaves it with a salvage or estimated residual value of only approximately 5% at the close of the original term of the lease.

4. Leasco no longer insures "against default for any reason whatsoever."

How and when should Mr. Steinberg have proclaimed these critical changes in his company's operating and related accounting methods? Undoubtedly he should have been as diligent in announcing the loss of innocence as he was in describing his company's virtues.

As to the when—it should have been forthwith. Thus, since the 1967 Auditor's Report (for the fiscal year ending September 30) was dated December 11, 1967, and makes no reference to the termination of the credit insurance, we might infer that INA did not make known its refusal to renew until some time between December 11, 1967, and January 1, 1968. Mr. Steinberg should have moved immediately to exorcise the prevailing myth, possibly as a rider to the 1967 report which was probably then in the process of being mailed "to our shareholders."

Critical Choice

Clearly, the choice of accounting alternatives—financing vs. operating—produces a critical distinction in the reported results. And contributing to the excitement created by the accounting for computer leasing companies is their universal use of the "flow through" method for the investment credit, which gives the first year's income a dramatic net-after-tax injection. It can be expected that this shot-in-the-arm at least can be perpetuated, and perhaps even expanded, so long as new properties are acquired and the investment credit retained. Otherwise, succeeding years may suffer grievously by comparison.

Another factor that somehow manages to get light treatment is the possibility of obsolescence. To compete financially with hardware manufacturers, the lessors have figured on a 12-year stretch-out of the computer's useful life. But is a 12-year period of wear-and-tear, and obsolescence, warranted for equipment which has been marked by rapid dramatic technological change? Thus, is it fair to schedule the depreciation charge so that after five years the balance sheet still shows a value equal to more than 50% of the original cost? It may well be that if the third-generation computer systems are the ultimate of modern man's creative process, such a deferral might be warranted. However, events of the past decade hardly support the view that computer technology will mark time.

How would we put an end to the fandangle? A "book of

rules" which might be established would at the very least pertain to depreciation policies and practices, to the accounting for the cost of borrowing, the compensation of executives, the accounting for taxes (including the investment credit), the fuller disclosure of prior liens given to banks and other lenders on the equipment owned by the corporation, showing rather fully the stockholder residual stake (if any) in the various pools of equipment, categorized by type and age, and the like. The standards should require the independent auditor on his own and direct responsibility to determine whether the carrying values for the receivables and equipment are consistent with all of the circumstances discernible by him (the auditor does have special expertise, since his firm is undoubtedly using sophisticated computer technology).

As we've seen, the computer-leasing accounting fandangle comprises spine-tingling fun and games. If the excitement were restricted to knowledgeable investors capable of absorbing major risks, we could have little quarrel. It is when we see the bedazzlement and the delusion spreading to ensnare the multitudes that it becomes necessary to call a halt to the game.

*   *   *

In writing this article (which also commented critically on Leasco's pooling of interests accounting, and the accounting practices followed by Levin-Townsend, another computer lessor) I didn't require a sixth sense in accountancy. The article merely called upon the accounting profession to recognize that they were perpetrating an obvious distortion by permitting the equipment costs to be written off over a long-attenuated period, a period which our professional conscience and consciousness undoubtedly told us was unreal, while the lessor was picking up the rentals from the hardware on a front-end-loaded basis, that is, in the early years of the equipment's life, when the equipment was undoubtedly in greater demand, and relatively more efficient.

Did Wall Street see this? I just can't see how they could possibly have missed it. But 1968 was a "Year of the Roaring Bull";

as a consequence reality, facts, and substance, like truth in war-time, became the first casualties—and the computer lessors were riding to their zenith. High riding undoubtedly helped Mr. Steinberg to believe the stuff being written about him, and in this expansive mood enter the lists against Chemical Bank, having just vanquished Reliance.

Have You Read Any Good Balance Sheets Lately?

Forbes' commentary was, as noted, predicated on their study of Leasco's 1970 income statement. When we pause to study their balance sheet at that date, we find a symmetrical state of lack of substance, absent Reliance. In other words (using phraseology paralleling *Forbes'*), excluding the $164 million of carrying value for Reliance Insurance acquired in 1968, Leasco had *no* net book value. In its nine-year history, its insurance-company acquisition aside, Leasco accumulated nothing—its computer-leasing profits (whatever they may have been) just evaporated or were diverted to various will-of-the-wisp investments, to Pergamon Press—and to an over $80 million payoff to the special group of investors who helped Steinberg get Reliance. They helped him get it on a highly questionable basis, even under the old accounting field rules, which permitted him to use pooling of interests accounting for that acquisition.

This conclusion, based on my analysis of the 1970 balance sheet, is supported by the configuration shown on the opposite page.

This summary is not a mere exercise in arithmetic in this context. In the Leasco case it might have been fairer for the shareholders to be given the corporation's *unconsolidated* balance sheet rather than the fully consolidated one found in the annual report. In most instances such a full consolidation is more meaningful, since it demonstrates the total resources available to the company for the fulfillment of its objectives. But it is usual for insurance-company subsidiaries to be left out of such a full consolidation since their resources are not generally

	Leasco's Fully Consolidated Balance Sheet	Reliance Insurance Company (Including its Life Insurance Subsidiary)	Leasco Excluding Reliance Insurance (cols. 1 minus 2)
	(1)	(2)	(3)

Assets:

(All amounts in millions)

	(1)	(2)	(3)
Common and preferred stock at cost	$ 174	$173	$ 1
Bonds at amortized cost	311	313	(2)*
Cash and certificates of deposit	110	29	81
Accounts and notes receivable	115	68	47
Finance lease receivables	60	—	60
Rental equipment (depreciated cost)	252	—	252
Prepaid expenses	50	47	3
Policy and first-mortgage loans	38	38	—
Real estate—at cost	26	17	9
Computers, furniture, and equipment (depreciated cost)	21	4	17
Goodwill	16	—	16
Other assets	29	38	(9)*
Total Assets	$1,202	$727	$475

Liabilities:

	(1)	(2)	(3)
Unearned insurance premiums	196	195	1
Unpaid insurance losses	220	218	2
Life policies and reserves	95	99	(4)*
Notes payable	292		292
Accounts payable and accruals	76	24	52
Federal and foreign taxes	21	24	(3)*
Due on purchase of securities**	33		33
Subordinated and convertible debt	99		99
Minority interests	7		7
Total Liabilities	1,039	560	479
Equity	$ 163	$167	$ (4)

* These incongruous balances undoubtedly result from the differences in classification and nomenclature used by Leasco, *et al.*, in the statement presentations.

** Represents the balance owing on the reacquisition of Leasco's preferred stock, described on pages 95-99.

available for the commercial and industrial operations of the parent company. This becomes evident when we realize that of the $710 million in liquid assets shown by Leasco's consolidated balance sheet (marketable securities, cash, and receivables), over 80 percent were not under Leasco's direct dominion and control, but instead were the property of its insurance subsidiaries. Nor may these "sequestered" liquid pools, comprising almost half of the gross assets of the Leasco complex, be diverted to the parent company except to the extent Reliance complies with the standards laid down by the insurance commissions of the states to which it is responsible.

Further, as I described in greater detail when considering Leasco's pooling proclivities, it borrowed $40 million for a period of two years from seven domestic banks under two term-credit agreements secured by 62 percent of Leasco's ownership of the stock of Reliance Insurance Company. The remaining $45 million was borrowed by two subsidiaries—$30 million secured by Leasco's computer hardware.

Thus, in view of the restrictions imposed by regulatory agencies and by the collateral agreement covering 62 percent of Reliance shares, I would recast Leasco's 1970 balance sheet along the following lines (thereby excluding its investments in Reliance) as follows (again, data in millions):

Assets:		Liabilities:	
Cash	$ 81	Notes payable	$292
Accounts and notes receivable	47	Due on reacquisition of preferred stock	33
Finance lease receivables	60	Accounts payable	52
Rental equipment	252		
Other assets (excluding goodwill)	20	Subordinated and convertible debt	99
Total	$460	Total	$476
		Equity (including the equity of minority interests)	nil

This "nil" for the Shareholders' Equity is especially disconcerting when we realize that the Convertible Preferred stockholders have a prior stake in the staggering amount of $197 million on Leasco's resources. The unaccounted-for-liability results from the preferred stock indenture requirement for a sinking fund and mandatory redemption by 1991–93—unless the shares are converted before then. In view of the prevailing deep discount from the conversion price such a conversion cannot be presently assumed. For a detailed analysis of this Damoclean phenomenon see the "$200 Million Question" in *Barron's*, December 18, 1972.

In short, my schematic balance sheet was intended to demonstrate the far more austere pools of resources available to Leasco for its traditional operations than those implied by the consolidated balance sheet generally disseminated by the company.

Again, I'm not denying the important value implicit in Reliance—but of what use is this value in Leasco's pursuit of its primary objective—that which gave it its birthright and name, namely, leasing data-processing equipment?

I have given inordinate consideration to a single corporation, both in this context as well as when considering some of the happenings during the halcyon days of the merger movement. But Leasco's accountings are especially fascinating, since in this single corporation's brief existence it demonstrated the ability to get revved up by the computer-leasing calculus; it used its high price/earnings multiple (applied to its exaggerated earnings, producing an exhilarating market price for its shares) as the catalyst for taking over Reliance; after the takeover it used Reliance's securities portfolio as a lever to produce still higher consolidated earnings. Leasco was also able to prevail upon its auditors to produce a 1970 balance sheet manifesting substantial affluence, albeit less than a year earlier in view of the $65 million pay-out on the put option given to some of the Reliance shareholders, a $30 million loss, and $9 million in preferred dividend. This manifestation of affluence is beyond what I would characterize as fair. Undoubtedly, though, Leasco's statements must be "fair in accordance with GAAP"—how else would the auditors and the SEC go along with them?

Having submitted this less than flattering commentary for inclusion in this work I was stunned to read later on in the December 1, 1971 *Wall Street Journal* that, "Leasco Corp. . . . said it arranged an $85 million six-year revolving credit term loan from 20 domestic and international banks, mostly to refinance current indebtedness." The article then told that the company was "initially borrowing $80 million. Of that, $48 million is to prepay [Leasco's] secured indebtedness . . . [principally] secured in 1970 by 62% of the stock of Reliance Insurance. . . ." And then, for me, the particularly dramatic announcement: "Leasco said the lien on the Stock has been released."

"It Can't Be"

My initial reaction was to say "this couldn't be—not in the light of my analysis." Surely, I surmised, the *Wall Street Journal* was fantasizing—they must have gotten the name of the company all wrong. But the receipt of the News Release from Leasco's Vice President-Corporate Affairs torpedoed that hypothesis. There, in black and white, was the underscored capitalized caption *"Leasco Completes $85 Million Unsecured, Six-Year Term Financing."*

I then presumed that the company's operations must have prospered since I developed my dismal calculus, whereupon I updated the configuration shown on page 150 by reference to the 1971 fiscal year data. The revised configuration (included in the notes section) did show an improvement from "nil" to $6 million, hardly enough to warrant this act of abject confidence on the part of the "20 domestic and international banks" who agreed to the release of the collateral held by them.

The unraveling thread is the second sentence of the News Release, "This six-year, revolving credit term loan extended to

two Leasco wholly-owned domestic financing subsidiaries. . . ."
[Emphasis supplied.] We must, then, look to see the stuff those subs are made of; we get a remarkably good glimpse of them in the form 8-K filed by Leasco "For the Month of November 1971." I trust each of you has convenient and ready access, on a continuous basis, to these forms. Just in case you don't, herewith some of the statements contained therein:

> Item 7(b). On November 30, 1971 (i) pursuant to a Loan Agreement, dated as of November 23, 1971, among Registrant, Leasco Borrowing Corporation ("Leasco Borrowing"), a Delaware corporation all of whose outstanding securities are owned by Registrant, Leasco Financial Services Corporation ("Leasco Financial"), a Delaware corporation all of whose outstanding securities are owned by Registrant, Continental Illinois National Bank and Trust Company of Chicago ("Continental Bank"), as Agent, and certain Banks which are parties to the Loan Agreement, a conformed copy of which is annexed hereto as Exhibit 13(b)(1), Leasco Borrowing borrowed $48,000,000 from such Banks and issued its Notes, guaranteed by the Registrant and Leasco Financial, to evidence such borrowings, and (ii) pursuant to a Credit Agreement, dated as of November 23, 1971, among Registrant, Leasco Financial, Continental Illinois, as Agent and certain Banks which are parties to the Credit Agreement, a conformed copy of which is annexed hereto as Exhibit 13(b)(2), Leasco Financial borrowed $32,000,000 from such Banks and issued its Notes, guaranteed by Registrant, to evidence such borrowings. Leasco Financial may borrow an additional $5,000,000 under the terms of the Credit Agreement.

Probably even more informative was the following item under "Other Materially Important Events":

> Item 12(a). Concurrently with the occurrence of the transactions described in [Item 7] . . . hereof, Registrant [Leasco] transferred 5,453,907 shares of common stock, par value $5 per share, of Reliance Insurance Company ("Reliance") to Leasco Financial in exchange for 1,000 shares of common stock, par value $.10 per share, of Leasco Financial and Leasco Financial transferred 3,260,000 of such shares of Reliance common stock to Leasco Bor-

rowing in exchange for 1,000 shares of common stock, par value $.10 per share, of Leasco Borrowing. The shares of Reliance common stock so owned by Leasco Financial and Leasco Borrowing constitute approximately 97% of the oustanding Reliance common stock. As a result of such transaction, Registrant now owns all of the outstanding common stock of Leasco Financial and Leasco Borrowing.

(b). The Loan Agreement and the Credit Agreement described in Item 7 hereof provide, among other things, that (i) the Registrant will not permit its consolidated net worth to be less than the sum of $165,000,000, plus $10,000,000 for each twelve month period elapsed since September 30, 1971, (ii) the Registrant may not incur indebtedness in connection with the acquisition of a new business and may not incur indebtedness in excess of $10,000,000 in connection with the making of loans, advances or investments in any new business in which any equity is owned by the Registrant, (iii) Registrant may not, after September 30, 1970, pay any cash dividends on its common stock or acquire shares of its capital stock unless after giving effect to such event, all payments so made after September 30, 1970 shall not exceed the consolidated net income of Registrant since October 1, 1970. . . .

Comfortably ensconced in the SEC library (where else does one find these 8-Ks unless you subscribe to the microfiche service provided, ironically, by Leasco?), I did turn to the Exhibits 13 (b)(1) and (2) referred to at Item 7(b). These two agreements—covering the "Unsecured" (sic) borrowings, permitting the shares evidencing 62 percent of Leasco's investment in Reliance to be released from the previous lien—aggregate some 30 pages of substantive matter (excluding another dozen or so for the protocol). These pages are so heavily loaded with "whereases," "warranties," "conditions to loans," "guarantees," "covenants," and "events of default" as to make it appear that Leasco was buying a television set on time—rather than merely borrowing $85 million on an unsecured basis. These guaranties, covenants, warranties, and other constraints relate to Leasco, per se, as well as these newly created financing subsidiaries.

Lest I've lost you in this maze of high finance here is the way the old loan secured by but 62 percent of Leasco's ownership of Reliance was, as I view the transaction, transmuted into one which gave the bankers a strangle-hold on 100 percent of that investment:

1. Leasco put all of its 5,453,907 shares of Reliance into a brand new Leasco subsidiary, Leasco Financial Services Corporation ("Leasco Financial").

2. Leasco Financial then took 3,260,000 of the aforementioned Reliance shares and put them into *its* newly created subsidiary, Leasco Borrowing Corporation ("Leasco Borrowing").

3. Leasco Financial then borrowed $32 million from a consortium of foreign or "international" banks; Leasco Borrowing (couldn't they have developed some more imaginative names?) borrowed $48 million from a consortium of domestic banks. (Continental Illinois is the "Agent" for both of these lending groups.)

4. The loans made to Leasco Borrowing were guaranteed by its parent, Leasco Financial and Leasco, per se. Those made to Leasco Financial were guaranteed by its parent, i.e., Leasco.

5. Pursuant to these "unsecured" loan agreements the newly created subsidiaries are categorically forbidden to engage "in any trade or business except that of borrowing money and lending money to [Leasco and its subsidiaries] and transactions directly related thereto."

6. To my lay mind, it appears that neither Financial nor Borrowing can breathe without prior consent from their "unsecured creditors"; and when one reads the paragraph after paragraph of limitations imposed on Leasco itself, one wonders whether it's the bankers or Steinberg who will be in the saddle.

By way of a tangential insight into this borrowing, it appears from a so-called "term sheet" developed by Leasco as an incident to this borrowing that balances are "To be maintained with each lender at 20% of their outstanding indebtedness." What this means is that of the $85 million credit only $68 million will really be available to Leasco—or slightly more than what Leasco had to apply to repaying the old indebtedness. It may be that the banks, with characteristic *noblesse oblige,* left Leasco with enough to pay for the expenses of this new financing. Of course, Leasco might be permitted to use $17 million of the money belonging to the policyholders and claimants of Reliance for these interest-free compensating balances required to be kept with the lending banks by these agreements. That, in turn, raises the question as to whether the regulatory agencies would or should permit such a sterilization of "other peoples' money"—but that's another story.

All this was, essentially, a critical commentary on the lack of forthrightness on the part of the company in the "managed and massaged" news release. Surely one would expect that the whole, unvarnished truth would be exposed for all to see in the certified financial statements promulgated for Leasco's year ended September 30, 1971. While it is true that this major borrowing transaction occurred after September 30, present standards require the certifying auditor to take cognizance of post-balance sheet events of such magnitude. And here things become even more confusing for me.

The certified public accountants' clean certificate was dated November 18, 1971. Footnote 5 of that report, as "additional information," tells us "Reference is made to the financial review section for additional information regarding . . . notes payable. . . ." Turning to that section, I did find a complete analysis of the notes payable as of September 30, 1971; especially significant in this context are the references to the promissory notes, credit notes and term loan notes aggregating $48 million. Thus, the $12 million in promissory notes due in instalments over 1972–1974, the $16 million in the October, 1972 credit notes, and $20 million in the October, 1972 term loan notes, all carry the legend "paid November 30, 1972."

This leads inexorably to the "new financing" section of the financial review which informs us that:

> On November 30, 1971, Leasco, through two wholly-owned domestic financing subsidiaries (which own Leasco's Reliance stock), completed financing of $85 million, unsecured, for a six-

year term at an interest rate of ¾% over prime in years one and two, and 1% over prime in years three through six. This extension of credit has been guaranteed by the parent company. $80 million has been borrowed and the proceeds were used to prepay the $48,000,000 parent company indebtedness outstanding at September 30, 1971. An additional $15,305,000 will be used to pay indebtedness of an international financing subsidiary maturing in March 1972, and the balance of $16,695,000 has been added to the general working funds of the company. $5 million remains available to be borrowed over the next two years. As a result of this financing, the parent company has no direct indebtedness. . . .

My aggravated confusion, of course, begins with my inability to comprehend how a November 18, 1971, clean certificate can incorporate by reference a most significant statement in the financial review section which speaks of a November 30, 1971, transaction in the past tense.

Going beyond this chronological incongruity, and turning to the substance of the statements in the financial review, I will, with some far-fetched rationalization, accept for the present the reiterated assertion that these new borrowings were unsecured. How could any responsible accountant, presumed to be familiar with concepts of debits and credits, assets, liabilities, and capital, swallow the pap about "As a result of this financing, the parent company has no direct indebtedness"? Surely, Leasco's borrowing from Leasco Financial and Leasco Borrowing are nothing but such *direct* indebtedness. And if they say these subsidiaries are merely Leasco's *alter egos* then, by the same token, the subsidiaries' borrowings are *direct* indebtedness of Leasco—yes, of the parent company.

As I view this nexus of transactions it adds up to the banks' increasing their hold on the Reliance shares from 62 percent to 100 percent of Leasco's holdings. And what may have prompted this very complicated borrowing arrangement was the desire of the banks to protect their position by relying almost exclusively on the Reliance shares, and thereby avoid getting their hands dirty with Leasco's computer hardware, container equipment,

158 UNACCOUNTABLE ACCOUNTING

and the like. Further, in the event of adversity the banks would not have to be distracted by the plethora of claims from the creditors and shareholders of the parent company; this kind of insulation, I understand, has been of some comfort to banks in the wake of the wreck at Penn Central.

All of which brings me back to where I began this extensive analysis of the Leasco standards of accountability, it's "All a Fandangle." I'm sorry to see that nothing has changed there, at least not for the betterment of their accounting standards, during the three intervening years.

The Lockheed Affair

May, 1971, brought forth a proposal from the President of the United States to the Congress for a quarter-of-a-billion-dollar bail-out loan for the besieged and beleaguered Lockheed Aircraft Corporation—a recommendation identical in amount with that proposed just a year previously for the Penn Central mess. From the published reports Lockheed's troubles are rooted in two crises which occurred in tandem—the C-5A fiasco followed by the Rolls Royce collapse.

I am not aware of any particular aberrations insofar as the Rolls Royce–TriStar crisis is concerned; however, the C-5A saga is a horse of another color.

Thus, on June 4, 1970, the Securities and Exchange Commission issued an order directing public proceedings in the "matter of disclosure by registrants engaged in defense contracting." The order asserted that, based on an inquiry by its staff in the matter of Lockheed Aircraft Corporation, "questions have arisen concerning the adequacy of the disclosures with respect to the costs incurred on major defense contracts of which the C-5A contract is a notable example."

The staff report, entitled "Report of Investigation in the Lockheed Aircraft Corporation—HO 423," in two parts, makes fascinating reading. Volume II deals with trading in Lockheed securities by members of its management and by ten "institutions," that is, mutual funds. The first volume is of particular interest to us for present purposes. After going into the history of the ill-fated C-5A contract, the report moves to question the timing and adequacy of the disclosures by management, and by Lockheed's independent auditors, of the huge cost overruns, and the resultant losses by Lockheed, on that contract. Here is the way the staff report described the central problem (not necessarily in the words used therein):

In September, 1965, the Air Force announced that it had awarded a contract for $1.4 billion to Lockheed to design and build 58 transport aircraft, designated as the C-5A.

Over the period subsequent to the announcement a number of substantial problems arose in connection with the contract, so that by mid-1968 costs had increased from the $1.3 billion projected in the contract to over $2.4 billion. This not only wiped out the anticipated profit but imposed on Lockheed the possibility of very significant losses, jeopardizing the company's overall financial condition.

From the Commission's point of view there is a question as to the adequacy of disclosure in annual and interim filings with the Commission, as well as information prepared for public distribution. There are also questions with respect to disclosures made in a registration statement filed with the Commission in March 1967, covering $125 million in convertible debentures issued by Lockheed.

This, then, was the reason for the Commission's ordering the hearings, which were scheduled and then adjourned—as far as I know, not to be heard of since. The staff's inquiry alluded to a "cure notice" from the Air Force going back to early 1967. Such notice is a formal contract procedure—the first step in a termination action; it enumerates the technical problems and tells the contractor that if the problems are not solved soon, termination procedures may be initiated.

There follows much discussion between the Air Force and Lockheed regarding the mounting cost patterns and projections. References are made to a new numbers game, the amount to be added to the budget for contingencies—the realists on the one hand, the Pollyannas and ostriches on the other. An interesting side note in the report (pages 37–38): The 1967 workpapers of Lockheed's independent auditors, Arthur Young, reflect a suggestion by the firm's Atlanta auditors that a qualified opinion be considered, since there was not a great deal of leeway between current estimates and ceiling or a loss position. However, Arthur Young's Los Angeles office, which directed the audit, decided against it. Also, "One of the Arthur Young auditors during the 1968 audit 'wondered' twice in his audit notes whether Lockheed had suspected trouble at the time of the audit the year before." It is to be emphasized that this was with regard to the 1967 audit—as will become apparent, the auditors didn't really make the magnitude of the crisis known until they issued the 1969 report (during 1970). By that time there was really no way in which the leaking coffins could be kept secret. It was this failure to disclose its difficulties as far back as 1967 that SEC Chairman Casey was alluding to in his June, 1971, testimony before the Congress (referred to in Chapter 2, when considering the canon of timeliness).

In the disclosure section of the report the SEC's staff makes some rather critical observations:

When commenting on the disclosures contained in the 1967 debenture bond prospectus:

> While there was a very general disclosure [of the points at issue] the statements made did not fully and adequately describe all pertinent factors and it requires much reading between the lines, with knowledge of the underlying circumstances, to catch the issues and the real risks facing this company.

The 1967 Annual Report:

This report went to shareholders, we are told, just a few days before the Air Force gave Lockheed some grim projections on its cost overruns, and where even the Corporation was constrained to concede "a small loss position." Nevertheless:

The cover of the report to shareholders showed the roll-out of the first C-5A and the report included various laudatory comments concerning the plane, made by celebrities present at the ceremony on March 2, 1968. Lockheed described the C-5A as "a star destined to play a prodigious role for the Air Force." Physical characteristics were outlined. The plane is on schedule. Production should extend into the late 1970's including derivatives. The report indicated that the first sales of the C-5A contract were recorded in 1967, a total of $117 million. The figure was expected to be nearly $500 million for 1968.

The 1968 Report:

By this time the Air Force was projecting a loss of $285 million. The auditors' footnotes steadfastly maintained "no loss is anticipated on the contract." But even the auditors couldn't persist in this assertion with a straight face (or in good conscience) since they added immediately thereafter: "However, complete realization of the inventory is dependent upon the accuracy of the estimated costs to complete and the legal interpretation of certain clauses in the contract. . . ."

The 1969 Report:

Here the auditors really "split their gut" to lay out the whole five years of history of turbulence surrounding the contract and Lockheed's performance thereon. While still claiming steadfastly that Lockheed could break even they do refer to the possibility of a $500 to $600 million loss (pre-tax, of course). In so doing the single audit note #2 took up about 180 column lines of type written in "footnote-ese."

Now, then, what's the point of all this, in this context? Simply to ask the same questions, once again: Where were the auditors in this mess? Where should they have been? Those who want a more extensive analysis of how everything went awry on this ill-fated expedition are referred to Berkeley Rice's *The C-5A Scandal.*

And so to put the lid on this Pandora's box, which contained the franchisors (Performance Systems *née* Minnie Pearl), National Student Marketing, Telex and Memorex, and the manufacturer-lessor tandem, Mill Factors, the computer lessors (principally Leasco), R. Hoe & Co., and finally Lockheed. The reader might ask, where are the bowling alley manufacturers, Continental Vending, Bar-Chris, Pioneer Finance, and a number of other glaring omissions? They're all in that Pandora's box—but we have to put the lid on some time or we'll never get to considering the shenanigans carried on by our land-office businesses—an Augean stable to which I turn in the succeeding chapter.

Leasco Down to Date

As it later developed, the November 1971 "unsecured" refinancing by Leasco was but prologue to a $50 million public bond offering effected the following year by Leasco Financial. "The proceeds of this offering," the cover page of the prospectus stated, "will be used to pay indebtedness which was originally incurred to repurchase certain securities of Leasco Corp. which had been issued in exchange for capital stock of Reliance Insurance Co."

This "revolving door" refinancing (i.e., public money goes in, the banks' money goes out) is described in detail in an article in *Barron's,* December 18, 1972, entitled "$200 Million Question." That article also described Leasco's unusual obligations under its preferred stock indenture (alluded to above, page 151), as well as the "unsecured" bank financing arrangements entered into by Leasco Computer, another Leasco subsidiary, in August 1972.

Unquestionably, with some companies "it takes all the running you can do" just to stand still.

Chapter 7

Accounting for the Land-Office Business

Iᴛ ᴡᴀѕ almost as though I had pronounced the nakedness of the Emperor—so devastating was Wall Street's response to my "Castles of Sand?" article in *Barron's* (February 2, 1970). All that the article did, as its subtitle made clear, was to "Question the Accounting Practices of Land Development Companies." There were "delayed openings" of trading in securities of these companies on the stock exchanges, followed by plunging prices, press releases containing scathing denunciations of the assertions made in the article (and of its author), and subsequently the activation of an Ad Hoc Committee of the American Institute of Certified Public Accountants to develop fairer standards for accounting by entities such as Amrep, Horizon, GAC, General Development, Deltona, Boise Cascade.

There was nothing profound about the accounting commentaries contained in that "Castles of Sand?" piece—all I said was that these companies were recognizing income in their accounts prematurely—as reported to the shareholders and not, of course, to the Internal Revenue; and that even if such premature recognition could be rationalized, the amounts shown on their balance sheets—again, purely for public consumption—were greatly in excess of their then realizable values.

This combination of "front-end loading" of income and the

exaggeration of the amounts being recognized, produced a most ebullient financial picture—making these companies the "love children" of 1969. So delectable were their reported operations that it was little wonder the conglomerators raced into the acquisition of existing land developers (General Development by City Investing, Gulf American by General Acceptance). Other conglomerators acquired land for development and sale, thereby generating this exciting income injection on their own; and some traditional companies diversified to mine this rich lode (at least rich insofar as appearances are concerned).

Essentially, the land developers buy huge quantities of undeveloped land in Florida, Arizona, California, and other exotic-sounding sunshine states. They then turn their agents, brokers, and salesmen (and salesladies) loose on vacationers who are in a mood to speculate on land values and on those dreaming of a retirement haven at the end of the rainbow. The sales techniques might well serve as a basis for movie scenarios—numerous articles have been written describing the hard sell after a day's outing by plane, boat, bus, with luncheon or dinner thrown in.

The lead article in the March 3, 1972, *Wall Street Journal* is especially relevant in this context, and especially pointed. Entitled "A New Leaf?" and subtitled "Land Firm That Once Drew Regulators' Fire Meets Trouble Again—Sales Tactics Bring Upsurge in Gripes About GAC Unit, Formerly Gulf American—Price Sure to Go Up 20%," relates these "examples of sales pitches" which the *Journal's* staff reporter experienced on "a recent visit to the sun-baked acres where some of the 1,000 odd salesmen peddle lots":

> In three years, your payments (on a River Ranch Shores lot selling for $6,150) will be $2,833. The property is sure to go up 20% a year. So in three years you will double the money you put into it."
>
> State law forbids land salesmen to predict precise increases in value. And a 20% increase is a long way from what has happened to prices in some other Florida land developments. GAC's own study, for example, shows that sales prices on land at its Cape

Coral development have risen only around 10% in 10 years. Some local real estate dealers paint an even bleaker picture. One says that some Cape Coral lots for which buyers paid $3,180 in 1960, 12 years ago, won't fetch $2,400 now. And if you bought a Cape Coral lot now at the asking price and sold a year from now, he contends, "You'd lose your shirt."

"Next year . . . that ($6,200 Cape Coral homesite) is going to be at least going up $620 in value. . . . You may say, 'Well, Bill, I want to sell next year.' . . . You might be selling too soon. But if you're happy at selling at, say, $7,000, we'll sell it for you."

In Florida, it's illegal to promise to resell a customer's lot unless the promise is in writing.

"We have no waterfront property left (for sale at River Ranch Shores). . . . (We do have) . . . 56 water-access (lots) left and . . . 200 (parcels of) nonwaterfront property left."

But GAC's own records show 273 waterfront lots and 406 with access to water among the 7,184 unsold lots at River Ranch Shores.

"We have nine property managers here (at River Ranch Shores). We're not salesmen. We get paid a salary."

The "property managers" are paid strictly on a commission basis. Each one recently was awarded a "personally engraved" gold medallion for "outstanding" monthly sales production figures ranging from $40,000 to $150,000 each.

"The population here (at Cape Coral) will double in the next two years" from about 17,000 people now.

A GAC official himself calls that "not realistic." He calculates that doubling is "possible" in four years but unlikely before six.

"Land prices go up every six months" and "are controlled by the state."

GAC hasn't raised prices for nearly a year, and the state has no control over prices.

In any event, I'm not sitting in judgment of their selling practices (nor commenting on the gullibility of their customers)—my frame of reference here is the accounting methods utilized by these companies which have the effect of revving up their reported earnings. Thus, we should know that the typical sales contract calls for a relatively minor down payment (1 or 2 percent or even less); the balance is payable over a long-extended period

—recently up to eleven years, with interest charged at a rate appreciably below the going rate for consumer credit.

With the contract in hand, and despite the fact that the purchaser generally has a right of rescission, and that the payments in the short range will inure principally to the salesman, agent, or broker (rather than to the land developer), the developer was able to reflect as revenue, in the year the contracts were written, the face amount of contracts with customers. Thus, it is picking up this revenue in its entirety (subject only to a loss reserve) even though, as noted, collection of the balance will extend as much as eleven years for over 90 percent of the contract amount. What's more, the land cannot be made use of immediately—it's still desert or infested with alligators.

A year after publication of the *Barron's* article, there were some dismal revelations. For example, from the *Wall Street Journal* for June 20, 1971: "Boise Cascade to Incur $44 Million Charge in 2nd Period on Writeoffs, Writedowns." This followed by several months a notice that Boise Cascade was making a study of its practices for accounting for revenues from its recreational-community subdivisions.

Then, too, the Amrep Corporation, whose president took especial umbrage at the "Castles" article in a letter published in *Barron's,* issued a press release (in April, 1971) saying: "AMREP Corporation, interstate land developer, announced today that it expects reduced sales and earnings in its fourth quarter and reduced earnings for the current fiscal year, ending April 30, 1971, as compared with the same periods last year. . . . Earlier this year . . . the Company announced a program . . . to enhance the quality of its receivables. [Amrep's president] said these moves, undertaken during a soft economy, had a greater than anticipated slowdown effect. . . ." This was hardly welcome news to the financial community; Boise Cascade and Amrep stock have been severely buffeted.

But now let's move on to my indictment of the land developers' accounting practices. To begin with, I cite a recent prospectus—that of GAC Properties Credit, Inc., in connection with the issuance of its 12% Senior Debentures due October 15, 1975. From this prospectus we learn that the land developers carry on various kinds of developments, thus: "Land in Golden Gate Estates is sold as improved acreage and also as homesites. . . . [GAC] Properties [the land development company, rather than the newly formed credit entity which was doing the borrowing under this prospectus] is obligated to develop the land plotted at Golden Gate Estates to the extent of providing roads and drainage canals." This enterprise differs from River Ranch Acres, where GAC Properties sells "unimproved acreage in its natural state for use as a sportsman's facility."

So within a single entity we find a range of undertakings regarding the product, the homesite or land tract to be delivered to the customers. The spectrum becomes wider yet when we include the various, varied land-development corporations included in these accounting deliberations.

As to GAC's terms of sale, the prospectus provides the following insights:

> Substantially all sales of land are made on an instalment basis.
>
> Instalments are usually payable over a period from seven to fourteen years with interest [at the rate of 7 percent at the time of the prospectus—just about the rate charged by banks to prime credit borrowers] charged on the unpaid balance.
>
> Sales are made without any credit investigation of the purchaser.
>
> In the event of a default in payment . . . the purchaser forfeits all payments made but cannot be compelled to make any further payments thereon.

We are then led to the description of the method of accounting for these sales transactions:

> [GAC] records a transaction as a sale when it has been paid an amount equivalent to two monthly instalments or 2½% of the sales price, whichever first occurs.
>
> Income is . . . charged with amounts deemed to be sufficient to provide for contract cancellations.

We note here that these signals for income reporting are completely switched for the preparation of the tax return. For example, for the year 1969 GAC's tax return showed a *loss* of almost $16 million, in sharp contrast with the $25 million profit reported to shareholders. For the years 1965, 1966, and 1967 the financial-statement income exceeded the amounts reported to the Director of Internal Revenue by $14, $20, and $10 million, respectively. The year 1968 was unusual for a number of reasons (made all the more so by the takeover by GAC of Gulf American)—in any event the tax return showed $5.5 million of taxable income (compared with a $1.6 million loss for statement purposes); undoubtedly the available loss carryovers obviated any need for sending any actual remittance to the Internal Revenue Service.

Because I will be alluding to the income tax accounting vs. financial statement accounting dichotomy in a number of instances throughout this work, let me digress to describe some of the principal factors contributing to this divergence.

In this special context of accountings by land developers the principal disparity arises from the fact that for financial statement purposes the companies will typically use the accrual method whereas on their tax returns they will opt for the instalment method. Thus, if the company effects a sale for $1,000 of land which cost it $200, it would show the entire $800 as pre-tax income on its financial statements even if it collected currently but $150 on account of that sale. On its tax returns only 15 percent of the entire gain would be reported, since it collected only that portion of the total sales price. Hence, a difference of $680 ($800 vs. $120) between the statements and the tax return on the gross profit line.

Then, too, these companies will undoubtedly be claiming immediate deductions for the mortgage interest and real estate taxes it is paying on land which it owns, whereas this interest and taxes will not be expensed on its books—instead they will be entered into the balance sheets as an asset of the business.

These are the principal differences for the land developers.

They don't really need much more to completely abort any tax payments to our government. Going to other companies in other industries we will find that some, for example those in the construction industries, will report to you profits in proportion to work in progress; to the tax collector, only when the work is completed and billed out.

More generally, we will find that on their tax returns companies will use highly souped-up depreciation write-offs, so that the acquired assets are written off aggressively and precipitously immediately after acquisition. For the financial statements the same companies presume the equipment will last and last and last—thereby reducing depreciation charges and correspondingly increasing the net income reported to you and me.

Similarly, for so-called research and development expenses, and sometimes sales, training, advertising expenses, and other "start-up" costs—all of which may be and are being deducted for tax purposes, but yet are capitalized (hence shown as an asset) on the balance sheets.

All this helps to explain Professor Eckstein's quandary described in Chapter 1, and will have an important bearing on the debits and credits of almost all of the companies described in this book, in this as well as in succeeding chapters.

This, then, is now the typical pattern of accounting for income from land sales and subsequent cancellations. Where, then, are my basic misgivings regarding these accounting practices?

Failing in the 3 R's

First: Remember the 3R standards alluded to in Chapter 2, regarding revenue, recognition and realization. We were there informed by the Accounting Principles Board's Statement 4, "Basic Concepts and Accounting Principles Underlying Financial Statements of Business Enterprises," that revenues (the top line of the income statement, the fountainhead from which income flows) may not be generally recognized until *both* of the following conditions are met: "(1) the earnings process is com-

plete or virtually complete, and (2) an exchange has taken place."
If the land which was ostensibly sold will typically not be developed for a decade or even longer, how can they say the "earnings process is complete or virtually complete," the essential precondition to revenue recognition?

Further in this connection, where there is but a $2\frac{1}{2}$ percent payment (or even less—two monthly instalments), how can they say there has been "an exchange"? This question is especially crucial when we realize that in a great many cases the customer has the right of rescinding the contract under various conditions dictated by consumer-protection laws.

Second: I find it most difficult to accept the developer's valuations of the customers' "paper" created on the sale at face value (subject, of course, to a cancellation reserve) in the light of the contingencies of cancellation and uncollectibility, and especially in view of the substandard interest rate generally charged thereon. For example, GAC was charging 7 percent, we were told, at the very time when it was made to pay 12 percent on an even better quality of obligation.

In short, the way in which these land developers' accountings have evolved has given to them a vested interest in income exaggeration. Revenue is picked up prematurely, and then in inordinate amounts. This induces a corresponding overstatement of the developer's year-to-year income—until there is a day of reckoning—as with Boise Cascade and Amrep.

As in so many other instances, a vested interest in an inequity cannot easily be exorcised—the best one can do is to endeavor to limit or confine it. And this is about the best the AICPA's Ad Hoc Committee will succeed in doing. Limitations undoubtedly will be effected by requiring the customer to demonstrate a greater likelihood of actually fulfilling his contract before the revenue may be booked by the developer, and then by providing somewhat stricter standards for the evaluation of the receivables resulting from the sale.

This tightening of the accounting requirements, especially when coupled with the expanded disclosure requirements expected of the Ad Hoc Committee, is most salutary. But the gnawing questions remain: Should these developers have been permitted their freewheeling ways in their early years? Should not the Accounting Principles Board and the independent auditors pursuing their examinations have moved peremptorily to strike down patent violations of the traditional wisdom of generally accepted accounting principles? Assuming that some of the evil spirits are put back into that Pandora's box, who can foretell what will next be let loose to make more trouble of the kind recently faced by the Boise Cascade and Amrep stockholders?

Against this background I express my premonition regarding the never-never land of accountings by firms engaged in various aspects of real-estate acquisition and development, other than the land subdividers discussed previously.

I turn to the consideration of a series of very special transactions, each one dramatic in and of itself, to demonstrate the ways in which our accounting communications process has been seriously confounded. Each of these transactions has been the subject of major criticism; most, if not all, have been (or are currently) the subject of critical inquiry by the Securities and Exchange Commission. But yet the questions remain: How could management have expected to get away with it in the first instance? Where the transactions were then reflected in the certified statements, how could the independent auditors have gone along with the charade?

Commonwealth United's New Year's Eve Ball

I will begin this segment by churning the not-yet-cold ashes of the recent past—those remaining from the 1968 New Year's Eve transactions of Commonwealth United (CU) in Beverly Hills—producing distortions involving the reporting of specious revenues simply because GAAP appeared to provide some rationalization for such reporting. Here, as will be seen, the distortion was rooted in the auditors being so obsessed with the "transaction" that they lost track of what was being transacted and the essential realities of the realization concept. The CU saga is not easy to unfold—since it needs to be pieced together from many sources, inducing in me a sense of consummate awe for cryptologists and archeologists. And, mind you, the Commonwealth United scrolls here in issue are no more than a few years old, and yet they must be unwound with care. Anyway, here's a brief re-telling of that saga:

The corporation's financial statements for 1968 were a most exciting production, reflecting all the glamour and exhilaration fitting for Beverly Hills—the corporation's home city. The rhetoric was inspired, telling us right off that: "The year 1968 was one of major change in the posture of Commonwealth United Corp. During the course of the year the company moved from a relatively obscure position to become one of the top 500 corporations in the country." And the epistle from the board chairman and president concluded: "Commonwealth United has a strong position for future growth." If only it were true, there would be far less grief among so many shareholders—individuals and institutional investors.

Alas—CU is now in disrepute. In the discard is the collage of euphoric data emphasized by the chairman. Thus, revenues up 43 percent, net income up 299 percent and on a per share basis up 151 percent—all of these ups are now up the creek, along with current assets of 30 percent (liabilities only 13 percent), working capital 54 percent, and equity 147 percent. The final index cited, "return on stockholders' equity up 66 percent" was all made of whole cloth—as it now turns out.

It took a whole year for all this to be brought out of the woodwork—in the meantime there were various actions by the SEC, suspension by the American Stock Exchange, CU's creditors (especially Bernie Cornfeld's IOS empire from whom they borrowed so heavily to give CU the necessary "vigorish") moved in, the author of the beautiful prose was dumped, and in late December, 1969, the corporation was compelled to issue a proxy statement running in excess of a hundred pages to tell shareholders that the 1968 "ups" notwithstanding, "For the six months ended June 30, 1969, the Company reported a loss before extraordinary items of $11,035,000, after adjustments and write-downs of $11,252,000 based upon decisions made in September and October [1969]. . . . The company also incurred extraordinary losses of $11,617,000, increasing the net loss for the period to $22,652,000. For the comparable 1968 period the company reported a net income of $3,906,000."

Tough luck—it could happen to anyone. It may be that 1969 was just a poor year for CU—would that the story ended there, insofar as our accounting profession is concerned. You see, the 1968 statements are put into very serious, and highly critical, question in the light of bits and pieces of information provided by the proxy statement.

Thus, the later-disclosed material tells how CU and Kleiner, Bell (CU's underwriter) got to be extremely cozy on New Year's Eve, 1968. Here's how they tell it:

> By reason of two real estate sales to principals of Kleiner, Bell, both of which closed on December 31, 1968, the company reported an aggregate gain of $3,363,200 in 1968. Such transactions contributed approximately 29 cents per share to the 98 cents per share earnings of the company reported for 1968. (For further details, see Real Estate Group—Year-End Transactions.)

Being of intrepid spirit, I looked where they told us to look, and there we have laid out the background of these year-end transactions. Regarding the "Sale of Hawaiian Land":

> After Commonwealth had agreed to purchase 4,000 acres of land in Hawaii (see Hawaiian Properties under this caption) and while arrangements for the formal closing thereof were pending, Commonwealth reviewed the alternatives. . . . Management concluded that a sale of the parcel was the desirable course. Accordingly, the company negotiated a sale of said Hawaiian acreage for a total price of $5,450,000 to a partnership composed of Messrs. Kleiner, Bell, and Shapiro (controlling stockholders of

Kleiner, Bell) and Richard A. Freling, Esq. [Mr. Freling was Dallas counsel for Kleiner, Bell and subsequently counsel for Commonwealth.] At the title closing held on December 31, 1968, the company received a cash payment of $541,000, comprising a $50,000 down payment and $491,000 advance interest on a note of $5,400,000 payable on June 30, 1970, and secured by the property. It was expressly stipulated that the purchasers would have no personal liability on the note and that, in the event of default thereunder, Commonwealth would look solely to the property.

Having never seen Hawaii, and having nothing better to do, I did go to see "Hawaiian Properties under this caption," only to find that:

On December 31, 1968, Commonweath also completed the acquisition of approximately 4,000 acres of unimproved land in Hawaii from Messrs. Crawford and their mother, Lillian Crawford, for a cash consideration of approximately $1,656,800. . . .

And so on New Year's Eve, Commonwealth bought unimproved land (through, as I understand it, the good offices of Kleiner, Bell—Commonwealth United's underwriter and apparently its Good Samaritan and patron) for $1,656,800 and before the revels began they resold the bonanza to Kleiner, Bell, Shapiro, and Freling (who must have thought it was Christmas Eve rather than New Year's Eve) for $5,450,000. There were some other pluses and minuses because the bottom line of that transaction (as the proxy statement tells it) reads: "By reason of this transaction, closed on December 31, 1968, Commonwealth recorded a 1968 profit of $2,963,000. . . ."

But the spirit of Christmas didn't end there; on the very same day Kleiner, Bell also bought the Worcester Office Buildings owned by Commonwealth. How much did this New Year's Eve deal put into the CU sock? Again from the proxy: "By reason of this transaction, closed on December 31, 1968, Commonwealth recorded a 1968 profit of $700,000." And where were the auditors in all this? Where should they have been? I have some pretty good ideas.

For me all this is an instant replay of the Westec game plan; for me there is serious question as to whether the very clear and compelling dictates of SEC Accounting Release 95 were considered and, if so, how the accounting for these transactions met these standards. There will, undoubtedly, be subsequent chapters written by the courts for this particular fiasco—for the present I leave the Commonwealth United saga with the question: Did they really realize the revenues which they booked on the basis of these incestuous goings-on on New Year's Eve, 1968?

A Major Realty Deal

I move on, then, to the transactions by another land operator —Major Realty Corporation. In September, 1970, the Securities and Exchange Commission ordered a public hearing (originally scheduled for that mid-October) regarding this company's report of a gain from the sale of land during the fiscal year ended May 31, 1968. That single transaction produced a most substantial gain for the year, and a correspondingly substantial receivable as of that May 31 (as well as the subsequent year-end). The transaction, the SEC said, contributed over $3 million to the company's income (more than 100 percent of the income for the year), and about 75 percent of its gross revenues from the sales of properties.

The notes to the financial statements for the year do make specific reference to this transaction, including a statement that: "The Company may rescind the sale if the buyer fails to commence construction for a regional shopping mall on or before June 1, 1969. If the buyer furnishes evidence of a lease or letter of intent to lease from at least one major department store, construction may be delayed as late as June 1, 1970." The Commission's complaint alleged that the income statement was untrue and misleading,

> ... in that registrant improperly treated the transaction ... as a reportable sale and thereby overstated sales with a resulting overstatement of net income, in view of the following:

1. Registrant received a down payment representing less than one percent of the purchase price.
2. Registrant retained the right to rescind the sale subsequent to closing.
3. No interest or principal payments were to be made until registrant's right to rescind was no longer extant.
4. The buyer had assets of a nominal amount.
5. The note given to the registrant by the buyer was a non-recourse note.

The SEC then challenged the fact that the receivable booked as of May 31, 1968, was carried over unabated into the 1969 fiscal balance sheet. In this challenge the Commission introduced certain additional facts which, they asserted, should have demonstrated the tenuous quality of this asset on Major Realty's 1969 balance sheet (even if the 1968 recording was rationalizable).

I cannot comprehend how Major Realty and their auditors believed they were satisfying the mandates of the SEC (again, its Accounting Series Release 95), or the precepts of our profession regarding the realization process, or of common sense and logic, by permitting this huge amount of income to be included in the fiscal 1968 report (even with a "subject to" clause in the opinion).

The proceedings ended with an April, 1971, Findings, Opinion and Order of the Securities and Exchange Commission informing us that Major Realty Corporation had "submitted an offer of settlement, pursuant to which it entered into a stipulation of facts, waived a hearing . . . and . . . consented to findings consistent with the allegations [of the SEC described above] that the annual reports were misleading and deficient." By way of atonement, Major Realty, "among other things, also agreed to file correcting amendments to such reports and to provide all its shareholders . . . with a copy of [the SEC's Findings and Opinions]."

Liberty Equities' Iniquities

The Liberty Equities Corporation, its auditors, and ten other defendants were the subjects of a complaint filed by the SEC in the District of Columbia in August, 1970. The complaint alleged:

> The consolidated income statement improperly reflected as ordinary income the purported profit of approximately $753,663 resulting from a transaction whereby defendant Liberty sold to Real Estate Investors of Iowa, Inc. a wholly owned subsidiary of Professional Investors of Iowa, Inc., for $808,663 certain options on real estate property located in Washington, D.C., which it had purchased for $45,000 shortly prior to this transaction.

The SEC complaint then noted that excepting for this very special transaction Liberty Equities would have shown a net operating loss for its 1968 year—$150,000, instead of the $610,000 income it reported. In addition, the financial statements failed to disclose, the SEC said, that:

(1) The transaction was unusual and non-recurring . . .
(2) The transaction took place on the last business day of defendant Liberty's fiscal year.
(3) Defendant White represented both parties to the option transaction (he was then a principal executive of both corporations).
(4) The transaction was consummated with a nonexistent entity.
(5) The transfer of these options in this transaction was the first active step by defendants Liberty . . . to form a joint venture in which defendant Liberty was to be an equal 50% participant with Real Estate Investors of Iowa, Inc.
(6) And the reason for entering into the transaction on the last business day of defendant Liberty's fiscal year ended March 31, 1968, was for the purpose of eliminating defendant Liberty's net operating loss and to "dress up" its financial statements.

Of the dozen defendants in this action for injunction, all immediately consented to the entry of a decree without admitting the correctness of the allegations. The auditors did file an answer; and what did they assert insofar as the foregoing issue is concerned?

To begin with, the auditors (through their counsel) assert that they submitted their report *"dated May 10, 1968,* of [their] examination as independent certified public accountants of the consolidated financial statements of Liberty as at March 31, 1968, and for the twelve months then ended" (emphasis added for reasons which will become clear.)

The answer repeated the statement in the "said report," namely, that the "examination of said financial statements was made in accordance with generally accepted auditing standards and accordingly included such tests of the accounting records of Liberty and such other auditing procedures as were considered necessary in the circumstances." Fair enough. In the course of this examination the auditors were informed by Liberty's officers that real-estate development was to be a significant part of Liberty's future operations—thereby making the gain from this particular real-estate deal part of its "ordinary, recurring items" (citing Accounting Principles Board Opinion No. 9).

What about the fact that the transaction was effected on the last day of the year? We'll let the auditors answer this one:

> Generally accepted accounting principles do not require disclosure of the fact that the sale of the real estate options was effective [sic] on the last day of Liberty's fiscal year. Prior to completion of its said examination [the auditors] received an opinion, dated July 12, 1968 [but remember the report was submitted May 10, 1968] from Liberty's counsel . . . which reflected that drafts of the real estate option sale agreement had been prepared by that law firm on March 15, 1968.

What about White's double-agent role? The answer referred to counsel's July 12, 1968, opinion which "specifically stated that during the negotiation of the transaction defendant White had acted solely on behalf of Liberty and was not an officer, director or shareholder of Professional Investors of Iowa, Inc. ('PI')." I'll return to Mr. White presently; in the meantime it should be noted that while PI signed a March 29, 1968, draft "instrument" regarding this transaction, this instrument was not signed by Liberty. As it turned out PI was not the eventual purchaser of the option; instead, the option was acquired by a subsidiary (Real Estate Investors of Iowa, Inc., "REI") formed by PI on April 12, 1968. As of March 31, 1968, the July, 1968, opinion of Liberty counsel makes clear, "no formal instrument had been signed in behalf of Liberty and there was no written agreement between Liberty and PI." As to whether PI could be held responsible for its oral undertaking as of March 31, 1968, is a question to be answered by reference to the applicable statute of limitations; the July 12, 1968, opinion of counsel believed they could be thus responsible. (Since REI was not in existence on March 31, 1968, it could not, of course, be charged with any undertaking as of that date.)

And so with that confused background (possibly relying on the opinion of Liberty's counsel in July, 1968) the auditors submitted their report on May 10, 1968. And since they "reasonably believed that the sale of the real estate options was properly classified as in the ordinary course of business in Liberty's consolidated income statement, and Liberty did so classify the transaction, generally accepted accounting principles required that the income therefrom be reflected in Liberty's earnings per share of common stock."

But that's not the end of my confusion regarding White or the standards of GAAP and/or GAAS (generally accepted auditing standards) which were here applied. Hopefully the assertions in the answer (page 15) will make everything fall into place. Thus spoke the auditors' answer:

> In the course of its said examination [the auditors] evaluated the collectibility of the note . . . of PI's subsidiary, REI, which Liberty received in the transaction involving the sale of real estate options to REI referred to . . . above. [The auditors] requested that Liberty obtain a copy of PI's financial statements. Such financial statements indicated that PI did not have sufficient net

assets (excluding the asset consisting of the options) to pay the note in full. [The auditors were] then informed by Liberty that PI intended to issue debentures to obtain such funds and that White & Co. (of which defendant White, a director and officer of Liberty, was President) would arrange for the purchase of said debentures by customers of White & Co. who wished to invest in real estate using PI and/or REI as the vehicle therefore. [The auditors] requested that White & Co. confirm this and received a telegram dated *June 21, 1968,* therefrom which stated that White & Co. had given a letter of intent to PI covering an issue of $750,000 of convertible debentures. [Emphasis mine—again remember the auditors' report was promulgated more than a month before this cold-comfort telegram.]

So Liberty's White (as the answer asserted earlier) now turns up as PI/REI's White. But more important: How could the June 21, 1968, telegram allay doubts as of March 31, 1968, where the auditors' report (issued, one might hope, only *after* important doubts were resolved) was submitted May 10, 1968? It may well be that we're taking time and chronology too literally; it may be that in this age of Aquarius June and July precede March and May. Of course, anyone versed in Alice's experiences in Wonderland will recognize the vagaries of time.

Did the auditors really need more than ordinary wisdom to see through Liberty's March 31, 1968, wizardry? Were they really so cozened by White and the other officers and directors of Liberty that they were oblivious to the transparency of the single transaction which produced a purported profit of $763,663—an amount equal to about 125% of the entire reported net income for the year?

One cannot be certain as to what produced a *volte-face* on the part of the auditors; conceivably, they too realized that their answer raised more questions than it answered. In any event, much to my surprise, the May 7, 1971, *Wall Street Journal* brought word that the auditors had joined the other defendants named by the SEC's complaint in a consent decree. The *Journal's* headline, "Peat-Marwick Enjoined From Future Violations of

U.S. Securities Law," and the subheadline, "Court Acts on Complaint of SEC That Firm Issued 'False' Data in Liberty Equity Statement," tell the story as far as the particular proceedings are concerned. As to whether this overt "consent to entry of the judgment without admitting liability in order to dispose of the SEC action" will prod the AICPA into a review of whether the best of GAAP/GAAS were here applied, I can only surmise.

In any event, we will be denied the court's response to what I have indicated are some incongruities in the chronology exposed by the auditors' aborted answer.

Occidental's Big Deals

In March, 1971, the Securities and Exchange Commission filed a "Complaint for Preliminary and Final Injunction" to which the defendants, Occidental Petroleum and its Board Chairman and Chief Executive Officer, Dr. Armand Hammer, entered their consent. (I'll bet Lewis Carroll would have enjoyed the curious phenomenon of the Consent Decree.) The SEC's complaint asserted that the corporation entered into several quick-injection land deals during the first two calendar quarters of 1970—deals which the SEC said were "acts, practices and a course of business which constitute violations of Section 10 (b) of the . . . Exchange Act . . . and Rule 10 b-5 . . . thereunder." What are these monstrous acts insofar as the land deals were involved?

First, more than 11 percent of the second quarter, 1970, profits stemmed from two purported land deals, as follows:

1. The Jenkins Ranch–Junction City Deal: On or about June 13, 1970, Occidental Land sold the Jenkins Ranch to Clout Realty (owned by someone called Nutter) for $7.6 million. (Less than a year earlier the property was booked by Oxy at $4.6 million.) Clout was to pay $760,000 on the purchase price as well as $1 million in "prepaid interest." (Nutter–Clout must have wanted a tax deduction.) Since neither Clout nor Nutter had the wherewithal (or a reasonable facsimile thereof) to make these payments, Oxy supplied it by a simultaneous cash purchase from

Clout of some Junction City Land for $2.6 million. Of that sum Clout paid Oxy the $1.8 million called for by the Jenkins Ranch contract; another $100,000 went to a broker who handled the tandem deals—leaving $714,000 for Clout. So it is that Oxy *paid out* a net of $814,000 and booked about $3 million in instant earnings.

2. The Dworman Deal: On or about June 30, 1970 (coincidentally the last day of the quarter), Occidental Land sold the Jones Ranch to the Security Alliance Corporation (owned by the Dwormans) for $5.3 million, for which Alliance paid $800,-000 down and a $4.5 million note; again, the purchaser also prepaid interest of $1,350,000. The Dwormans (like Nutter) apparently didn't have the necessary funds either, whereupon Occidental bought some land from them for about $5 million—$3,050,000 in cash went, so that the Dwormans ended up with $900,000 of Occidental's money, and Oxy picked up a $3 million profit on its sale.

Second, more than 10 percent of the first quarter, 1970, profits were derived from two purported land deals, as follows:

1. The Rhodell Farms Deal: On or about March 31, 1970 (damned coincidence!) Occidental Land bought 1,240 acres of land from Rhodell (owned by Rhodes) for $2.5 million cash. On the same day Occidental sold 1,000 of these same acres to Arizona Construction for $4.1 million—with a reported purported profit of $2.1 million (the arithmetic is correct). Arizona paid Oxy $800,000 in cash—the rest of the purchase was on a note secured by the 1,000 acres and other land owned by Rhodes (who owned half of Arizona Construction before the Occidental deal—and borrowed another $75,000 from Occidental to buy out his other 50 percent partner). How did Rhodell use the $2.5 million it got from Occidental? Well, $800,000 went to Arizona—and we can trace that; another $1.4 million went to pay off some Rhodell debts; the remaining $284,000 was used by Rhodell for working capital. In sum, Occidental paid out $1.7 million net and picked

up a bookkeeping plus of $2.1 million—that was a very busy last day of a quarter.

2. The Agro-Hobbs Deal: On or about March 31, 1970 (doesn't Occidental ever rest on the last of the quarter?), it bought some land from Agro Resources Inc. for $5.8 million and immediately resold it to Hobbs Land for $7.9 million—yes, Virginia, Santa put $2.1 million into Oxy's stock. Only it couldn't spend it because the shell game went like this: (*a*) Oxy paid Agro $2 million cash and assumed existing obligations on the acquired land for the $3.8 million balance of the purchase price; whereas (*b*) Hobbs paid Oxy $1 million in cash, took on the $3.8 million in existing debt, and gave its $3.1 million note to round out the $7.9 million purchase price.

Oh yes, you need one more piece to this puzzle: Agro is owned 20 percent by Schultz and 80 percent by a syndicate; Hobbs is Schultz's wholly owned *alter ego*. To explain the deal to his fellow Agroites, Schultz wrote (June 12, 1970): "In substance Agro borrowed $1,000,000 from Occidental but must repay $3,200,000 in five years at 10% interest on the unpaid balance. For cogent reasons Occidental could not make a pure loan. . . ."

Anyway, as I've observed, the defendants in this action entered into a consent decree; and if you then read their concurrent press release it might appear that they did that just to get rid of the pesty madmen at the SEC, with Oxy and Dr. Hammer insisting that they weren't going to change a thing. Why the SEC goes along with this charade is beyond me.

Cornfeld New Math: $17 Million Equals $119 Million

An especially tangled and spectacular land office *tour de force* was engineered by Bernard Cornfeld—undoubtedly the most tangled and spectacular financial tycoon of recent, if not blessed, memory, in behalf of his Investors Overseas Services empire. It will not be easy to unravel this most intriguing saga; I will take hold of the Ariadne thread by tugging at the 1969 Annual Report of IOS, Ltd., the parent company for the Cornfeld empire.

This report is Spartan and dull in appearance—particularly when we compare it with the report for the year preceding. Absent are the portraits of the *dramatis personae*—all so studied and posed with proper mood and lighting; absent also are the exhilarating growth curves and projections. Instead, in nought but black and white, we are given some data and assertions, thus:

1. Net income for 1969 amounted to $10,282,000; that for the year before was $14,369,000. It is important that we bear the 1969 income figure of about $10 million in mind—it is crucial for this epic.

2. As the accompanying letter from Sir Eric Wyndham White, Cornfeld's successor as Chairman of the Board, pointed out, 1969 was a momentous year for IOS: "Perhaps the single most significant event of your Company's year was the public offering of I.O.S., Ltd. Common Shares. This issue was the largest such offering ever conducted outside the United States."

3. Turning to the review of the income decline Sir Eric observed (and this too is significant for this tale):

> Profit-sharing management fees for security portfolios which provided the bulk of net income from Proprietary Fund Operations in 1968 made a negligible contribution in 1969 because of generally declining market values. *In 1969 this was more than compensated for by performance-based management fees received with respect to non-market linked investments.* [Emphasis supplied.]

4. Finding this "non-market linked" investment fee income was not difficult since the 1969 Statement of Consolidated Income reported under Income from Proprietary Funds: "Advisory fees, in 1969 principally from Natural Funds Ltd. . . . $9,830,000." (Note how closely this single item aproximates the empire's entire income for the year of $10,282,000.) We are told to go to Note 6—to which we jog.

5. That footnote, captioned "Income from Proprietary Funds" informs us, *inter alia*:

   a. Subsidiaries of IOS act as portfolio managers for a series of mutual funds subsumed under Fund of Funds (sometimes referred to as FOF).

b. As such manager IOS is entitled to management fees including "10% of the net realized and unrealized investment gains on the investments maintained in the fund account. . . ."

c. With respect to the Natural Resources Fund (one of the FOF enterprises) the aforementioned 10 percent compensation included $9,737,000 attributable to:

. . . an interest in certain Canadian Arctic oil and gas exploration permits. Based upon the terms of the sale outlined below, as approved by the Boards of Directors of FOF, FOF Prop. and IOS Growth Fund Limited, which included outside directors as well as certain officers and directors of IOS and its affiliates, this investment was valued by the Funds at $119,000,000 in December 1969. This was an increase in value of $102,000,000, as to which the advisory fees were receivable by IOS and were subsequently paid by the Funds.

6. How did they figure this $119 million for something which the Funds bought only relatively recently (six months or so for the most part) for $17 million? Well, we saw that it was "based upon the terms of the sale" which are outlined as follows:

The sale referred to above was concluded in January 1970 and was made to the operator of the permit interests, King Resources Company . . . covering a 10% interest in the Funds' investment on the same basis and terms as a December 1969 sale by such operator of a 9.375% interest to outside third parties.

7. The $119 million, we were told, was predicated on a gross valuation for those Canadian permits of $156 million with some discounting (to make the result more conservative) and to account for a King Resources' profit participation.

8. Finally we have the Auditors' Report dated in Zurich, Switzerland, on June 1, 1970 (interestingly, they were able to date the prior year's report on April 15), which tells us that:

In our opinion, subject to the effect on the consolidated financial statements as of December 31, 1969, of (a) certain investment valuations underlying the determination of advisory funds discussed in Note 6 . . . the accompanying consolidated financial statements present fairly the financial position of I.O.S., Ltd. and subsidiaries as of December 31, 1969 and 1968, and the results of their operations for the years then ended, in conformity with generally accepted accounting principles consistently applied during the period.

This, then, is as far as the official version goes on this Canadian iceberg. That we may have been shown only the tip thereof is indicated by some revelations by Charles Raw, Bruce Page and Godfrey Hodgson in their *"Do You Sincerely Want to Be Rich?" The Full Story of Bernard Cornfeld and I.O.S.*

As they tell it the trail of these particular land transactions is labyrinthine; it involves a symbiotic relationship which developed between two super salesmen, two super egos, two imperious characters, Bernard Cornfeld and John M. King. By a most remarkable coincidence the independent audit responsibility for the IOS empire as well as King Resources was vested in Arthur Andersen & Co., one of our Big Eight accounting firms.

Here are some of the trail markers noted by Raw, *et al.* (in some measure paraphrased by me):

1. On March 4, 1968, the Fund of Funds, one of the IOS nexus of entities, created a "Natural Resources Account." This account was managed by IOS, Ltd.

> Although no fee was fixed formally, IOS proposed to reward itself for running the Natural Resources Account by taking 10 percent of any appreciation in the value of the account's investment whether that appreciation was realized in a sale, or simply entered in the books.

2. By the end of 1969, $60 million from the Fund of Funds had flowed into John King's companies. No list was published showing the disposition of these monies; however, a news story disclosed that "More than 45 percent of the money had gone into King's companies operating in the United States, chiefly to acquire oil and gas prospects. Another 39 percent had gone to Canada, $11 million having been spent on oil-exploration rights in the Arctic."

3. The Cornfeld empire was, in essence, built on a mammoth mutual fund requiring continuous evaluation of the assets comprising that monster. "The great point about natural resources investments, however, was that unlike stocks and shares, there was no widely quoted and established market to put a value on unrealized appreciation. It was up to IOS itself, with the aid of King Resources, to assess increases in the value. . . ." The higher the values estimated, the greater the amount diverted to Cornfeld and his colleagues (who, through IOS, Ltd. owned most of the IOS management company); this would be accomplished by the 10 percent skimming process.

4. By the end of 1969 Cornfeld was telling his salesmen that these Canadian permits were "our most spectacular investment." This is, of course, entirely consistent with the felicitous data incorporated in the annual report.

5. The mathematical process by which an investment of less than $20 million is extrapolated to $156 million (and discounted to only $119 million) in the space of months ran something like this (again essentially according to Raw, *et al.*):

   a. A logical method of revaluing a natural-resources holding which, as Sir Eric pointed out, was a "non-market linked" investment "is to sell part of it . . . it may be fair to apply the [value on this sale] to the complete holding. But the validity of the technique obviously depends upon the independence of the buyer and the scope of his purchase. . . ."

   b. How does one go about selling part of it in such a manner as to permit the valuation of the whole by extrapolation?

In early November 1969 Arthur Andersen . . . suggested to King Resources that an increase could be allowed if supported by an arm's length sale to knowledgeable outside parties. If King Resources Company sold a 25 per cent interest in all of the Arctic permits to Texaco or another major oil Company, the auditors believed it would be appropriate to give proportionate value to the 75 per cent retained. Where to draw the line was the problem: the auditors at this stage regarded a 10 per cent sale as a bare minimum.

c. All that Cornfeld apparently heard was the "10 percent sale as a bare minimum." He used that as the catalyst, apparently supplying his own notion of what represented "an arm's length sale to knowledgeable outside parties." Before we proceed further with this unraveling we should be made aware that the FOF interest in the deep freeze was matched by an identical interest owned by King Resources. In other words, FOF and King were 50-50 partners.

d. In December, 1969, King did manage to get off 9.375 percent of its interests to what were ostensibly "outside third parties." The terms of sale, as is all too common in realty transactions, called for very little hard money—but a lot of paper. King Resources was not able to use that paper for anything much, since, as it soon turned out, one of these outside "third parties" who bought in December, 1969, was "in deep financial trouble" and the other was "in dispute with King Resources over the deal."

e. Nevertheless, in December, 1969, these induced sales by King were at a $15 per acre price—a price which was, of course, immensely greater than the original cost.

f. Then the grand slam by IOS—it sold to King Resources one-tenth of its interest in the iceberg (that is, the 10 percent floor suggested by the auditors back in November, 1969) by reference to the $15 outside "third parties" arm's length price (how long, how short, the arm is not revealed).

g. The foregoing calculus produced a $156 million valuation which, as the financial statements pointed out, were brought down to but $119 million—producing the $102 million unrealized appreciation for FOF and a real cash advantage to IOS (and Cornfeld, *et al.*) of 10 percent thereof.

To my simplistic mind this kind of a deal is so patently transparent it should not require the perceptive talents and intrepid independence of a major accounting firm to have told these clients at both ends of the axis what they could do with all the paper shuttling between them. Even if such auditors were responsible for the independent attest function for but one of these emperors they should have spoken out the way Andersen (Hans Christian, that is) did to the scoundrels in the *Emperor's New Clothes*—"The emperor is naked!!"

What are the principal Raw-Page-Hodgson conclusions regarding this fantasy land?

> IOS was the creation of Bernard Cornfeld and Edward M. Cowett. Together these men built up an organization so steeped in financial and intellectual dishonesty and directed so recklessly that it was absurd that it should have been entrusted with so much of other people's money, let alone praise for the brilliance with which it was managed.
>
> . . . IOS was not a respectable financial institution. It was an international swindle . . . one which acquired control over more than two and a half billion dollars of other people's moneys.

It may well be that the whole IOS operation can be best, even if indelicately, described in the words used by Cowett, Cornfeld's principal collaborator, to describe the German branch. He is quoted in the book as saying, "I always used to say that it was built on a unique foundation of shit and quicksand."

The Ice Age can evaporate just as stealthily as it was formed. This is dramatically demonstrated by the interface between the accountings for a single transaction which took place on August 7, 1970 between two IOS-controlled corporations.

On that date Fund of Funds' subsidiary, F.O.F. Proprietary Funds Ltd., the owner of the arctic lands being carried on its books at the inflated book values established as of December 31, 1969, transferred its investments in the Natural Resources Fund Account, as well as in Investment Properties International, Limited to a newly formed, wholly owned subsidiary, Global Natural Resources Properties Limited. These investments, then on FOF's books at about $165 million and $28 million respectively (together with $17 million in cash)—an aggregate of $209,515,600—were exchanged, as footnote 11 to FOF's 1970 report informs us, "for all of the outstanding shares of Global, a newly formed corporation whose total net assets at that time were represented by these assets acquired from the Fund."

The footnote then gives us some assurance regarding the numbers involved in the exchange, thus:

> Management has made inquiries and has been informed that Global's management is not aware of any subsequent developments which would have a material effect on the August 7, 1970 valuation of the assets transferred and therefore as of the date of this report [January 29, 1971], the Boards of Directors have no knowledge of facts that would, in their opinion, indicate the need for any material change in their basis of valuation of natural resource interests transferred to Global as described above.

Then, with specific reference to the Investment Properties International ("IPI") investment, the footnote continues:

> On August 7, 1970, Proprietary held . . . approximately 47% of IPI's outstanding stock. These shares were valued at the average of the quoted bid and asked prices. Management believes that this is an appropriate price for the purpose of reporting net asset value.

So once more the tally men proceeded with their assigned chores and quantified the transfer to Global at $209,515,600. And since FOF distributed these newly acquired Global shares to the FOF shareholders as a dividend, the certified Consolidated Statement of Changes in Net Assets for the year 1970 shows a subtraction of precisely this amount from FOF's capital account. This, then, purged the FOF accounts of the Canadian deep freeze, as well as the IPI investment.

Vesco New Math $209 Million Equals $65 Million

Now we turn to the 1970 report of Global Natural Resources Properties Limited. It must have been a really difficult report to prepare since it was not completed until September 22, 1971, according to the auditors' certificate.

Let us read Global's version of the same August 7, 1970, transaction. Its footnote 1 first relates some facts which are consistent with those discerned from the FOF report; the footnote goes on to say:

> The underlying oil, gas and mineral properties received as of August 7, 1970 were recorded at the acquisition cost of the Predecessor [FOF], as adjusted for abandonment of properties and other adjustments. . . . The investment in [IPI] was recorded at $27,866-933, the quoted market basis carried by the Predecessor . . . less a reduction of approximately $6,000,000 to give consideration to the limited marketability of the . . . shares. [This, of course, means that the number entered into Global's books for IPI at August 7, 1970, was $21.9 million.]

As a consequence of the radical surgery performed by Global on the August 7, 1970 "values," it put the bundle of acquired assets on its books at $65,324,807, which is only about 30 percent of the "values" which the FOF report said were in existence at that exact same date. What it comes down to is the question as to "who was kidding whom" on that critical date, and even as late as January 29, 1971, when the FOF auditors assured us all managements (of FOF, Proprietary as well as Global) were in agreement that $209,515,600 was the correct number?

Clearly, we have a credibility gap amounting to $144 million —a gap wide enough to induce a crisis in confidence for any sensitive viewer of the accounting scene.

The reader should be apprised of two additional facts which might help account for this otherwise unaccountable accounting. Thus, between January 29, 1971 and September 22, 1971 (i.e., the dates of the respective reports) there were two critical changes made in the IOS complex, to wit: Robert L. Vesco moved into the position of ultimate control of that empire; and possibly of greater import, the Global tale was told by Lybrand while FOF's was, as we already know, Andersen's. But most certainly the successor auditors should have read the notes to the financial statements promulgated by their predecessors, and carefully studied the workpapers which led to these earlier promulgations.

Most fortuitously, as of this writing the incumbent President of the American Institute of Certified Public Accountants is a distinguished partner of the firm responsible for these 1969 and earlier audits of IOS. I can think of no greater service which he could perform, or a more effective way of demonstrating his and his firm's commitment to fairness and intrepid independence (even if it hurts), than to convene a Select Committee of distinguished persons (not necessarily all CPAs) to probe the whole IOS mess including the apparent total breakdown in their internal controls, their prospectuses, and compliance with laws and regulations, with a special mandate to answer the oft-repeated queries: "Where were the auditors in that case? Where should they have been?"

Such a committee would not have an easy task—probing a dung heap built on quicksand is never sweet smelling or easy. But yet it is the kind of probes undertaken in Canada and England, respectively, in the wake of the Atlantic Acceptance and Pergamon Press fiascos—so why not here and now?

Such a Select Committee could then serve as the prototype for corresponding probes into the big busts or deflated bosoms at: Commonwealth United, Penn Central, Performance Systems, Westec, Mill Factors, Perfect Film, the Wall Street Back-Office Mess (thereby retaining the symmetry of the octagon), and whatever else the future may yet hold in store for our profession.

In the succeeding chapter I will describe what has turned out to be the most dramatic utilization of generally accepted accounting principles pertaining to realty transactions, namely, the ways in which Penn Central and its realty subsidiaries (Great Southwest and Macco) utilized these principles and transactions as the critical ploy in their fulfillment of their very special game plan.

Chapter 8

Great (and Not So Great) Southwest Land Deals

T<small>HESE</small> land-office deals raise serious questions as to whether the duly appointed independent tally-men fulfilled the important responsibilities with which they are vested. Because of its dramatic import and continuing repercussions, I am here introducing "Six Flags at Half Mast?" essentially as it appeared in the January 11, 1971, issue of *Barron's* (subsequently introduced into the *Congressional Record*).

*   *   *

In view of the plight of its corporate parent, the bankrupt Penn Central, Great Southwest Corp. and its troubles might rate hardly more than a footnote to financial history. However, the losses suffered by public shareholders in the railroad's 90%-owned realty subsidiary are real enough—the stock, which hit a peak 41½ in '69 (after a 10-for-1 split), now trades around 2. Moreover, Great Southwest's difficulties are far from over. A little over a month ago, the new management which took over last summer disclosed that Great Southwest was faced with a fresh cash squeeze. It was entering the new year, they were told, with all funds committed and the company urgently in need of an infusion of capital. First National City and other lenders were being asked to advance Great Southwest another $8 million to keep going. To add to the woes, the company has warned, "substantial adjustments" are in prospect in the value of certain properties.

Yet, while Great Southwest faces an uncertain future, a critical glance back at some of the goings-on, especially in 1969, seems in order. For one thing, it may help shed some light as to how the company reached its present dismal state. For another, and even more important, it reveals clearly how the results of Great Southwest were inextricably woven into the Penn Central's finances. The appearance of Penn Central's financial viability, I submit, was achieved with the aid of some accounting procedures, which, to put it mildly, raise serious questions. Indeed, there is reason to question the underlying theory on which these accountings were based, as well as the auditing standards applied in the verification of the accounts.

I am mindful, of course, that *Fortune* magazine got into a controversy when it presumed to attack Penn Central's accounting practices. Let's begin, ironically, by quoting from a letter sent by the auditors, Peat, Marwick, Mitchell & Co., in which they took umbrage at *Fortune*'s article.

In response to *Fortune*'s assertion that "sales of real estate, which should have been designated as extraordinary items, were credited to normal income, . . ." the auditors said:

"*Fortune* states that gains and losses from sale of real estate . . . are an extraordinary part of Penn Central's operations. This is untrue. Penn Central is one of the largest real estate companies in the world and has substantial real estate transactions every year. . . . Obviously, therefore, as required by Opinion No. 9 of the Accounting Principles Board, these items must be shown as part of ordinary income. *Fortune* could have avoided this error by simply reading the APB Opinion. Even without the Opinion, common sense and simple logic dictate that something which recurs annually cannot, by definition, be extraordinary."

Now, I have read Opinion No. 9, as well as a very perceptive analysis and critical commentary on it by my colleague, Professor Leopold Bernstein, of the Baruch College. I profess a modicum of common sense and simple logic. And I assert that a gerrymandered, contrived transaction, even if it is made to recur annually, need not, *ipso facto,* be ordinary.

Actually, in a limited respect, I agree with *both Fortune* and the aggrieved auditors. Thus, on the one hand, I agree with the magazine's writers that at least $25 million of Penn Central's 1969 real estate income should not have gone into ordinary income. On the other hand, as the auditors maintain, neither should it have gone into extraordinary income. My "common sense and simple logic" tell me that at least $25 million of that reported income from real estate transactions didn't really exist; including that amount in income makes sense and is logical only if we are willing to presume that our generally accepted accounting principles (GAAP) are nonsensical and preposterous.

At the center of this particular issue is Great Southwest Corp. (GSC). It owns large real estate holdings in Texas, Georgia, California and Hawaii, and as a result of a 1969 merger absorbed the operations of Macco Corp. (formerly an almost wholly owned Penn Central realty subsidiary).

A Few Misgivings

In '69, Great Southwest was a prime factor in keeping Penn Central's (the railroad's parent holding company) operating (i.e., "ordinary") income out of the red. Thus, while Penn Central's 1969 "earnings from ordinary operations" were reported to be $4.4 million, it included consolidated profits from real estate property sales and operations of about $82 million. My misgivings here are not with that full sum, of course (some of it came from hotel operations and the like). However, I do quarrel with about $29 million, or 35%, of the total.

Further, while not all the real estate income came from Great Southwest, that unit did contribute most felicitously to Penn Central's reported earnings. As the Penn Central report noted: "Net earnings for Great Southwest Corp. last year set another new high of $34,364,000 after taxes, an increase of 25.3% over 1968 earnings of $27,425,000."

Actually, the statement regarding GSC's contribution to Penn Central's earnings for 1969 may have been understated. Unless I misinterpret the footnotes, the parent washed out the tax reserves established by GSC, which increased the subsidiary's earnings to $51 million, not $34 million. After allowing for the 10% minority interest in the public's hands, Penn Central could be seen to have included net of about $46 million of GSC profits in arriving at its $4.4 million net ordinary operating income for '69.

Let's turn to my "$29 million" complaint. Thus, of GSC's $51 million pre-tax income, about $29 million, or almost 60%, came from a transaction involving the Six Flags Over Texas Amusement Park, a thematic park in the Fort Worth-Dallas area. The Amusement Park was constructed and owned by Great Southwest. In June, 1969, however, it was sold to a newly created limited partnership, comprising 152 individuals.

In June, 1969, the partnership—called The Six Flags Over Texas Fund Ltd. (to be referred to as "Fund")—sold publicly subscriptions aggregating $5,950,000 in limited partnership interests. The proceeds were used to purchase the amusement park from GSC on June 30, 1969, coincidentally the last day of GSC's (and Penn Central's) quarterly accounting period. Immediately after the purchase, Fund contributed the property to another partnership ("Flags") in which a new Great Southwest subsidiary, SFOT, became the general partner (with a $1,000 contribution). Fund was the limited partner in the Flags venture. SFOT thereafter became the "sole and exclusive manager of the partnership business."

The nearly $6 million Fund raised among its 152 limited partners was disbursed as follows: $1.5 million as a down payment; another $3,932,670 for "the prepayment of interest"; the next $416,500 covered the underwriter's commission; and the rest (yes, there was something left over—exactly $100,830) to Fund's working capital.

The price tag for the Amusement Park and a covenant by GSC not to compete in that area was set at $40 million. That contrasts with the gross cost of the Amusement Park to GSC of $14,183,175 as of April 30, 1969; after allowing for accumulated depreciation on the Amusement Park of $4,842,647, GSC's carrying value was about $9.3 million. According to the Fund prospectus: "The price of the Amusement Park and consideration for the covenant not to compete was determined through negotiations between Property Research Corp. and GSC. Fund did not participate in any negotiations relating to such price or such consideration for the covenant not to compete. . . ."

The $40 million total purchase price was allocated as follows: land, $5,000,000; buildings and improvements and personal property, $25,000,000; GSC's covenant not to compete, $8,000,000; goodwill and license to use the name "Six Flags Over Texas," $2,000,000.

GSC wound up with the $1.5 million cash down payment, plus an "Amusement Park note" for the remaining $38,500,000. The indebtedness is vital to the accounting analysis which will follow, so let's study it closely. The note carries an interest rate of 6.5% per annum (when money was going for 8% or more to prime borrowers), with principal and interest payable in the combined amount of $2,315,685 annually. The indebtedness would be liquidated by the year 2005 A.D.

Lest I be accused of being "chintzy," and caviling over whether the rate should have been 6.5% or more, let's read on about the Amusement Park Note. Thus, under "limited liability," the Fund prospectus makes the following point:

"The sole recourse of such holder for the collection of the Amusement Park Note shall be against the property covered by the Amusement Park Mortgage. The Amusement Park Note will provide that neither Fund nor any general or limited partner of Fund shall be liable personally for the payment of the

Amusement Park Note or for the payment of any deficiency upon foreclosure under and sale of the property covered by the Amusement Park mortgage."

This, then, is the way GSC sold to Fund the land, buildings, improvements and equipment (which, as duly noted in a 14-page exhibit to the prospectus, included a Merry-go-Round complete with 1 Band Organ, a cannon range with 8 cannons, a Crazy Horse, and a "Casa Magnetica" complete with 1 bed).

Despite the questionable "quality" of the paper taken back on the sale, GSC picked up (with its auditor's blessing) $17.5 million in after-tax income (and about $29 million in pre-tax income) on that $40 million transaction. By way of an aside, it's worthwhile pointing out that the limited partners, who "anted up" almost $6 million (so that GSC could enjoy this $29 million of bookkeeping income) also got a nice slice of pie—but not from GSC; the slice will come out of IRS's hide (to switch the metaphor).

Tax Gimmicks

At first blush, it might appear they were euchred. Thus, when one looks at Fund's 1969 Form 10K, it's clear that the *entire* $6 million of investment was eliminated by a loss of about $6 million so that the limited partners ended up with a *capital deficit* after six months of playing in the park—all duly certified by Fund's independent certified public accountants. As a result, the limited partners hope to enjoy huge tax write-offs.

Clearly, what attracted the limited partners was that they were being let in on a tax-gimmicked deal. The prospectus informs the potential "investor" that for tax purposes the first $32 million (with certain adjustments) of accumulated net losses (computed without depreciation) will be deemed to be for the account of Fund's limited partners. Further, and especially essential to the tax maneuver, "for tax purposes, all depreciation allowable in respect of the property of Flags and all amortization of intangibles allowable to Flags . . . and all credits allowed to Flags (as investment credits, for example) will be allocated to the Flags Limited Partner" (and thereby to the Fund limited partners who provided the $5,950,000 lubricant).

Also in the prospectus, limited partners are informed that: "In the opinion of counsel for Fund, at least $3,734,405 of the interest to be prepaid on the Amusement Park Note on the Closing Date ($3,932,670), will be deductible by Fund in computing its net income or loss for the year of payment. . . ."

There is some equivocation, as is appropriate for a proper opinion from tax counsel, that this conclusion might be challenged by the Internal Revenue Service. For example, this expert opinion is predicated "upon assumptions and representations to the effect that the consideration for the covenant on the part of GSC not to compete and the purchase price of the amusement park are their respective fair market values arrived at through arm's length negotiations by unrelated parties. . . ."

It's abundantly clear that the sophisticated syndicate investors were not a party to the negotiations leading to the $40 million price. As far as they were concerned, they'd probably say "the bigger the price, the merrier" because they would then be getting even bigger tax write-offs. In fact, they were not paying the $6 million just to become Texas entrepreneurs. This simply was their price for admission to the Tax Planning Gravy Train (not one of the rides open to the general public in the Texas amusement park); as it turned out, they got a handsome return on their investment by the 1969 write-offs alone.

At this point, we should more fully identify Property Research Corp., which conducted the negotiations with GSC leading to the fixing of the $40 million price and its allocation. As noted, Fund's limited partners were not privy to these deliberations and determinations. They were handed a *fait accompli*. The opinion from tax counsel made explicit that their conclusions were predicated on the assumption that the price and allocations were made at arm's length and hence were done independently and objectively. But were they? Judge for yourself regarding the length of the arm:

First, it should be pointed out, Property Research was not licensed as real estate brokers in Texas (GSC, in fact, had to pay a James L. Flowers, Jr., an honorarium to lend his professional credentials to the transaction). Property Research Corp. happens to be the sole owner of Property Research Interstate Inc. (PRI), underwriters of Fund's limited partnership offering. As noted earlier, PRI realized over $400,000 on that sale. And even more interesting (and sweeter), GSC was obliged to pay PRI's parent, Property Research Corp., $1.2 million in cash plus a promissory note in the original principal amount of $750,000 for compensation for services performed by it in connection with the sale of the Amusement Park, if the deal was consummated.

But back to our main theme, which is: Should Penn Central have recognized this whopping sum as income—extraordinary or ordinary? To be sure, since a similar transaction took place on a smaller scale in 1968 with Six Flags Over Georgia, Peat, Marwick, auditors for both Great Southwest and Penn Central, were able to say that this was recurring annual ordinary income. But, to repeat, was this really income of any kind? (For the record, the Georgia deal was reported in 1968 as extraordinary income. Then, sometime in 1969, it was decided such transactions were now going to be perennial, whereupon the auditors deemed the gains to be ordinary and accordingly restated the 1968 accounts.)

Meeting the Projection

In all this, I have been using Great Southwest and Penn Central financial statements for the calendar year 1969 as the frame of reference. However, it is probable that the primary focus should be on the interim financial statements. What appeared in the annual reports may really have been entirely anticlimactic. It should be emphasized that there is no indication that the independent auditors knew of, or concurred in, the reporting of the transactions in the interim disclosures. Just when they first learned of them, and their reaction, are not known to me. But it's worth noting that at their May, 1969, annual meeting, Penn Central shareholders were told by Board Chairman Stuart Saunders that Penn Central "will have a favorable showing in its second quarter."

As it turned out, Penn Central reported a 7.5% drop in second quarter (1969) earnings, including a loss from its railroad system. On a consolidated basis, Penn Central said it earned $21.9 million, down from $23.6 million in the June quarter of 1968.

If, then, after picking up Penn Central's share of the Amusement Park income (which must have been more than $25 million, after deducting the minority interest) Penn Central could show only $21.9 million, it is safe to say that the consolidated second quarter operations would have shown a deficit absent the Amusement Park deal and such a loss would have been inconsistent, to put it mildly, with Chairman Saunders' prophecy to shareholders.

The fundamental question, though, is whether this $40 million transaction stands up as a sale. Great Southwest, after all, still acts (through SFOT) as the general partner and is solely and exclusively responsible for the management of the operation. Furthermore, was this $38.5 million of non-recourse, 6.5% paper taken on the sale, entitled to be entered in the balance sheet as an asset and, even if so, should it have been carried at face value? Further, should not the auditors at least have spread the $8,000,000 explicitly attributed by the sales contract to the 10-year covenant over the decade in which GSC is constrained not to compete?

And while one might sense the tenuous quality of the GSC earnings in the GSC footnotes, who would be expected to read them since Penn Central owned over 90% of that subsidiary? How, then, could the reader of the ultimately significant Penn Central consolidated statements get even the slightest inkling of this contrived income even after the most careful study of the financial statements and all 15 footnotes, or the euphoric statements of Chairman Saunders included with the 1969 annual report? Should not the independent auditors at least have had the humility to carry over to the Penn Central collage the footnotes (however inadequate in my view) shown by the GSC statement?

What's more, the independent auditors could not here take a "cop-out" by asserting they were merely the auditors for the Penn Central parent and were, therefore, very much like the piano player who had no idea what was going on upstairs. No, the same auditors who certified to the Penn Central statements were the independent auditors for GSC as well. They are also listed as the accounting experts in the Six Flags Over Texas Fund prospectus, and it was they who certified the 1969 statements for that limited partnership.

I cannot but feel that had the GSC auditors stepped back to look at this tangled web as a whole they would have recognized the absurdity of reporting a $29 million profit on this maneuver. They would have seen that the very most that GSC could have realized was the $5 million paid by their new partners, of which $2 million went to the underwriters. They would have seen that at best the extrapolation from $3 million to $29 million was fair only to the extent that GAAP was unfair.

Peat, Marwick's partners have shown some sensitivity to questions regarding the GSC accountings. One partner is quoted as saying that the facts were all in the footnotes. But they were surely not in the Penn Central statements—since there was nothing there regarding this crucial transaction. It wasn't in Penn Central's statements to shareholders nor in the 10K filed with the SEC. As to the GSC statements, statements to which few excepting the most morbidly curious (like this writer) would turn, my response is that it's *not all* there either. The GSC notes disclose naught but the tip of the iceberg—the rest is submerged in the murky waters of GAAP.

This leads to what might well be the crux of this essay. How did the auditors square the absence of any disclosure on the Penn Central statements (and in my view less than full disclosure on those of its subsidiary) with Rule 2.02 of our Code of Professional Ethics, whereby a CPA is enjoined from expressing an opinion on representations in financial statements if he fails "to disclose a material fact known to him which is not disclosed in the financial statements but disclosure of which is necessary to make the financial statements not misleading . . ."?

In the Wake of the Wreck

In the wake of this publication much has happened. The House of Representatives Committee on Banking and Currency issued a series of Staff Reports on "The Penn Central Failure and the Role of Financial Institutions"—which make interesting reading. News articles have, with great frequency, documented the agonies of Penn Central and its subsidiaries in their endeavors to bring together their 1970 accountings and reduce some of the confusion regarding the accounts for the preceding years. Further, on April 19, 1971, the Interstate Commerce Commission's Bureau of Enforcement filed a series of verified statements concerning Penn Central's financial and diversification practices which it compiled in its "Investigation into the Management of the Business of the Penn Central Transportation Company and Affiliated Companies—(Docket No. 35291)."

Undoubtedly anticlimactic, but a significant footnote to this saga, is an article in the June 21, 1971, *Wall Street Journal* headlined "Penn Central's Great Southwest Reports $143.1 Million Loss for '70; Suit Is Filed":

> Great Southwest . . . said it had a $143.1 million loss in 1970, mainly from write-downs of its real estate operations. . . . The net loss . . . compares to a profit of $34.4 million . . . in 1969. . . . "We hope we've properly reserved for the bad news of 1970, and can look forward to a positive year in 1971," said Bruce Juell, Great Southwest executive vice president. . . .
>
> Great Southwest said the present figures are subject to the . . . ultimate effect of pending litigation and certain investigations by

governmental agencies, including a review by the Securities and Exchange Commission of its 1968 and 1969 financial statements.

As to the lawsuit, most of the 125-page complaint, we are told, deals "with a so-called tax-sharing agreement between Great Southwest and its parent company, and the 1969 merger of Macco Corp. into Great Southwest."

Regarding the merger the lawsuit is "seeking $368.5 million in damages. . . . The plaintiffs contend that Glore Forgan and Pennsylvania Co. were unjustly enriched by $260.5 million in the Macco merger when Pennsylvania Co. forced Great Southwest to pay $285.5 million in securities for Macco, whose 'true actual value' wasn't any more than $25 million." Also, Glore Forgan was given 10,000 shares of GSC stock for services and "that the merger decreased Great Southwest's net worth by $108 million."

As to the tax sharing agreement, the shareholders claim that the Pennsylvania Co. "used misrepresentation and fraud" to impose that agreement on GSC.

But of more immediate and direct interest, the March, 1971, Peat, Marwick, Mitchell & Co. *Staff Memo* carried the following as its feature story:

PMM TAKES BRILOFF BEFORE AICPA ETHICS DIVISION

Dr. Abraham J. Briloff, critic of the accounting profession, is being brought before the Ethics Division of the AICPA by PMM & Co. because of his article, "Six Flags at Half-Mast? Great Southwest Corp. Hasn't Exactly Raised Accounting Standards." The article appeared in the January 11 issue of the financial weekly *Barron's*.

In a letter to Donald Schneeman, director—AICPA Division of Professional Ethics, PMM & Co. general counsel Victor M. Earle, III, states that "the Firm charges Briloff with publishing a sensational, defamatory, and unfounded article—in an effort to discredit fellow members [of the Institute]."

The Division, further, is asked "to look into and to dispose of this matter with all deliberate speed because of the gravity of the charges contained in the *Barron's* piece. . . ."

In his article, Briloff, professor of accounting at the Baruch College of the City University of New York, focuses on the Great Southwest Corp.'s sale of The Six Flags Over Texas Amusement Park, located in the Forth Worth—Dallas area, to a newly-created limited partnership.

Briloff charges that the sale was "a gerrymandered, contrived transaction" and, therefore, recording a gain "makes sense and is logical only if we are willing to presume that our generally accepted accounting principles (GAAP) are nonsensical and preposterous."

In a refutation of several thousand words submitted to the Ethics Division, senior partner Walter E. Hanson replies to Briloff's allegations in detail. He sums up by saying that, "Not only is he [Briloff] totally wrong about that [The Six Flags] transaction, but in addition he goes beyond all limits of credulity by suggesting that the accounting for it by one subsidiary somehow led to Penn Central's collapse."

There are a number of serious errors of omission and commission in this story; be that as it may, some weeks subsequent to publishing this staff story Peat, Marwick did get around to submitting a complaint to the AICPA Ethics Division, making its article something of a self-fulfilling prophecy. The complaint was accompanied by their "Analysis of the Accounting Aspects of the Sale by Great Southwest Corporation of Six Flags Over Texas."

PMM to the Defense

In this analysis, after recapitulating their version of the facts and summarizing "Briloff's Complaints" and presenting theoretical argument pertaining to "When Is a Sale a Sale?" and "When Is Revenue Earned?" followed by a section on the subsequent "Operation of the Amusement Park," PMM turns to the "Arm's Length Aspects of [the] Transaction," as follows (paragraph numbers are those used by PMM in its analysis):

33. Briloff implies the sales price was not determined at arm's length because Property Research, the underwriter, was well paid.

To our knowledge, Property Research was not affiliated with GSC and GSC was not affiliated with the 152 investors. GSC had obtained an appraisal indicating a fair value of about $38 million. The price was set at $40 million and accepted by 152 investors in a public offering. We had and have absolutely no reason to question the arm's lentgh aspect of the transaction, and the appropriateness of the amount GSC paid Property Research was not a matter for us to judge.

Then, following brief discussions of "Measurement of the Revenue" and the "Noncompete Covenant," the PMM Analysis proceeds to the response to the crucial "disclosure" complaint in the "Six Flags" article. Under the caption "Disclosure and Materiality" they state the following:

41. He complains without explanation, of the "inadequate" disclosure in GSC's statement.

42. It is difficult to imagine what more Briloff could demand of GSC's footnote treatment of the Six Flags transaction. Note Sixteen of the 1969 annual report reads as follows:

On December 31, 1968, Great Southwest Atlanta Corp., a subsidiary of the Company, sold all of the property and equipment of Six Flags Over Georgia, an amusement park, for $22,980,157 resulting in a net gain of $4,813,400. Upon completion of the sale, the purchaser, Six Flags Fund, Ltd., contributed the amusement park to a limited partnership in which Great Southwest Atlanta Corp. is the General Partner and operator. As partial consideration for the sale, Great Southwest Atlanta Corp. received a 7% mortgage note in the original amount of $21,000,000 which is secured by the amusement park. The note is payable in annual principal instalments of $700,000 beginning in March 1975 and is subject to optional prepayments without penalty.

On June 30, 1969, Great Southwest Corporation sold all of the property and equipment of Six Flags Over Texas, an amusement park, for $40,000,000 resulting in a net gain of $17,530,170. Upon completion of the sale, the purchaser, Six Flags Over Texas Fund, Ltd., contributed the amusement park to a limited partnership in which Six Flags Over Texas, Inc., a wholly-owned subsidiary of Great Southwest Corporation, is the General Partner and operator. As partial consideration for the sale, the Company received a 6½% mortgage note in the amount of $38,301,585 which is secured by the amusement park. The note is payable in annual principal instalments of $1,094,-331 beginning in March 1971 and is subject to optional prepayments without penalty.

Subsequent to the sale of Six Flags Over Georgia, the Company changed its policy toward amusement parks from one of constructing and operating such parks to one of constructing, developing, selling and operating such parks. Accordingly, the sale of the amusement park known as Six Flags Over Georgia in 1968 has been reclassified from amounts previously reported to reflect the transaction as an ordinary sale rather than as an extraordinary item.

43. Interestingly, the first paragraph of that Note 16 is almost identical to the disclosure the year before in the 1968 annual report regarding the sale of Six Flags Over Georgia.

44. Of even greater interest is the fact that the 1968 financial statements were incorporated by reference into GSC's proxy statement dated April 11, 1969. . . .

45. The 1968 financial statements of GSC were reviewed by the staff of the Securities and Exchange Commission. The staff did not question the accounting treatment of the sale of Six Flags Over Georgia or the adequacy of the disclosure.

46. Aside from the fact that the amounts were different, the sale of Six Flags Over Texas was almost identical to the sale of Six Flags Over Georgia.

47. Finally, in the *crux of his essay*, Briloff complains of no disclosure of this transaction in Penn Central's financial statements. . . .

48. GSC, Penn Central, and Peat, Marwick had absolutely no reason to hide or bury this transaction in Penn Central's financial statements. Any such intent is irreconcilable with the record. The sale was reported in *The Wall Street Journal* on July 1, 1969. . . . Penn Central's press release on July 28, 1969 . . . and it was mentioned by David Bevan (Chairman of Penn Central's Finance Committee) at Penn Central's annual meeting in May 1969.

49. When we reported on Penn Central's financial statements, we obviously did not rely on the fact that the transaction had been disclosed publicly in not requiring disclosure in the financial statements. The question of disclosure of this transaction in the financial statements was specifically discussed by our partners, and the conclusion was that the transaction was not of the character or magnitude to require specific disclosure—it was not material.

50. Disclosure was made in GSC's financial statements, for obviously the sale of the Amusement Park, while in the ordinary course of business, was a material matter to be considered with respect to GSC.

51. But was it of a magnitude requiring separate disclosure in Penn Central's financial statements? Was one ordinary transaction netting $25 or $30 million to Penn Central material? It's less than 1% of shareholders' equity of $2.8 billion. It's 1+% of total revenues of $2.3 billion. It's about 25% of net income from real estate and related operations, the revenues and costs of which were clearly set forth in the statement of earnings. It's about 25% of the net loss of $122 million. There were total property sales of $186 million—why single this one transaction out for special mention? Why talk about one property sale netting $25 or $30 million but not about the snowstorm that cost just as much when both are in the ordinary course of each year's events?

52. Briloff relates the gain to earnings of $4.4 million from ordinary operations and concludes the gain was material. If $4.4 million is the beacon, literally dozens of items were material and should have been separately mentioned. That would be preposterous.

53. And to say, as Briloff does, that the ". . . appearance of Penn Central's financial viability . . . was achieved . . ." (paragraph 2) through the accounting for this one transaction and to suggest that the accounting for this one transaction somehow contributed to Penn Central's ". . . present dismal state" (paragraph 2) is utterly absurd. No matter what Briloff or anyone else says, $25 million more or less in Penn Central's balance sheet at December 31, 1969 cannot achieve the appearance of financial viability of Penn Central. Just look at the balance sheet.

It would, of course, be entirely inappropriate to enter into the controversy with Peat, Marwick regarding their ethics complaint against me; nor will I here take issue with them regarding the theoretical arguments or the standards of materiality and disclosure advanced in their analysis. To the contrary, I here and now confess and proclaim *Mea culpa!!* I could not know it at the time I wrote the article that in actuality the Six Flags deal was really "no big deal" by the Penn Central–Great Southwest–Peat, Marwick lights. I did not then know that what I thought was an extraordinary, material, unusual dramatic transaction by the Penn Central complex (requiring important and agonizing deliberation by their auditors with resultant disclosure in Penn Central's published statements) was really nothing more than business as usual. I beg forgiveness for thinking $29 million was a lot of money for Penn Central's 1969 second quarter income, and their reported 1969 full-year operations. I was thereby manifesting a limited-focus, gimlet-eye view of $29 million of income.

I now see how, as the analysis puts it, the PMM partners could "specifically discuss" the "question of disclosure of this transaction in the [Penn Central] financial statements" and come up with "the conclusion . . . that the transaction was not of the character or magnitude to require specific disclosure—it was not material." Similarly, I can now better understand how from their ethereal heights the PMM partners could determine that the transaction was not "of a magnitude requiring separate disclosure in Penn Central's financial statements." After all, I can now see that this was just "one ordinary transaction netting $25 or $30 million to Penn Central" and therefore not "material." I can now, with the greater wisdom acquired since my original "Six Flags" broodings, recognize that I should not have "single[d] this one transaction out for special mention."

The ICC Investigates

Whence cometh this new wisdom? No, it was not from the PMM analysis; instead, I have been much informed by the verified statements (specially those numbered 9 and 13) and the supporting exhibits filed by the investigators for the Interstate Commerce Commission in April, 1971.

So it is that in his verified statement No. 13, George K. Deller, an auditor assigned to the ICC's Philadelphia regional office, reported on his investigation of "the circumstances of Penn Central's investments in Great Southwest Corp. and Macco Corp." In the course of his investigation Mr. Deller "reviewed documentary material pertaining to Great Southwest and Macco . . . maintained in Penn Central's Philadelphia office. In addition [he] visited Great Southwest's offices in New Beach, California and Arlington, Texas . . . [where he] reviewed the books of account and corporate records of Great Southwest and its subsidiary companies, including Macco."

Based on his review, Deller's affidavit gave us the following insights regarding the Great Southwest–Macco goings on:

1. The 1965–1969 profits from these two companies reported by Penn Central:

	GSC	Macco	Total
1965	$ 2,132,000	$ 3,703,000	$ 5,835,000
1966	3,007,000	4,331,000	7,338,000
1967	5,014,000	7,566,000	12,580,000
1968	9,654,000	21,021,000	30,675,000
1969	34,364,000	*	34,364,000
Totals	$54,171,000	$36,621,000	$90,792,000

* Merged into GSC during 1969.

2. The affidavit then goes on to describe the most salutary effect which the GSC-Macco *modus operandi* has had on the Penn Central accountings. This phenomenon was especially apparent in a September 20, 1969, memorandum from Basil Cole, Penn Central's Vice President—Executive Department, to Penn Central's Chairman Stuart Saunders. It appears that the operations for the third quarter of 1969 (the quarter immediately following the Six Flags Over Texas deal) were in the red; Cole was concerned, whereupon he wrote to Saunders pointing up the dramatic possibility of another of the "Great Southwest

deals"—this time using "some of the assets of Merchants Dispatch" as the catalyst. In describing this possibility for "changing the color" of the quarterly report, the Cole memorandum provided the following insights:

> It will be necessary to give [this kind of a deal] highest priority if anything is to be accomplished in the seven working days remaining in this quarter. Concluding a sale to another railroad or a car-leasing company seems out of the question, but based on discussions with Harry Beeman, Ted Warner, Sam Hellenbrand and others, it seems to be technically feasible to structure a transaction patterned after one of the Great Southwest deals. (Bryant Ranch was sold to a limited partnership for $100,000 cash and a promissory note for $30,900,000.) MDT has a fleet of 4,000 to 5,000 refrigerator cars and several repair shops which are virtually debt-free. I see no real difficulty in finding an investor to purchase these assets and then contract with MDT for their operation. More difficult will be the technical problem of putting together a transaction that will satisfy PM&M and avoid the label of gimmick if exposed to public scrutiny. As to this, Charlie Hill's ideas and views will be indispensable.

3. The Deller affidavit then goes into great detail regarding the Bryant Ranch transaction, the one referred to by the Cole memorandum as the prototype of the Great Southwest deals. It seems that proprietorship of the 4,928-acre ranch in Orange County, California, went along a rather tortuous trail prior to the real big income injection in 1968. All or parts of it were traded back and forth among Macco and its subsidiaries as follows:

a. In 1964 the property was sold to a partnership (Canada Oaks) in which Macco kept a two-thirds stake in profits.

b. In 1967 it was sold to another partnership, Highlands Investment Company.

Property Research Corp. (PRC), a securities and real estate broker, an officer of PRC and its legal counsel together held 45% of the ownership interest in Highlands Investment Company. [Macco] paid to PRC a commission of $565,000. . . .

[Macco] recorded a gain of $4,939,726 on the sale to Highlands. As indicated earlier, Penn Central reported to its stockholders that Macco earned $7,566,000 in 1967.

c. In 1968 (after reacquiring the Ranch from Highlands) Macco Valley sold the entire Bryant tract to Saddleback Investment Company for $31 million.

This was the sale referred to in Basil Cole's memorandum of September 20, 1969, to Stuart Saunders. As consideration, Bonnie Valley was to receive at closing $100,000 as a principal down payment, an unsecured note in the amount of $5.4 million representing Saddleback's obligation to prepay interest in that amount in 1968, and a note in the amount of $30.9 million, payable over 20 years and secured by a deed of trust on the Bryant property. The latter note contained a provision obligating Saddleback to make a principal payment of $500,000 before December 31, 1968.

Saddleback Investment Company was organized the same day it purchased the Bryant Ranch from Bonnie Valley. Formed as a limited partnership under California law, Saddleback's sole general partner was Dennis E. Carpenter. Its sole limited partner was Property Research Corporation, the firm involved in the 1967 sale of 1,800 acres of Bryant land to Highlands Investment Company.

For its part in the sale of the Bryant Ranch Property to Saddleback, Property Research received a $2 million real estate brokerage commission from [Macco].

Macco recorded on its books a pretax gain of $11,780,000 on the sale of Bryant Ranch to Saddleback. In recognition of Jamboree Land Co.'s investment in Saddleback [because PRC could not dispose of all of the limited partnership units in Saddleback so one of Macco's subsidiaries, Jamboree Land Co. "warehoused" the unsold units until 1969], $1,786,000 of the gain was deferred until 1969, when Jamboree disposed of its interests in Saddleback.

For 1968, as noted above, Penn Central's shareholders were advised that Macco had consolidated earnings of $21,021,000—we now know over half of it came from the Bryant Ranch deal.

4. There were other major real-estate deals, as Deller's affidavit goes on to inform us. He lists five such deals in 1968 and 1969, as follows:

	Purchaser	Reported Profit
1968	J.T. Pool	$3,400,000
	Tampa Investment Co.	2,242,000
	Abe Reider, *et al.*	2,863,000
	Subtotal	8,505,000
1969	Turmac Investment	1,001,000
	Lake California Funds	1,910,000
	Subtotal	2,911,000
1968–69	Total	$11,416,000

According to the affidavit all of these deals had similar terms and conditions, to wit: (*a*) down payment of less than 5 percent of principal; (*b*) a two-to seven-year moratorium on principal payments; and (*c*) one year's prepayment of interest at the closing.

He then pointed out that the aggregate selling price involved in this handful of transactions was about $20 million and only "$441,375 cash was received as principal down payments"; the "notes received as consideration had maturities extending from seven to twelve years."

What we see here are some very rich profit mixes (over 50 percent of the sales prices) even though only about 2½ percent is paid in cash. The affidavit doesn't point this up, but notice how closely the Bryant Ranch "profit" together with the "profits" on the three special 1968 transactions just about account for all of Macco's profits, as reported by its parent Penn Central. Little wonder Mr. Cole was enthralled by the idea of another "Great Southwest deal" to salvage Penn Central's third-quarter 1969 income collage.

Not that it's that important, but for the sake of completeness the Deller affidavit calculates that Macco's 1968–69 profits from those five deals would have been less than $300,000 rather than over $11 million if they had been reported on the so-called instalment method, that is, proportionate to the principal collections.

5. The Deller verified statement No. 13 then goes into some detail to explain the 1968 Six Flags Over Georgia sale as well as the corresponding one Over Texas the following year. But we're experts on the structuring of that kind of transaction, so we'll pass them by.

This single affidavit gave me insights into the real-estate transactions and accountings by Penn Central which I never dreamed possible; as the ICC's investigator pointed out so dramatically, these Great Southwest land deals were as ordinary and commonplace as Penn Central selling tickets to Pittsburgh.

And to proceed even further with this confession, I should not have even presumed to probe and then to criticize the whole accounting process created by Penn Central for its reports to shareholders. I came to this sorry conclusion after careful study of the disclosures contained in verified statement No. 9 submitted by Thomas J. Russo of the ICC's Bureau of Accounts. It was his responsibility, in connection with the Penn Central investigation, to review and investigate "various accounting practices followed by the carrier's previous management." In his sworn statement, based on his review and investigation, Mr. Russo makes the following assertions:

1. *Maximization of Reported Earnings.* In general, the management of the merged Penn Central adopted the former Pennsylvania Railroad's policy of maximizing income. The result was an increase in income without a corresponding increase in cash flow, thus obscuring the carrier's true financial condition.

Even before the merger the widening difference between the PRR's reported income and its cash flow caused David Bevan to state in a November 21, 1966, memorandum to Stuart Saunders:

The policy may be instituted of maximizing earnings to the greatest extent possible within the limits of good accounting practices. In the last years, this has been done on the Pennsylvania in accordance with your expressed desires. It does mean, however, that we tend to create a wider and wider difference as between reported income and cash flow. Today the cash flow of the Pennsylvania Railroad is substantially less than its reported income. We changed the basis of consolidation and, therefore, a substantial amount of earnings of subsidiaries are now included in our reported income but are not actually available to us from the standpoint of dividends. . . .

Over the short term today the New York Central earnings as reported are much more real and tangible from the standpoint of an ability to pay dividends than are these of the Pennsylvania. . . .

When these facts are borne in mind, it is easy to see that New York Central is paying dividends well within its capacity whereas in the case of Pennsylvania, we are stretching our financial resources to the limit.

As indicated, this emphasis on reported earnings was carried forward by the merged Penn Central. In a memorandum to Stuart Saunders dated January 15, 1969, Basil Cole, former Vice President–Staff, suggested that auditors from Peat, Marwick, Mitchell & Co. be encouraged to uncover areas, overlooked by Penn Central accountants, where profitability might be improved.

Following for your consideration, are three subjects that you may wish to cover with Walter Hanson [of Peat, Marwick, Mitchell & Co.] during your luncheon tomorrow. . . .

2. *Earnings Improvement Opportunities.* The primary function of PM&M is to police the accounts against abuses, but in many cases they are in a position to uncover situations where advantageous items tending to improve profitability have been overlooked by our accountants. In such cases it would be very helpful if the information were brought to the attention of the Comptroller, or the appropriate accounting representative, to provide an opportunity to maximize net income.

That the Penn Central was "earning profits" in the accounting offices rather than in operations is evidenced by a letter from the former controller to Mr. Bevan with reference to the individual who became the eventual controller. The letter states in part:

"His imaginative accounting is adding millions of dollars annually to our net income."

The affidavit then goes on to detail a number of important "steps undertaken by Penn Central to maximize reported income." While they are of great magnitude and interest, they are not especially germane to Penn Central's land-office operations; accordingly I shall not relate them here.

Insights from an Insider

Some further insights into the land-office maneuvers of Penn Central via Great Southwest (and these might well complement Russo's findings) are provided by a complaint filed in mid-July, 1971, with the United States District Court in Dallas, Texas. In that case the plaintiff, Byron Williams, sued as a shareholder of Great Southwest claiming that he (and other shareholders) had been defrauded by the practices perpetrated by the Pennsylvania Company, Penn Central, Glore Forgan and others. In his affidavit verifying the complaint, Williams describes his intimate knowledge of the transactions complained of since, at varying times, he was a member of the law firm of which GSC's chief executive's father was the principal partner, and that he represented that executive "in his personal bankruptcy proceedings growing out of his involvement with the 'Texas Pavilion' at the 1964–1965 New York World's Fair." More directly, and more significantly, Williams was the "Assistant to the President" at Great Southwest.

As such an insider, Williams describes the following pattern of land transactions contrived for GSC's subsidiary, Macco, by its management under a "perform or get fired" mandate from Penco (the railroad's holding company). Under this edict Macco had "to produce book profits and improve the cash-flow deficiency . . . all without borrowing from Penco and without any kind of equity financing. . . ." How did the ingenious GSC-Macco management fulfill its mandate? Here's the sequence described by Williams in his complaint:

A. Macco would contract to sell a tract of real estate to a third-party speculator for a relatively small cash down payment (usually taking the form of pre-paid interest) and a promissory note for the balance.

B. The promissory note given by the purchaser to Macco for the balance of the purchase was "non-recourse" and carried with it no personal liability to the maker. . . .

C. Since the purchaser was not assuming personal liability on the purchase money note (but was merely speculating and hoping for a price rise, and his pre-paid interest "down payment" was deductible in the year paid, he could afford to pay a much greater price for the real estate than a "user-purchaser."

D. Simultaneouly, Macco as a professional land developer, would contract to develop the property for the purchaser . . . within a given period, to the purchaser's satisfaction.

E. Such contract would provide that if Macco did not complete the development obligations within the specified period, it was obligated to rescind the sale (or repurchase the property); returning to the purchaser the amount of money . . . actually paid in, plus a return thereon at some specified rate as, for example, 7% per annum.

F. Thus, if Macco did not perform its development obligations and had to repurchase under the contract, the net effect (after it was over) was that Macco had borrowed the purchaser's money for a given period at 7%.

So impressed was Penn Central's Finance Committee Chairman with this charade that he acclaimed it as "ingenious" because it (as the complaint goes on) "not only obtained financing for Macco at no cost or risk of equity dilution . . . but Penco also found that the transactions so structured met SEC and professional accounting standards for booking profits on each such sale."

In his supporting affidavit Byron William gives us some rather intimate and highly personal details of how GSC fitted the Penn Central game plan so admirably, viz:

On or about March 20, 1969 . . . I received a telephone call from {Macco President] Baker in which he informed me that [Penn

Central Chairman] Saunders had telephoned him with an emergency request for as many dollars profit as could be produced by GSC and/or Macco before the end of the quarter (March 31, 1969), and he asked me to supervise the GSC efforts to accomplish same.

*   *   *

From the time of Baker's call until 11 o'clock P.M. on the night of March 31, 1969, I worked some 12 to 20 hours per day meeting the profit goals, and literally had no time for any other endeavor.

It goes without saying that had I known all this I would have realized that the Six Flags deal was so much a part of the standard operating routine of creating the appearance of profits in the last moments of a calendar quarter that, as its auditors steadfastly maintain, it became an integral part of its normal operations—you know, like selling Metroliner tickets to passengers in a hurry. In retrospect, it is hard to see why the erstwhile Assistant to the President at GSC fell into the same trap; he should have known better since he was such an integral part of the "earnings factory." So we'll give forth with yet another *Mea Culpa!!* this time in behalf of both Byron Williams and myself.

It follows inexorably, therefore, that I must apologize abjectly to Peat, Marwick for my having singled out the Six Flags Over Texas deal as if it were a "big deal" and thereby implying that there was something so exceptional, unique, or extraordinary about it as to raise the eyebrows of any auditor. From what Peat, Marwick's analysis submitted to the AICPA in connection with their ethics complaint against me, but more dramatically from what was revealed to me by the report of the ICC Enforcement Division, the Six Flags Over Texas transaction was clearly subsumed under the "game plan" devised by Penn Central's management, apparently after active and regular consultation with their auditors.

I apologize, also, to Property Research Corporation for even implying that their masterminding of the Six Flags Over Texas limited partnership involved something other than an arm's-length, clear, cold, objective appraisal of the Six Flags Over Texas properties so that they were worth exactly $40 million. After all, they have been part of a symbiotic relationship with Penn Central's subsidiaries in their "subdeployment" practices for a number of years.

I know now that my criticism stemmed from my naïve presumption that the auditors would probe the *substance* of transactions and exorcise those which were structured to accommodate management's plan for "maximization of reported earnings," that is, the plan referred to by Mr. Russo, to wit: "In general, the management of the merged Penn Central adopted the former Pennsylvania Railroad's policy of maximizing income."

The SEC Orders Hearings

Then, too, on December 9, 1971, the Securities and Exchange Commission "ordered public administrative proceedings . . . involving Great Southwest Corporation . . . 91.44% . . . owned by Pennsylvania Company which is wholly owned by Penn Central Transportation Company [which, in turn] is a wholly owned subsidiary of Penn Central Company." (SEC Release No. 9418.)

These hearings were to begin January 5, 1972, on the SEC staff's allegations that the Great Southwest financial statements for 1968 and 1969 contained "materially misleading statements" and omitted "material information required . . . to make the statements . . . not misleading." In an accompanying statement the SEC's Division of Corporation Finance detailed the ways in which Great Southwest went about creating bookkeeping profits on its dispositions (under the questionable circumstances with which we are already intimately familiar) of the Bryant Ranch and Six Flags Over Georgia during 1968, and of the Texas counterpart in 1969.

These hearing were then postponed from time to time—most recently to Valentine's Day, 1972.

I was looking forward to the revelations at these hearings; I was confident that they would further clarify a great deal of my confusion regarding the accountings of Great Southwest and its Penn Central parent. I was especially hopeful that these proceedings would fill important gaps in my understanding because, in addition to the SEC's own usual careful preparation for the hearings, they were counselled by Congressman Wright Patman, as Chairman of the House Committee on Banking and Currency, to initiate "certain lines of questioning . . . in order to insure that the total picture emerges from the hearings." The lines of questioning suggested by Chairman Patman to William J. Casey, Chairman of the Securities and Exchange Commission, were as follows:

1. The roles played by the various parties in the transactions including:
   a. Great Southwest officers
   b. Pennsylvania Company officers.
   c. Penn Central officers and directors
   d. Commercial banks
   e. Peat, Marwick, Mitchell & Co.
   f. Property Research Management
2. The real nature of the cash flow from the purchasers of the properties to Great Southwest to the Pennsylvania Company to Penn Central.
3. What was the basis of the payback by the purchasers? Where were the funds to come from?
4. What was the true financial condition of the syndicates (purchasers) who allegedly acquired the properties?
5. Were the purchasers enticed into the transactions on the basis that their participation would provide them with a tax shelter for a very small cash investment?
6. What pressures were brought to bear on Peat, Marwick, Mitchell & Co. by Penn Central management? Did Peat, Marwick, Mitchell & Co. exercise the proper degree of independence

in their dealings with the managements of Great Southwest, the Pennsylvania Co., and Penn Central?

7. What were the reasons behind the Penn Central management's attempts to distort the financial data?

8. How can Peat, Marwick, Mitchell & Co. justify its standards for verifying the "Accounts Receivable" in the three transactions involving Great Southwest with its answer to the SEC complaint in the Liberty Equity case.

9. What fees did Peat, Marwick, Mitchell & Co. receive from Great Southwest, the Pennsylvania Co., and Penn Central for its services? Were these fees reasonable in relation to the work performed by Peat, Marwick, Mitchell & Co.?

But lo! my hopes and expectations were dashed moments before the postponed hearing date. For reasons not yet officially disclosed, the SEC withdrew its order for the hearings; accordingly, this source of important enlightenment is foreclosed to me—at least for the present.

The *Wall Street Journal* for March 3, 1972, did give us some inkling as to what's in the works, thus:

> Great Southwest continues to be involved in major litigation and currently is discussing with the Securities and Exchange Commission the financial reporting of certain transactions in 1968 and 1969, Mr. Palmieri said. The SEC's staff alleged in December that Great Southwest's annual 10K reports for 1968 and 1969 "materially" overstated sales and net. The SEC alleged that the overstatement had resulted from "improperly including" in sales revenue the contract price of three real estate transactions.
>
> If a settlement is reached along lines being discussed, Mr. Palmieri said, it will result in a substantial reduction of Great Southwest's net worth, possibly resulting in a deficit figure for the company's net worth. About $20 million of profit is involved for the two years in the discussions, Mr. Palmieri said. He emphasized that the SEC discussions won't affect 1971 earnings.

Regrettably, publication of this book cannot be delayed until this epic is concluded. It will be especially interesting to see whether the incumbent management exculpates itself by putting the onus onto its predecessors, and the company's auditors. In turn, how will the auditors react to a determination that the silk purse to which they certified in 1969 and 1970 (for the years 1968 and 1969 respectively) were nought but you know what.

In the light of all this new enlightenment, while I plead *mea culpa* I cannot refrain from adding *E pur si muove.*

My anguished pleas for forgiveness were heard and granted. Thus, in late October, 1971, the Executive Committee of the Ethics Division of the American Institute of Certified Public Accountants informed me that there was no basis to the Peat, Marwick complaint against me. Can there be a more fitting ending to a morality play?

Great Southwest Laid to Rest

On January 15, 1973, the Securities and Exchange Commission promulgated its Findings and Opinion in the Great Southwest administrative proceedings. Incorporated in this most recent promulgation was the Commission's order, issued May 30, 1972, directing GSC to restate its 1968 and 1969 accounts so as to exclude the profits attributable to both Six Flags deals, as well as the Bryant Ranch raw land transaction. According to the Commission:

> Where financial statement . . . treated certain real estate transactions as sales and recorded profits in connection therewith, but it appeared that, though transactions may have met formal, legal requirements of sale, corporation retained control over management of properties and retained substantially all risk of loss and opportunity for gain, *held,* financial statements [were] materially misleading in treating transactions as sales for accounting purposes. . . .

> The accounting principles involved are not new or unique. Ten years ago we issued Accounting Series Release No. 95 ("ASR 95") to provide guidance in the application of generally accepted accounting principles to real estate transactions reported in financial statements. . . . In our opinion, the real estate transactions in question in this proceeding involved circumstances of the type discussed in ASR 95 . . . dictating that there be no recognition of profit.

Chapter 9

A House Is Not a Home

THE week preceding July 19, 1971, was hectic—for the home-builders and for me. A dispatch by Reuters conveying the flavor of that frenetic period reads as follows, with only typographical errors corrected:

Professor Critical of Market Action

on

Rumors of His Real Estate Study

"Talking Point"

New York, July 16—Real-estate stocks got hammered yesterday when a rumor circulated that yet another report was due to be issued on their sometimes controversial accounting methods.

But the man said to be responsible for the report told Reuters that the flurry of selling developed over an unwarranted nervousness in the market and had nothing to do with his work in the area.

Professor Abraham Briloff, a well-known lecturer at New York's City University, denied that the report was even ready and called the market's reaction a sickening circumstance.

Rumors that Briloff's report was on the way hit some of the stocks for big losses.

U.S. Home Corp. dropped $6\frac{7}{8}$ to $63\frac{1}{8}$; Development Corp. of America plunged $4\frac{1}{2}$ to $63\frac{3}{4}$.

U.S. Financial Corp. was halted most of the session after los-
ing one point to 46¾ on an imbalance of orders.

Briloff explained that "A couple of weeks ago, I made some
inquiries of a few security analysts concerning the real-estate field.
As a result . . . this all happens."

Briloff said he has no idea of what the content of the report
will be. "I have no preconceived conclusions on the real-estate
industry's accounting methods," he said. "The study is far from
fruition," adding that it might not be ready for months.

The professor, who also travels the lecture circuit appearing
before professional groups and has written for financial publica-
tions, noted that in the course of a year he prepares "maybe a
dozen papers . . . and this is only one."

He blamed the stocks' collapse on the market's "nervousness
and tension over the real-estate group and how the rumors flew
just thick and fast as a result of these very preliminary questions."

A source on the trading floor said that it was undoubtedly concerned over Briloff's report that set off the selling.

He noted that some analysts understood that excerpts from a
longer report would appear this weekend in a financial paper and
that it would be highly critical of the handling of real-estate sales
by some development companies, who in the past have taken a
substantial portion of the purchase price into the income figures
although only a small part of the price has been paid by the
buyer.

But Briloff said he found it hard to understand how the market could react so quickly to rumors when he hadn't yet determined himself what the report would conclude.

References to this flap appeared in *The New York Times* and
Wall Street Journal on successive days. Subsequently (late July)
a "Heard on the Street" column of the *Journal* began as follows:

The recent drubbing of the fast-stepping homebuilding stocks,
still painful to many investors, is leading to a sweeping reassess-
ment of some of these securities.

It's generally agreed that many companies in the field should
continue to display above-average earnings growth. At least over
the next year or so. But the consensus among several analysts is

that the perplexing questions surrounding some homebuilding industry accounting procedures may well have an inhibiting effect on future stock-price advances during the next few months.

About 10 days ago, homebuilding stocks ran into brisk selling amid rumors that *Barron's* had an unfavorable article in preparation on the industry's accounting practices. Some stocks, such as U.S. Financial and U.S. Home, were stung by quick declines . . . in market value. What scared some pros was the rumor that the article would be written by Abraham Briloff, a professor of accountancy at the City University of New York. Last year, the professor wrote a critical review of the accounting practices of land-development companies in *Barron's*. That article had a devastating effect. It sent the shares of many such concerns skidding, and the group has yet to fully recover.

In fact, Mr. Briloff doesn't have any article in preparation at this time. However, he is in the early stages of a study on the accounting practices of homebuilders. And his findings may be included in a book on accounting that he's planning to have published this fall. In any event, whether his findings do or don't make the book, several analysts think the homebuilding group faces uncertainty until the study's conclusions are unveiled.

Market letters prepared by various Wall Street houses entered into the controversy regarding the pros and cons of the accounting of the homebuilders. One such newsletter, written by a professor of accountancy and published by an important brokerage firm, sought to allay the investors' concerns. Thus, after taking note of the lowering of "the accounting boom . . . on another industry—homebuilders" in the "past few weeks," that letter continued: "As a professor and an accountant, this writer takes pride in the clout we have recently achieved. Nevertheless, it is not clear that in this instance the evidence justified the reaction."

Inflators vs. Programmers

That "professor and accountant" proceeds to an invidious distinction between "earning inflators" (he cites the franchisors as an illustration) and the "earnings programmers" (i.e., the homebuilders). In the former instances the companies "were systematically inflating reported income. They reported sales and profits well before they were apparently earned. . . . The bubble burst only when the accounting rules were changed to require much slower reporting."

Homebuilders, on the other hand, are engaged in programming their earnings, which means "income smoothing" rather than "simple inflation." There is "an almost infinite variety of methods" available for this smoothing process; he lists: "Arbitrarily allocating high and low values to different plots of land"; "swapping tracts of low-cost land with other companies, at inflated prices" (but, in his view, this is acceptable since "at some future time the high costs will have to be absorbed"); "being excessively optimistic about the degree of completion on large projects accounted for on the percentage-of-completion method"; "using second or purchase-money mortgages to inflate the apparent sales price of properties sold."

That professor and accountant is so right—the homebuilders are "merely" programming, rather than inflating, as he sees it. However, had he paused for a moment he would have realized that barring outright fraud, or at least lying, all inflation is nought but programming which somehow didn't work out according to the program. Unquestionably, the franchisors, land developers, manufacturer-lessors, and computer lessors were all "programming"—until they had to proceed with the "take-a-bath" accountings of the late 1960s.

Under the circumstances, anything I might then have said or written might well have proven anticlimactic. But silence might have been the ultimate disservice to the homebuilding industry as well as to those who try to understand its fiscal operations and maneuvers incident to their vital investment decisions for themselves or for their clients. Further, if there are any major accounting aberrations, then my profession should be made aware of them so that the wheels of the gods might be set in motion for their slow, even if not especially fine, grinding.

What triggered my original curiosity regarding the account-ings in this essentially new industry (new, at least, as far as the public securities markets are concerned)? In part, it was a normal and logical outgrowth of my earlier inquiries into the flam-boyant accounting practices of the land-office business and, later, of the Great Southwest Corporation and the interrelationship between its realty sales accountings and those of its once-omnipo-tent and still-ubiquitous parent, Penn Central. But more prob-ably my interest was aroused by the fact that the stocks of the homebuilders were enjoying an extraordinary felicity despite a rather desultory market generally.

The sophisticated performance-oriented money managers were swarming to the shares of these companies (and it was not too long ago that I hardly knew the names of the companies thus involved) the way ants swarm to the honey pot. In this mad rush, the shares of these companies were attaining historic heights, permitting them to use their shares as "funny money" for ac-quiring other companies (frequently within the industry, some-times outside). Concurrently, there was a mad rush of mom and pop builders (or father and son builders) to transmute their sole proprietorships or partnerships into corporations as the initial step to "going public."

There Ought to Be a Law

And now put it down as Briloff's Law that wherever ants swarm, the pot will not only contain a bit of honey, but will also be filled with accounting gimmicks.

This law was demonstrated to be applicable to the bowling alleys, franchisors, nursing homes, land developers, conglomer-ates, computer lessors, computer peripheral manufacturers, fi-nance companies, and National Student Marketing (I can't quite figure out to which industry it belongs). In each instance, there was the same swarming, with a corresponding massive allocation of capital resources to the new stellar phenomenon—"smart money," it's called—and then poof! the bubble gets pricked. In fact, it may well be that the very success of the few is what sows the seeds of destruction for the many. This is so, first, because there are so many amateurs who get into the act. Possibly of greater import, there are the cynics who really want to examine the honey pot promising year-to-year growth rates of 25 percent and more; there are still a few who put some credence in the "law of diminishing returns," which is even older than Briloff's Law.

Ironically, it may well be that the sophisticated performance-oriented money managers—"Adam Smith" calls them the "gun-slingers"—and the reputable independent auditors who certified the accounts of the companies in the homebuilding industry knew, long before any accounting academician asked for the prospectuses and statements of the companies, just what the honey pot really contained. In fact, it was that knowledge, or hunch, which produced the weird happenings of the "week that was" to which I alluded.

In any event, this is the way the October 25 *Barron's* carried the results of my probe into the accounting practices of three of the leading homebuilders, under the caption "Gimme Shelter."

*   *   *

Whatever its other claims to fame, 1971 will go down as the year of the housing boom. Something like two million homes were expected to be built that year; if mobile homes are added in, the total would exceed by some 22 percent the previous peak of 2,050,000 units set in 1950. The outlook for 1972 is for more of the same. Scant wonder that Wall Street has showered its favor on the equities of homebuilding concerns.

Their popularity isn't especially hard to understand. Long a business dominated by family-run, undercapitalized, local outfits, the homebuilding industry today boasts a far more professional look. Dominating the field today are rapidly growing corporations able to buy huge tracts of land and commanding the where-withal to finance massive construction programs. Not least, the homebuilders have been able to count on a generous helping hand from Washington, which has aggressively cut costs and expanded the availability of mortgage money for home buyers.

Because of their investment prominence, a hard look at the accounting employed by the homebuilders seems in order. My probing of their techniques reveals several discernible patterns which have contributed importantly to their growth. I will consider, first, the ways in which they employ the old business-combinations accounting field rules—the methods which produced the "go-go" economics of conglomerates. I will then turn to a special *modus operandi* in this industry, the joint venture, and describe the ways in which it has been used for producing distortions and obfuscations in the reported income of our homebuilders. I also will consider the ways in which the corporations in this industry are especially capable of making the numbers come out however they might choose. It all adds up to a phenomenon I call "massaged earnings."

In this analysis, I concentrate on the three kingpins in the homebuilding trade—Kaufman & Broad, Inc., U.S. Home Corp., and U.S. Financial Inc. They boast both size and stature—and, in addition, listings on the New York Stock Exchange, a factor which we assume would make their standards of accountability of the highest.

These companies, of course, build homes. But, it would appear, that's only their primary role. On closer inspection, the trio might more nearly resemble financial conglomerates. Thus, they are extensively involved in financing (of the activities of others in land acquisition and development as well as the construction and ownership of homes, apartments, and commercial properties). They also underwrite insurance and insure titles and escrows. They have also branched off into other endeavors—the manufacture or sale of mobile homes and mobile home parks, conducting cable television operations, and leasing of equipment.

All of which, to be sure, has made for dramatic growth. Thus, Kaufman & Broad in 1970 racked up sales of $152.3 million, compared with $8.75 million in 1960. Pre-tax profits over the same span shot up to $12.4 million, from $669,000, while net soared to $6.5 million, from $319,000. At U.S. Financial, 1970 revenues of $125.7 million compared with $35.1 million in 1966. The gain in profits was more eye-popping. In that five-year stretch, reported earnings before taxes rose to $12.2 million, from $663,000, with net scooting to $6.5 million, from $383,000. Not far behind has been U.S. Home, fiscal year 1971 sales of which amounted to $91.6 million, up from $26.6 million a half-decade earlier. Its pre-tax net, meanwhile, climbed to $9 million and after-tax profits to $4.6 million, from $349,190 and $227,475, respectively in 1966.

Aware of the awesome burden I undertake in criticizing these mighty attainments, I move to probing the accounting practices which contributed importantly to these geometric (they have not yet reached an exponential rate) growth curves. Not the least of the techniques has been the accounting for business combinations, which has been roundly discredited in the great conglomerate orgy of the sixties.

Generally unrecognized are the ways in which homebuilders have used this pernicious accounting process. In fact, business combinations accounting is especially important with homebuilders because all of them were—it seems almost yesterday—tiny, limited operations. But by consolidating their little building activities into a corporate complex they have been able to carry over relatively huge submerged values which have enhanced their stunning growth.

The Accounting Principles Board undoubtedly did not recognize the cynicism it was demonstrating when, in Opinion No. 20 (July, 1971), it included a "special exemption for (companies effecting) an initial public distribution." That opinion set forth the rather detailed field rules applicable to situations where accounting changes are effected during a particular year. There are rather elaborate provisions describing the kinds of restatement, retrospective, pro forma, and the like, which are required. There is, however, a one-shot exception—when a closely held entity first determines to join the big time and go public. Then, the formal complex restatement and adjustment procedures may be dispensed with.

What the APB is saying is that a closely held enterprise has one set of accounting principles and practices; a publicly held company has its own. Undoubtedly, the former are the "Twiggy-oriented" precepts, committed to conservative balance sheets and income statements (to avoid being taxed excessively, naturally). The publicly owned-entity precepts, on the other hand, are of the "full-bosom" variety. Hence to allow the switchover from one set of books to the other, the APB provided for a one-shot amnesty, so that the company does not have to go through the process of purgatory otherwise required by Opinion 20.

Under some circumstances, the old "mom and pop" business might well be counseled not to change its practice if it plans to merge. Chances are an acquiring company might be willing to pay even more for a dollar of value "off the balance sheet" than for one which has surfaced.

To see how it works, let's start with U.S. Home. That company really got "plugged into the big time" when it took over Imperial Land Corp. during 1968. Through this transaction, U.S. Home acquired an operation which was generating (in its latest full fiscal year) sales of nearly $19 million and net of almost a million, pre-tax. This was a hefty injection, since in fiscal 1968 (prior to this merger) U.S. Home sales were less than $8 million and pre-tax profits roughly $600,000. After joining the fold, Imperial thus contributed about 60 percent of the gross and more than half of the combined net. Correspondingly, Imperial contributed an important management component to the combined empires. In brief, under the rules, it was a real pooling.

But what about the numbers used on the combination? The acquisition was accomplished by U.S. Home swapping 850,000 of its shares for "all of the outstanding capital stock of Imperial Land Corp. and its subsidiaries and affiliated companies." Since U.S. Home common was trading in a range of 12 to 15 in February, 1969, when the swap was effected, the acquisition really cost about $11.5 million. How much of this went on the books? Less than one-tenth, or just $925,000.

The arithmetic used by U.S. Home on the Imperial acquisition is intriguing. U.S. Home issued 850,000 shares of new common with a par value of 10 cents a share; capital stock was credited with $85,000. Simple enough. Then, U.S. Home picked up Imperial's retained earnings of $1,099,000—making a total credit of $1,184,000. How, then, do I come up with "only $925,-000"? The answer lay in a charge to capital surplus.

Proof of the Pooling

On the pooling, U.S. Home buried hard costs in the capital surplus account of $259,000. By subtracting the $259,000 in the capital surplus debit from the $1,184,000 toted up above, you come up with the $925,000 which U.S. Home put on its books—instead of the over $11 million it really paid for Imperial's shares and its real assets.

A look at Imperial's balance sheet discloses, as might be expected, inventories (valued at the lower of cost or market), real estate held for investment, and property and equipment used in operations. There's not a clue to the "off balance sheet" items which a nice, conservatively managed family-owned business picks up over the years.

Nor is there anything fancy in Imperial's accountings. Its audited statements (same auditors as U.S. Home's) do not contain cryptic notes about percentage-of-completion accounting or deferred income taxes or other manifestations of possibly "iffy" income. No—according to a 1969 prospectus, its sales are booked only "when construction and payment are substantially completed."

As a consequence, on this acquisition alone, U.S. Home succeeded in suppressing about $10 million in value for which it paid—maybe not in coin of the realm, but paid for nevertheless.

This single suppression was equal at the time to over four times U.S. Home's net worth.

Let's remember, though, U.S. Home was an aggressive acquisitor. During its fiscal year ended February 28, 1971, it pooled no fewer than five separate operations—Port Builders Inc., Soble Construction Co., First Development Corp., Ellis Suggs Construction Co. and affiliate, and East Construction Co. and affiliates. All told, U.S. Home immediately gave up a bundle of securities including 604,397 common and 20,000 preferred shares (which I count as 66,666 common, since they are immediately convertible)—so that the total was 671,063 shares. Add to that another 845,334 common shares either held in escrow or contingently issuable based on various earn-out formulas, and the bundle could come to 1,516,397 shares.

Taking the minimum number of shares (to avoid controversy) and the then prevailing approximate average market value of $25 a share for the 671,063 U.S. Home shares, we have an aggregate cost of $16.8 million. How much did U.S. Home enter into their books for this $16.8 million bundle? Less than one-twelfth, credited thusly: preferred stock, $20,000; common stock, $122,-879; earned surplus, $1,150,053; capital surplus (net) $20,453; a total of $1,313,385.

And, mind you, the foregoing bookkeeping credits are not only for the shares paid initially but also reflect 624,397 of the 845,334 shares still to be delivered. If I were to have used the total 1,516,397-share package, and applied the $25 market value which prevailed at about the time U.S. Home paid out the shares, the cost to U.S. Home of these five companies would work out to about $38 million. In short, take a number between $15 million and $36 million and that is the real economic cost incurred by U.S. Home which it *didn't* and *never will* show on its books. In exchange, U.S. Home got real assets from Port–Soble–First–Suggs and East; it also got land, work in process (all undoubtedly conservatively valued) and other inventories. All of these real assets have flourished in U.S. Home's 1971 report, or will come to fruition in the years ahead—however and whenever its "programmed earnings game plan" calls for these suppressed values to sprout.

Lest one infer that U.S. Home is oblivious of the advantages that can flow from purchase (as contrasted with pooling) accounting, let's set the record straight. In late November, 1970, the company disclosed that it was acquiring Orrin E. Thompson Construction Corp. in a $12 million transaction. It may be difficult to believe, but the auditors figured this transaction at $5 million. They shut their eyes to $1 million in stock payable in 13 months (permitting the Thompson sellers to defer income taxes), to say nothing of $6 million contingently payable (200,-000 shares valued at $30) over the next five years.

What special advantage is derived from U.S. Home's *purchasing* rather than *pooling* Thompson? Simply this: it will pick up this subsidiary's post-acquisition sales and profits without requiring the restatement of the earlier years' operations. By avoiding the restatement, U.S. Home's "growth curves," and related managerial rhetoric, will be a source of ever greater delight to shareholders and professional money managers.

This does not imply that the auditors allowed anything that was not consistent with GAAP (Generally Accepted Accounting Principles). To the contrary, judging from the extensive briefs and other published statements which they promulgated in defense of the pooling process and their especially extensive experience in these matters, I defer abjectly to their astuteness in this field. But consistent with GAAP or not, are these huge suppressions in such contexts conducive to a fair presentation?

We move along to Kaufman & Broad. It's a company which has manifested a rejection of the cheap pooling coin; its acquisitions regularly go into its books as purchases. Hence, the full cost, without diminution, is supposed to get itself entered on the K&B books.

All too frequently, the purchase-accounting game plan calls for major build-ups in the goodwill account. Or, as we will soon see, in such other intangibles as trademarks and dealer distribution systems, since these "assets" may not require amortization whereas goodwill now does. Besides, goodwill is sometimes seen as a combination of two "four-letter words."

What's nice about K&B's merger accountings is that they got through 1968 without any of that intangibles stuff getting on their books. And that wasn't easy, especially in view of the complexities of their '68 acquisition of Kay Homes.

But after 1968, the K&B acquisition accountings became less imaginative. Thus, in 1969, when it acquired 80 percent of Leisure Industries for stock and Biltmore Mobile Homes for cash, a sum of $3,001,000, largely for the latter, went into "intangible assets . . . which are not being amortized." This was subsequently reclassified via Solomonic wisdom—half to trademarks, half to dealer distribution systems. One year later, when K&B picked up Victoria Wood (chiefly from Revenue Properties, the embarrassed Canadian land-office operation) and Wayside Homes, there was a "cost of investments in excess of the equity of those companies" aggregating $8,149,000 which K&B classified as:

Trademarks and brand names (not to be amortized) $2,349,-000; dealer distribution systems (also not to be amortized) $681,000; goodwill (to be amortized at the rate of $130,000 a year for 40 years) $5,119,000; for a total of $8,149,000.

K&B thus picked up about $12 million of intangibles. This is a sizable chunk, representing almost 30 percent of its November 30, 1970, book value.

Let's look at those intangibles booked in 1970. Would that I could tell you how much of these millions stemmed from the Wayside acquisition (as distinguished from Victoria Wood). However, the answer is not to be found—neither in corporate statements nor in prospectuses. However, my review of these leads me to assume that the attribution to Wayside could not have been very much. Nevertheless, I will assume the trademarks and dealer distribution items to be entirely Wayside's and the $5 million in goodwill to be entirely for Victoria Wood.

If that were the case, I hope the CPA team at K&B could give us their definition of goodwill. I always presumed that this euphemism related to the capitalized value of the excess profit being earned by a company. In Victoria Wood, one has to look awfully hard to find important earnings. For the two years ending August 31, 1970, from the information given in the November 30, 1970, prospectus, Victoria Wood averaged about $500,000 annually in after-tax income. This is a return on its shareholders' equity of about 8 percent. Is that the kind of return justifying goodwill to any extent? If anything, standing on its own, I would say there was negative goodwill rather than $5 million worth of real value—to say nothing of any portions of the Victoria Wood cost that may have been charged on K&B's books to trademarks, brand names, and dealer distribution systems.

Real-Estate Holdings

I'm not implying that K&B overpaid. Doubtless they made a careful study of the properties in Canada before they put all that money into the operation. But I just cannot believe they paid anything for goodwill, as such. Of course, Victoria Wood has huge amounts of real estate in various stages of development—almost $25 million at the time of the takeover. It undoubtedly also had some land under option—real estate which may have appreciated, producing an added value.

But then we must understand that a greater attribution of K&B's cost for Victoria Wood to land, improvements, and other real assets would have necessitated their being written off as these assets were disposed of. And that would have produced a bigger adverse impact on K&B's earnings than the 2½ percent annual write-off of goodwill—on a straight-line basis.

Let me now zero in on the Leisure Industries acquisition—it has some remarkable ramifications and implications. Back in December, 1968, K&B acquired 80 percent of Leisure Industries through the issuance of 32,000 shares of common with a then market value of $952,000. In addition, the sellers of the Leisure stock were entitled to earn out an additional 32,000 shares (which would be 96,000 present shares as a result of stock splits), based on cash flow and profits formulas contained in the October, 1968, agreement.

The SEC files include the following as the balance sheet of Leisure at the time of acquisition:

Assets		Liabilities and Capital	
Cash	$ 12,628	Note Payable (Secured)	...$8,400,000
Land for Resale	8,420,000	Capital Stock (100 Shares).	50,000
Improvements	17,372	Total Liabilities	
Total Assets	$8,450,000	and Capital	$8,450,000

The balance sheet is so simple, even my freshman accounting students could prepare and understand it. For 80 of Leisure Industries' 100 shares, K&B paid $952,000 in stock (forgetting the contingent shares).

The public K&B files do not provide an answer as to what accounts were debited with that $952,000, which, according to the 1969 report, were credited to capital stock ($32,000) and capital surplus ($920,000). It should be noted that the book value of the Leisure acquisition was $40,000 (80 percent of $50,000). There was, then, an additional debit of $912,000 made somewhere. My searching leads me to believe this excess over book value was charged to inventories; in fact, the indications are that this charge was in the amount of $927,000—I shall use that larger figure for what follows. This, of course, permits me to give K&B a good grade for this acquisition since they *did not* bury the excess cost in goodwill or suppress it via pooling.

But, in this context, I'm raising the Leisure question in terms of the K&B assertion that it is essentially uncontaminated by land dealings. (I can understand its sensitivity on that score in view of the controversy regarding the accountings by land developers who sell their wares at the retail level on a long-attenuated payout basis.) As of August 31, 1970, the spread in the inventories item was $819,000, a reduction of $108,000 from the November 30, 1969, balance of $927,000. A registration statement filed in September, 1971, in connection with the proposed takeover of Sun Life Insurance Co. tells us that as of November

30, 1970, this spread had been further reduced to $793,000, or a total of $134,000 for the entire fiscal year ended November 30, 1970.

Now what do I make of this $134,000 write-down? Simply this, assuming that my hypothesis and resultant inferences are correct: Since this write-down may have represented about one-seventh of the total original land cost spread on the Leisure acquisition, I concluded that about one-seventh of the Leisure-owned land (costing $8,420,000 on its books) was sold during this fiscal year ended November 30, 1970. If that is so, then Leisure sold land costing about $1,200,000 that year—and using a 20 per-cent land cost (as being appropriate for a "recreational land" operation), I come up with assumed Leisure sales of $6 million ($1,200,000 ÷ 20 percent). On these sales, taking an estimated net after-tax profit of only 15 percent, we have something like $900,000 (subject to reduction for the minority interest in Lei-sure) coming from the kind of operations which have been the subject of a major accounting controversy and caused earnings flip-flops (and agonizing reappraisals) by many companies in the land-development industry.

This probing of the Leisure Industries acquisition and subse-quent operations leads to another accounting phenomenon which the sophisticated investor should understand—that of de-ferred income taxes. I will digress to consider this phenomenon with particular reference to Leisure. Briefly, "deferred income taxes" is a term of art which means that for bookkeeping purposes we show an amount for income taxes computed on the basis of what the financial statements show; if we assume a 50 percent federal and state tax rate, then on pre-tax income of $2 million our computer tells us the tax would be $1 million. We then go to the tax returns (federal and state) and there our taxable income turns out to be a penurious $100,000, so that the tax checks go out in the amount of $50,000.

Thus, the current tax would be shown as $50,000, the deferred tax at $950,000; total income tax $1 million, net after tax, ditto. Now whence cometh the spread between the bookkeeper's pre-tax $2 million and the tax accountant's $100,000? This is a question too frequently ignored—at the investor's peril.

Let's look at K&B's annual report for 1970 where the footnotes explain these deferred taxes as "resulting principally from instalment sales and accelerating certain expenses for tax purposes." As another compass point, as of November 30, 1970, K&B's deferred taxes aggregated $7,011,000. Since its accumulated earnings at that date were $16,161,000, I infer that more than 40 percent of all of K&B earnings through 1970 were merely such for bookkeeping purposes as distinguished from its tax records. Surely, since K&B's home sales, as they say, are booked only when title passes, so that K&B gets paid then and there, these sales could not have generated these "rich mixes" of instalment sales to permit the tax deferral. And to confound me further, K&B's management maintains it has "used the same accounting methods since our founding."

Now I'm certain management knows of what it speaks; after all, K&B's board chairman is a highly regarded certified public accountant. But then there are the haunting questions: If there was no change in accounting methods, then whence cometh the new phenomenon in 1969, of huge pockets of tax-deferred or tax-sheltered income? Does this mean that while K&B management does not "speculate or invest in land (and) normally purchase unimproved land . . . to meet planned needs for the next 18 months," things have changed drastically since 1969 so that K&B found that it had inordinate amounts of "remnants of land which have non-residential uses or do not meet (K&B's) present needs or criteria"? To what extent did the Kay Homes and Victoria Woods acquisitions provide this land, possibly land entered in K&B's books at suppressed values (to the extent that my commentary on K&B's acquisition accounting methods is fair)?

K&B's land sales may have generated these deferred taxes in yet one other way. In 1969, we saw that K&B acquired 80 percent of Leisure Industries and all of the Biltmore Mobile Homes, Inc. Since the latter was not acquired until October, 1969, I assume that it could not have had any effect on the 1969 operations, which leaves Leisure Industries as the most likely fountainhead for these tax deferrals.

Major Misgiving

Anyone who has been exposed to the accountings by land-development companies, and Leisure is just such a company, knows that these companies create two things: long-deferred receivables (which are, nevertheless, picked up as real assets forthwith) and long-deferred taxes (since the income is reported for tax purposes under the instalment method).

My misgiving in accepting this new acquisition as the primary source of the mushrooming in K&B's deferred taxes stems from the very magnitude of this deferral. Thus, each of the years 1969 and 1970 produced over $3 million in such taxes; taking a 50 percent rate, it would mean that over $3 million of K&B's net-after-tax income in each year was derived from its leisure-land operations. Such a conclusion is much too staggering, since it is appreciably in excess of what I computed previously as Leisure's gains from recreational land sales by applying some rules of thumb regarding profit expectations. My reluctance is all the more understandable by an assertion in the November 30, 1970, prospectus, to wit: "The minority interest in the net income of Leisure Industries, Inc., which is not significant, is included in other income in the accompanying statement of consolidated income."

In short, there is but one categoric conclusion to be made regarding K&B's deferred tax dynamics. Namely, it's difficult to determine fully the major contributing factors to this phenomenon. To the extent there are disclosures which may have a bearing thereon, the data are confusing and frequently contradictory. This failure goes to the heart of the "quality of earnings" issue.

But back to the mainstream of business-combinations accounting where we still have to study U.S. Financial's practices. In 1970, the company acquired three outfits—Development Creators, Inc.; Shelter Corp.; and Mosser Construction, Inc. The auditors do not say so explicitly but the first two—Development and Shelter—were apparently accounted for as purchases, though originally, as a NYSE listing application indicates, they were to be treated as "poolings" (which accounting treatment, it then said, "has been reviewed and approved by Touche, Ross & Co., the company's independent auditors"). Oh well, many a change in signals can occur in our most uncertain world, so why should things be different with USF and their independent accountants?

Let's just note that for DCI–Shelter, USF gave up $2,005,000 in preferred stock. However, since half of these shares are in escrow "contingent upon the attainment of certain levels of future earnings" USF booked only half of this bundle, or precisely $1,003,000. Even of this half, only $325,000 they said represented real assets—the rest was charged to "intangibles . . . (which) amounts are not being amortized."

In Under the Wire

Now to Mosser. This deal was accounted for as a pooling, which gave the 1970 income statement "beefed-up" gross revenues. In the notes to the Mosser financial statements (certified by different independent accountants from those doing USF's books): "On October 30, 1970, the majority shareholder of the Company agreed in principle to exchange his shares for shares in U.S. Financial, San Diego, California." That date was critical—if it had been but two days later, new Accounting Principles Board Opinion 16 would have banned this swap as a pooling, requiring that it be accounted for as a purchase.

USF beat the Halloween, 1970, deadline by a day (probably because the thirty-first was a Saturday). In consequence, the $10 million worth of convertible preferred stock given to Mosser was, the auditors assured us, permitted to be entered as a pooling. Consequently, USF need not, did not, and will not record this $10 million as $10 million. Instead, my arithmetic tells me that the net entry after all is said and done will be about $2.3

million. How does this switch from $10 million to $2.3 million come about? Simple enough:

We start with a credit to the preferred-stock account for the $10 million par value and another $2.2 million credit to retained earnings for the surplus carried over from Mosser's books —a total of $12.2 million. But then subtract from that total $9.9 million charged to the paid-in capital account (including the $2.5 million to be charged there when the escrowed shares are released) and we have a net credit for the Mosser deal of but $2.3 million.

Lest I be accused once again of "straining at gnats" by complaining about a suppression of only about $7.7 million, let us remember that this single suppression was a quarter of 1969 shareholders' equity even after restatement for this pooling. Relate these proportions to the corresponding antics of our once-awesome conglomerates and you can see these erstwhile giants were merely squirreling away "penny ante" sums. And we know how advantageously these giants were capable of utilizing their suppressions for "instant earnings" injections.

Moving away from the business-combinations complaint, let's analyze a very special kind of situation which pervades the home-building industry—namely, their obsession for entering into joint ventures to achieve their *raison d'être*.

The prevalence of this phenomenon is evidenced by the following contained in a March, 1971, USF prospectus:

"USF conducts a significant portion of its single-family home production as a participant in joint ventures. Typically, USF's joint venturer is an independent general contractor and developer who is familiar with local industry conditions and regulations. Such joint venturer contributes half the equity capital (which may be borrowed from USF, if secured by the pledge of collateral), his skill as general contractor and administrator of the project, and, in some instances, the land to be developed. USF typically invests the remainder of the equity capital and provides interim financing and related services. USF controls the design of construction, the rate of development, cash disbursements and accounting, and performs a variety of other related services. At December 31, 1970, USF was a participant in 67 joint ventures."

If you were to stand back and see what so many of our homebuilders are doing in this regard, especially in their accounting practices, they can be seen to be essentially franchisers. But what gives me a special sense of concern is that our accounting principles and practices have developed a lacuna regarding these amorphous entities. We tend to use the corporate entity as our primary frame of reference, and have evolved standards for accounting generally, consolidation, and disclosure regarding such entities. Most recently, when our Accounting Principles Board promulgated Opinion 18 governing the so-called "Equity Method of Accounting," to require corporations to pick up the operating results of their investments in subordinate entities where there is less than a 50 percent consolidating interest, they limited this new dogma to "investments in common stock" and clarified (they said) "the applicability of the equity method of accounting . . . to investments in common stock of subsidiaries and extends the applicability of the equity method of accounting to investments in *common stock of corporate* joint ventures and certain other investments in *common* stock." (Emphasis mine.) So, while the APB must have known of this burgeoning phenomenon of unincorporated joint ventures, it determined to stand mute.

At any rate, let's get into the implications of these loopholes. Take footnote C of USF's 1970 report: "Joint venture operations are not consolidated. Investments in joint ventures are stated at cost plus equity in earnings less withdrawals. . . . Certain interest and fees earned by the Company from joint ventures and all overhead and administrative costs applicable to such interest and fees are recognized as received or incurred."

Why, that's almost innocuous, assuming that it's comprehensible. But let's see what it really adds up to. The USF March, 1971, prospectus includes the following statement in Note (2), which is *not* included (at least so far as I can see with my vision growing dim from my study of footnotes) in the statements which went to shareholders: "Start-up costs, overhead, and administrative costs of joint ventures are deferred and subsequently expensed on a pro-rata basis as sales of the new projects are recorded." Aha! USF's accounts are fine as far as they go—but the joint venture then picks up the overhead, start-up, and administrative costs, which are not written off. Instead, they're deferred.

But let's go further—because that's not the only kind of front-end loading of income which is feasible with joint-venture accounting. As we've previously noted, "in some instances" USF's co-venturers will also contribute "the land to be developed" to this joint venture. Where might this co-venturer—the contractor generally who is being "franchised" by USF—get the land? Well, USF sometimes puts on another hat—that of the land developer and seller.

In nonaccounting terms, it suggests that USF is front-end loading by going through the back end. It sells the land to its co-venturer and not to the joint venture in which it's a partner. It is the partner (and not USF) who then puts the land into the joint venture. Where does the partner frequently get the money to pay for the land? You guessed it. If the particular venture goes "up the creek," who gets stuck with the land and the losses? Again, you've got the answer. In the meantime, though, USF has the income on its books.

If such a transaction were done under the aegis of a consolidation of corporate entities, the roundabout profit on the land sales would have to be excluded or eliminated in view of the internally generated financing. But maybe I'm expecting too much fairness from our generally accepted accounting principles and our related auditing standards.

But to go on. In its 1969 report, USF shareholders are informed that "The heart of U.S. Financial's production is the joint-venture arrangement with local builders." Particularly singled out is an arrangement USF entered into with Hallcraft Homes, Inc., in which it put up $3 million of senior debt and

Hallcraft put in the bulk of its assets. The USF report, in discussing this liaison, says: "Hallcraft has scheduled the production of 9,850 residential units during the years 1970, 1971, and 1972 in the areas of Arizona, Colorado, and California. Also included in this partnership is Hallcraft's 'Data Core' which franchises builders of townhouses in 17 major U.S. cities. This partnership is financially self-sufficient and generates its own credit sources."

But now we move along in time. In a mid-1970 audit (presumably for its NYSE listing) the accountants tell us: "In June, 1969, the Company entered into a limited partnership agreement with Hallcraft Homes Inc., of Phoenix, Ariz., under which the Company made a cash contribution of $3,000,000 and Hallcraft contributed substantially all of its assets and liabilities. *Under a separate agreement* an option was granted to Hallcraft for the purchase of the Company's interest for $5,000,000 . . . together with warrants. . . .

"This option was exercised by Hallcraft as of June 18, 1970, and income of $1,500,000 was recognized by the Company. . . ."

Hit or Myth?

The italics are, of course, mine. Did the auditors know of this "separate agreement" when they certified the 1969 statements? Did USF's management know of this agreement when they made those euphoric predictions for the shareholders in the 1969 report? Does not this "separate agreement" make something of a myth out of all of the glowing commentaries regarding the USF-Hallcraft hookup?

But let's probe further. Footnote C to the 1970 year-end report reiterates that "During 1970, Hallcraft exercised its option to purchase the Company's interest for $5,000,000 in cash," and goes on to tell us "Income of $1,750,000 was recognized in 1970 representing the Company's share of the unrealized profit on work in progress at the time of the repurchase by Hallcraft." (An additional $250,000 was picked up by USF after June 30, so that the mid-year figure of $1,500,000 became $1,750,000 at year-end.)

The point, bluntly, is how much of that $1,750,000 should have been accounted for as ordinary income from housing operations during 1970. This misgiving stems principally from a reading of the June, 1971, Hallcraft Homes, Inc., prospectus (prepared a year after Hallcraft had emancipated itself). There, under "USF Partnership" are some important insights: "The partnership operated from an effective date of May 1, 1969, to June 19, 1970, at which time the Company (Hallcraft) exercised its option to terminate the partnership, believing that the relationship would no longer be equitable from the Company's standpoint. As required by the partnership documentation, the termination was effected through the purchase of the USF interest by the Company for a consideration consisting of its $5,000,000 subordinated and promissory note and a warrant for the purchase of shares of the Company's Common Stock. The $5,000,000 amount of the note had been negotiated on the basis of returning to USF its $3,000,000 capital contribution plus its share of anticipated partnership profits; such profits were calculated to include not only those which would have accrued to USF's account by the time of termination, *but also those which would eventually arise out of partnership projects in process at the time of termination* (a similar profit projection having been made in computing the amount of the Company's original capital contribution to the partnership, represented by the business and assets transferred by it, in relation to that made by USF). . . .

"As indicated in Note 1 of Notes to Financial Statements, the excess in consideration received by USF upon termination of the partnership (comprised of the $5,000,000 note plus the $25,000 value assigned to the warrant) over its equity in the partnership (comprised of its $3,000,000 original capital contribution plus $296,000 representing its share of undistributed profits) was added by the Company to its recorded cost of the assets freed from USF's minority interest by the termination.

Between the June 19, 1970, termination date and the April 30, 1971, fiscal year-end, $956,000 of such added cost had been reflected in the Company's reported cost of sales, leaving a balance of approximately $773,000 thereafter to be retired." [Emphasis supplied.]

What does this mean? Far from USF's entitlement to consider the $1,750,000 of 1970 income as ordinary, routine income, I find that for 1970, USF would really have earned out no more than $232,400 from the joint venture with Hallcraft had it remained in effect throughout the year. It works out like this:

According to the Hallcraft prospectus, USF's share of the partnership profits for the period from May 1, 1969, through June 19, 1970, was $296,000. USF had already picked up as its share of these partnership profits in its 1969 report (for May 1, 1969, through December 31, 1969) some $250,000. This indicates that the USF profit share from January 1, 1970, through June 19, 1970, must have been $46,000.

Add to that the profits USF would have earned after June 19, 1970, if the partnership had been continued. Hallcraft reported its profits for the period from May 1, 1970, through January 31, 1971, as $1,874,000. In addition, about $650,000 of extra costs were booked by Hallcraft because of the termination of the partnership, so that we would have a restated profit of $2,524,000. The most USF might have earned by December 31, 1970, would have been 10 percent, or $252,400. Thus, the maximum USF share of profits from this partnership which would have been reported in 1970 if the partnership had continued throughout the year would be $298,400.

Even putting USF's position in the most favorable light, based on the Hallcraft prospectus, USF's 1970 share could have been no more than $631,000, as follows: The balance of USF's share through June 19, 1970, as above, was $46,000. The portion of overplus paid by Hallcraft included by it in its operations from June 19, 1970, through April 30, 1971, was $956,000, or at the rate of about $90,000 each month, so that for the 6½ months of USF's year to December 31, 1970, the accrued profit would be $585,000, for a total of $631,000.

In short, from the foregoing relatively simple, two-dimensional arithmetic I come up with an indicated overstatement of ordinary operating income for the year 1970 (if we are to believe the Hallcraft prospectus and their independent certifying accountants) of at least $1 million and possibly $1.5 million. In fact, a September 14, 1971, Hallcraft prospectus discloses that as late as July 31, 1971, there was still $446,000 of the USF payment not yet attributed to its sales costs (hence would not have been "earned out" by USF if the divorce had not occurred).

This is more than quibbling over a mere million and a half dollars. For recognition of this $1.5 million, as of USF's June 30, 1970, statement date, represented almost all of the year-to-year gain in USF's six-month pre-tax earnings ($5,181,272 versus $3,557,554). And on a full-year basis, the $1,750,000 garnered on the Hallcraft termination exceeded the increase in USF's pre-tax income ($12,208,000 for 1970 versus $10,848,000). Without the Hallcraft injection, USF would have had to report almost flat earnings. The comparison would have been even more invidious on a per-share basis, since there was an increase in the number of "Common and Equivalent Shares" from 3,314,000 to 4,019,000 during the years 1969 to 1970 (and on a fully diluted basis from 3,915,000 to 4,107,000 shares).

Questions of Disclosure

Having thus considered the areas of accounting for business combinations and joint ventures and partnerships, I turn to a number of other misgivings which I have regarding the accountings by our "three crowns."

Here I refer to a *terra incognita* in K&B's accountings—namely, "Investments and Advances: Unconsolidated subsidiaries—investment at equity." (The other two such tenuous areas are the Intangibles and "Investment and Advances: Joint ventures and partnerships.")

The balance-sheet amount for this K&B item is a whopping $10,425,000 in 1970, compared with $4,997,000 the year before. Note 1 tells us that the unconsolidated subsidiaries were "Nation Wide Cablevision, Inc. . . . International Mortgage Co., First Northern Mortgage Co., and other insignificant subsidiaries."

The footnote gives us a combined, condensed balance sheet as of November 30, 1970—but it's only for the "unconsolidated *mortgage* companies" (emphasis mine) and not for all of K&B's unconsolidated subsidiaries by any means. That this tiny balance sheet is nowhere near the whole "vital center" for these unconsolidated companies is demonstrated by the fact that it shows the shareholders' equity and intercompany payables to aggregate but $2,565,000—a far cry from $10,425,000.

That raises the question: In which unconsolidated subsidiaries did K&B sink about $8 million, over and above its mortgage subs? It could be the cable-television companies, which might be something of a cash drain for K&B. Furthermore, the agreements pursuant to which K&B's subsidiary, Nation Wide Cablevision, acquired Total Telecable in late 1968, tend to indicate that K&B undertook substantial contingent obligations by guaranteeing Nation Wide's debts and giving its creditors a contingent right to obtain warrants to acquire K&B stock. These guarantees and contingencies are alluded to in a K&B November 30, 1970, prospectus: "To fund the 1968 acquisition and future CATV development, Nation Wide placed a $3 million . . . note . . . with an institutional investor with warrants to purchase . . . under certain conditions K&B Common Stock. It also obtained a seven-year term loan from the Bank of America in the amount of $9.7 million (supported by a commitment from the Company to the Bank to make Nation Wide's instalment payments to the Bank if necessary)."

Yet despite these K&B undertakings regarding its capital stock and debt, the 1970 annual report nowhere makes mention of them. Here this professor might be accused of having succumbed to myopia since, clear as day, note 7 says: "Commitments and contingent liabilities include the obligations incurred in the ordinary course of business such as . . . guarantor of certain obligations of its unconsolidated subsidiaries aggregating approximately $6,000,000 at November 30, 1970." But, delving further, it's clear that the $6 million had nothing to do with the Nation Wide contingency. I make this assertion on the following evidence: (1) the Nation Wide contingency exceeded $6 million—it was probably in excess of $9 million at November 30; and (2) excepting for an unexplained word change the 1970 note is the counterpart of one in the 1969 report which read: "The Company is also contingently liable as guarantor of certain obligations of its unconsolidated *mortgage* companies aggregating approximately $7,000,000." [Emphasis supplied.]

Maybe K&B and its auditors felt that the $9 million wasn't material. But then is $6 million more so? And if $9 million isn't material, why were they so meticulous in spelling out annual lease obligations "ranging from approximately $525,000 in 1971 to approximately $300,000 in 1975. . . ."?

However, there are other items of less than complete disclosure discerned by my study. They include:

1. USF's failure to describe the nature of its leasing activities; at the end of 1970 it had over $3 million in deferred income which appears to have come from these activities.

2. K&B's "netting" of its "no recourse" liabilities for land purchases against the cost of the land. This practice fails to reveal the magnitude of the company's risk from its land operations. (It's very much like buying a commodity future on margin; while you might only lose the amount of the margin, the risk extends to the price movement on the contract as a whole).

3. K&B's failure to disclose the extent of its contingent liability to its mobile-home dealers from whom K&B is obligated to repurchase any unsold units. Conceivably, these agreements

may put into question K&B's right to book income at the time it makes shipments.

4. And then, of course, we have the universal problems pertaining to the use of the so-called "percentage of completion" accounting method and the uncertainties surrounding the allocation of land cost to sales. But I have to stop this essay somewhere—leaving these matters, however important, for another day.

Where does all this lead to? Clearly, there is a compelling need for a drastic revision in the standards governing the accounting and disclosure of the financial condition and results from operations in the homebuilding industry. I selected the financial statements of the three principal companies in this industry on the supposition that these "Tiffanies" would be at least as revealing and as of good a quality as other companies in the business. But the analysis prompts only grave concern for the standards of accounting that are being applied by my professional colleagues.

*   *   *

Chapter 10

Is There a Termite Nest in the House?

The point has been made in many contexts in this work: Accountancy is not a "zero-sum numbers game." Instead, any over-heating of the earnings collage for a particular industry attracts a correspondingly dramatic inflow of resources and concurrently permits the affected entities to use their exaggerated price/earnings ratios in aggressive acquisitions programs. I have described this phenomenon in great detail in the chapters on business combinations; we saw how this dynamics produced the conglomerate movement of the past decade and how, when their game was fully understood, there was the inevitable fall.

Our homebuilders are, at least as of this writing, still moving along their upward trajectory and, accordingly, attaining power over increasingly large pools of other people's money. This metastatic process takes on many different forms; for present purposes I shall limit my discussion to three manifestations thereof, namely, "incest trusts" of the kind created by U.S. Financial; the real-estate joint-venture epidemic, which was principally conceived as a tax shelter for the super-rich but which has been vulgarized so as to make it almost as commonly available as shares in a mutual fund; and the takeover of insurance companies which, as we know, was an important maneuver by the conglomerates just about the time they were at apogee.

Let's turn to the "incest-trust" idea as exemplified by the successful offering during the summer of 1971 of $50 million worth of shares of beneficial interest (with warrants, to be sure) by USF Investors—a "real-estate investment trust" created and effectively controlled by U.S. Financial. The intimate ties between the homebuilder and its captive trust are evidenced by the initial pool of mortgages and real-estate interests taken over from U.S. Financial, and by the following caveats contained in the trust's initial prospectus:

> U.S. Financial has agreed to afford the Trust the right to participate to the extent of 50 percent in each mortgage and real-property investment originated by, or available to, U.S. Financial and its subsidiaries in which the Trust desires to participate. With respect to any development, construction, or other interim mortgage loan secured by a property in which U.S. Financial or any affiliate has any interest as owner, lender, lessee, or builder, U.S. Financial will be obligated to acquire 15 percent of such loan, provide a commitment for the permanent financing for such loan, or issue a guarantee as to the Trust's interest in such loan. For a discussion of the circumstances in which the Trust may engage in transactions with U.S. Financial and other affiliated persons or in which the Trust has rights to have investment opportunities presented to it by such persons, and the possible conflicts of interest presented thereby and certain provisions which have been adopted to reduce, but which will not eliminate, the possibility of such conflicts, see "Adviser and Advisory Agreement." Notwithstanding such provisions and the restrictions as to transactions between the Trust and the Adviser, and affiliates thereof, the transactions permitted between such parties may be considered not to be made at arm's length, and the Adviser may be in a position to influence the decisions of the Trust. The Adviser and its affiliates may, from time to time, deal independently with entities borrowing from, or otherwise doing business with, the Trust.

In this connection an article in the *Financial Analysts Journal* for May/June, 1971, entitled "Real Estate Investment Trusts," by Peter A. Schulkin, an economist with the Boston Federal

Reserve Bank, is especially significant. It considers at great length the very serious conflicts of interest which may arise where the trust's adviser has an interest in the properties in which the trust is making a mortgage loan. Thus: ". . . The potential for sacrificing some of the [trust's] shareholders' interests is clearly present as the adviser may give itself financing on terms it could not obtain from other sources. The favorable terms may not be easy for the shareholders to detect, since they can take non-price forms—for example, a mortgage might be given for a larger amount than could be obtained elsewhere." To Schulkin this kind of a controlled situation can also lead to "tie-in business" and excessive compensation for the adviser, which in the USF case is 84 percent owned by U.S. Financial—our homebuilder. This, in his view, may dictate a need for legislation seeking a strict separation of these varied, conflicting interests. Clearly I share Schulkin's concern and consider the circumstances to be especially aggravated where the trust is controlled by the homebuilder desirous of selling its property most advantageously.

Being of a generation which still remembers the mortgage-bond scandals of two score years ago—scandals frequently rooted in banks "laying off" their rotten or rotting eggs in their captive trusts loaded with "other people's money"—I turned, pretty much at random, to a rather musty book on the library shelves published in 1932, Ernest Allan Barbeau's *The Mortgage Bond Racket*. Running down the captions should give you the flavor of what then went awry, and what might lay in the future for these captive trusts:

Chapter 1: "Holding the Bag"—A Ten Billion Dollar Racket
Chapter 2: "Dissolving the Smoke Screen"—Investors Out on a Limb, The Open Door to Loot, Symbols of Safety??? Insolvency Cleverly Concealed, Criminal Looseness
Chapter 4: "Giving the Public 'the Works'"—High Appraised Values, Main Cause of Losses, The Come-On, Shearing the Lambs, Made Their Own Appraisals

Chapter 6: "Baiting the Hook"—Safety Slogans Grossly Abused, "Trustees" Only Window Dressing, Robbing Peter to Pay Paul

And so it goes—how much have we learned during the two score years? But then Santayana provided the key: We don't learn from history because we don't read it.

Joint Ventures and Syndication

Moving to the syndicate syndrome, we can see where joint ventures have a very special place in the operations of our home-builders, especially in connection with their multifamily apartment construction. In this context we will see how home-builders are concurrently capable of building termite nests. No, I am not here implying that they implant the insects in the foundations of their homes; instead, the nesting is in the foundations of our government's tax structure.

By way of background, the Summer, 1971, *Real Estate Review* includes an article by a tax attorney, Sheldon Schwartz, entitled "How to Find Tax Shelter As a Limited Partner"; its opening gambit: "The quest for tax-sheltered income has brought the limited partnership into the limelight as a favored investment vehicle. The business and tax features which accompany the limited partnership are well suited to real-estate shelters."

Why is a real-estate syndicate so "ideally suited to bring these tax advantages to the investor"? According to Schwartz, it provides the following: (1) permits high-bracket (non-real-estate-oriented) investors to participate in a project without any managerial responsibility, with limited liability for partnership obligations, and with a degree of anonymity which may be most desirable; (2) allows the pass-through of net operating losses generated from large depreciation deductions, and liberal recapture, both of which specifically are sanctioned by Congressional act; and (3) permits the builder-sponsor to erect the project without any investment by "selling" the anticipated tax losses to the limited partners in exchange for a cash investment in the partnership which is sufficient to furnish the funds necessary to make up the difference between the government-insured financing and the full construction costs.

One's first reaction to all this is that our government is euchred from both ends. At one end, it subsidizes the builders with loans at bargain-basement interest rates, and then on the other subsidizes the "high-tax-bracket investor" through huge tax write-offs. But that isn't the principal thrust of this essay—let's go back to our homebuilders, those who are the builder-sponsors in the Schwartz article. This kind of an arrangement suits their accounting game plan most admirably.

First, we must bear in mind that when these limited partners are buying the property, they are not particularly concerned with the price tag on the property. All they want to be assured of is that there is a favorable "discounted cash flow." This computation seeks to reduce to present values the future inflows of cash value to the tax-obsessed investor; this future inflow, in turn, is derived, at least in the especially significant early years, from the huge anticipated tax savings rather than from the operation of the property per se. This feature permits an artificial price tag to be put on the project by the builder-sponsor; through this inflation the profit from the venture to the builder is expanded.

But that's the overall, total picture. In addition the builder-sponsor can "front-end load" its profit in a great many ways, namely: It can immediately sell to the syndicate the "package" or concept for the project, including the financing arrangements, and thereupon "book" the profit; it can immediately sell to the syndicate the land which is to be built upon—another profit injection; it can start in with picking up the construction profit on the "percentage-of-completion" basis—an accounting procedure which I will consider presently.

So it is that long before anyone has moved into the project our homebuilder has already booked a number of layers of profits. Proceeding from there, imaginative tax planners have figured out especially dramatic ways in which the builder-sponsor will be able to "sell" even bigger "anticipated tax losses to the limited partners," to use Schwartz's phraseology, and thereby to increase the project price or the package price even more.

Our tax laws are most flexible especially when it comes to partnerships. For example, the partners could agree among themselves that where, say, the income from rentals minus operating expenses is $200,000 and the depreciation allowable is $300,000, the sponsor-builder could agree to pick up on its tax return a $200,000 plus factor (the income before depreciation), while the high-bracketed limited partners get a $300,000 minus amount for the depreciation. Now you might say that overall the partnership lost $100,000—how can one partner show $200,000 plus while the others show $300,000 minus? Simple—and it doesn't take synergism or advanced calculus; just simple arithmetic—and inverted tax logic.

Nor does the builder-sponsor get any of that $200,000 in cash—none of the partners will probably get it. That sum will be going toward the amortization of the mortgage, so that the only real cash flow comes through the high-bracketed limited partners' egregious tax savings.

Ah! you might still ask, doesn't the builder-sponsor then have a huge tax to pay on that $200,000 of taxable income from the partnership? It would, and maybe should—if we had a logical tax structure. But as we now know, homebuilders have developed various kinds of tax shelters of their own—to which I alluded in my discussion of the deferred-tax mechanism. And so the builder-sponsor can serve as the agreeable accommodator of the limited partners' tax-avoidance proclivities without sustaining any current out-of-pocket tax cost. Only the government has an out-of-pocket cost; the most surprising thing about all this is that its fiscal deficit is at but a $25 to $30 billion rate. Maybe the government also is "cooking its books."

An especially dramatic and cynical manifestation of this "euchring the government from both ends" operation is discernible in a prospectus promulgated in the summer of 1971 by a prominent investment house, E. F. Hutton, Inc., in connection with an underwriting of 7,000 shares ($1,000 each) of "Limited Partner Interests" in American Housing Partners.

I want to emphasize at the outset that the cynicism referred to above is not with the prospectus, per se; quite the contrary, it's so unqualifiedly open and above board as to warrant the highest approbation from those of us committed to full and fair disclosure. It tells us right off, in italicized type, that the "shares should only be purchased by investors with significant taxable income. . . . Shares should not be purchased for cash distributions. . . . Management fees will absorb a substantial portion of cash return"; and that there is a "high leverage increase [in] risk" and a "risk of loss."

Finding the Termite Nests

Why should anyone be willing to buy these 7,000 shares potentially to lose $7 million? Well, gather round and see how our homebuilders can become termite-nest builders.

Let me back up a bit and note that in its prospectus promulgated for the Sun Life acquisition (to be discussed below), Kaufman & Broad unveiled the following, under "Asset Management":

> Kaufman and Broad Asset Management, Inc., a wholly owned subsidiary, was formed in July, 1971, to acquire, sell, and manage tax-sheltered housing for investors. The company performs two primary activities: (1) to acquire and manage federally subsidized housing developments, primarily low and moderate income housing under the 236 Program of the Federal Housing Administration, for American Housing Partners, a public limited partnership offered in August, 1971; and, (2) to sell Kaufman and Broad's conventional multifamily housing developments (apartments and mobile-home parks) and to provide management for these communities when required.

Here, then, is the clearly marked trail from K&B to this limited partnership. In the partnership prospectus we are told about the "Federal Housing Investment Incentives," to wit:

> In order to stimulate private investment in moderate-income housing, the Federal government provides significant tax incentives, interest and rent subsidies, mortgage insurance and other measures which are intended to reduce the risks and afford investors the prospect of tax deductions, cash distributions, and possible long-term capital gains. . . . The tax deductions, which are the primary benefit to investors, diminish over the years. . . .

This partnership being sponsored by Hutton "has been formed to invest in such federally assisted housing," and thereby to achieve certain "professional management" (via K&B, for appropriate "management fees," to be considered presently) and, especially felicitously, to attain a nexus of "tax consequences" including: "Tax Consequences: Deductions"; "Tax Consequences: Depreciation Recapture Avoidable"; "Tax Consequences: Capital Gains Tax Deferrable." It is the first of these "consequences" which is intended to bait the hook, thus:

> It is anticipated that over 85 percent of the cost of such projects will be financed with FHA-insured mortgages, and that the original tax basis for depreciation purposes will be approximately $5,700 per share since each shareholder's tax basis will be the price he paid for his shares plus his share of the mortgage debt on the projects in which the partnership invests (*where no one has any personal liability for such mortgages*). Under special provisions of the Internal Revenue Code and regulations (the "Tax Code"), new residential rental properties for qualified tenants can be depreciated at much faster rates than other properties, i.e., under the 200 percent declining balance or sum-of-the-years' digits methods. Accelerated depreciation deductions begin when a project is completed. There will also be substantial deductions during the initial construction period, apportioned over approximately 2½ years. Shareholders, who can utilize deductions, will be able to realize tax savings by applying such deductions against their taxable income from other sources. [Emphasis supplied.]

This tax-avoidance process is then spelled out in the American Housing Partners prospectus in greater detail under "Federal Tax Status":

The partnership anticipates that it will incur substantial net tax losses which will be initially larger, will decline over the years, and will be virtually exhausted after 20 years. A shareholder may deduct his share of such losses from his other taxable income to the extent of his tax basis for his shares. Each shareholder's tax basis will be the price he paid for his shares, plus his share of the mortgage debt on the projects in which the partnership invests *(where no one has any personal liability for such mortgages)* adjusted for his share of partnership income, losses, and cash distributions. It is anticipated that over 85 percent of the cost of projects will be financed with FHA-insured mortgages. On this basis, shareholders' tax bases for depreciation purposes will be approximately $5,700 per share. [Emphasis supplied.]

The partnership may depreciate new residential rental projects under the 200 percent declining balance or sum-of-the-years-digits' methods, as compared with the 150 percent maximum rate applicable to nonresidential real property. In addition, certain rehabilitation expenditures incurred before January 1, 1975, on moderate-income housing may be deducted ratably over a five-year period.

A significant amount of the expenditures during construction is also expected to be deductible, including construction loan interest and fees, interim commitment fees, rent-up fees, FHA mortgage and other insurance premiums, and real-estate taxes. The amount of the foregoing items will vary with the length of the construction period, interest rates, and other factors. The $275 per apartment unit rent-up fees are payable to the management company. The availability of these expense deductions during the initial years of investment should result in significant tax deductions prior to completion of projects and the commencement of depreciation deductions. While the partnership will be advised by qualified tax and legal counsel, there can of course be no assurance that some deductions may not be challenged or disallowed.

One doesn't have to look very far to find the particular "shtik" which K&B is putting forward to its potential "partners," and the reason I'm putting that noun into quotes is to indicate that they're really partners with the government rather than with K&B. The fact is that for every $1,000 invested the limited partner will derive a basis for depreciation of up to $5,700 in addition to the pattern of quickie deductions to which I have alluded. If, then, you happen to be in a 50 percent tax bracket, you will get back something up to $2,850 (conceivably even more) in *tax savings* for every $1,000 put in. There may, of course, be a day of reckoning—estimated to be a score of years from now; in the meantime, all systems are "A–OK."

The reader might be pardoned if at this juncture he asks, "How can an 'investment' of only $1,000 (without any possibility of losing more than that sum) get the partner tax savings of as much as $2,850 or even more?" The answer to such a guileless question lies in the clauses which I emphasized when quoting from the prospectus. Longer ago than anyone remembers there was introduced into the Income Tax Regulations [Section 1.752-1(*e*)] an abomination permitting just such a leveraging or extrapolation of basis by reference to a mortgage taken on by the partnership provided *none* of the partners is liable for that indebtedness. This aneurism in our tax structure may have been justifiable in some distant past—the sweep of subsequent decisions in the tax realm, in my view, has made this leakage unwarranted and unjustifiable. But as Alice knows, the Cheshire Cat may have gone but pussy's smile lingers on and on, and this aneurism is contributing to the hemorrhaging of government revenues that should be derived from the affluent.

Where and how does K&B get its compensation for pandering to the tax-avoidance proclivities of Modern American Man? At pages 10 and 11 of the prospectus we are told of a "Management Contract" between the American Housing Partners and a management company called "KB Management Partners." This company, in turn, is a partnership of K&B Asset Management, Inc. (96 percent voting interest) and "a corporate affiliate of E. F. Hutton & Company, Inc. (4 percent). The emoluments flowing to this management company include: up to $795,000 for "finding, appraising, negotiating, and acquiring interests in projects and monitoring construction"; a "$275 per apartment

unit rent-up fee"; upon total or partial liquidation and distribution of the proceeds, a liquidation fee equal to 1 percent of the
sales price plus 3 percent of the net-after-tax proceeds.

But what is of very special interest to us in this Age of Aquarius is the incentive program provided by the agreement with
the management company. Follow this "K&B kicker" very carefully lest you get lost in the thicket.

As is evident from the foregoing, the competent management
would not want to be compensated by reference to its profit-
producing astuteness; remember, the *sine qua non* of this partnership is to manufacture losses. As a consequence, the bigger
the "average annual tax deduction plus cash distributions per
share," the bigger the "annual management fee expressed as a
fraction of 1 percent of invested assets." So it is that if the tax
losses for 1972 or 1973 amount to over $450 per share, manage-
ment gets 25/100 of 1 percent of the invested assets; but if,
perish the thought, the losses are less than $415 per share, the
managerial rewards are cut back by 60 percent.

To make matters even more agonizing for the K&B management pool, they might be terminated—yes, *fired*—if in *any year*
the losses per share fall below certain limits. For example, if the
1972 or 1973 losses are less than $360 per share, then manage-
ment can be "canned"—at a meeting of the partners called for
that purpose. (It is true, I here allude to losses, whereas the
agreement calls for "losses plus cash distributions." But since
the latter is intended to be *de minimis,* I have ignored them in
this exposition.)

It should be noted, if only in passing, that K&B may derive
yet another advantage from this tax-gimmicked partnership;
this one is described most innocuously at page 13: "It is not contemplated that KB or its affiliates will develop projects in which
the partnership invests, but if a project is acquired from (or
sold to) KB or its affiliates, the management company will not
receive any acquisition, rent-up, or liquidation fees for such
services, and the purchase price will be not more than (nor the
sale price less than) that paid to (or received from) disinterested

third parties for comparable interests, as established by independent appraisers." (I would, of course, expect these independent appraisers to match the independence of the independent auditors.)

What do we then see in this Alice in Wonderland perversion? The government, under section 236 of the National Housing Act of 1968, provides for the federal insurance of up to 90 percent of the certified costs of a project; it provides for mortgage subsidies as well as for federal payments to project owners on behalf of qualified low-income residents. These as well as other programs are designed as subsidies to alleviate the housing shortage of the nation. But then, little noticed by our citizenry (and possibly even unnoticed by our legislators), for every $1,000 of investment induced by these generous subsidies the government may be called upon to shell out (via tax rebates to its affluent citizens) as much as $3,000 or more by way of year-to-year tax savings.

It should be emphasized that the decision makers at the highest levels of our government are not oblivious to this monstrous erosion in its tax revenues. They took direct and overt notice of a corresponding perversion in the wake of the "Six Flags" article —this notice and suggestions for reform notwithstanding, they were apparently determined to pursue a "don't make waves" policy. For whose benefit and at whose behest?

But the mere loss of urgently needed tax revenues is not the only social cost imposed upon us by the American Housing Partners, and corresponding syndicates. Thus, as an angry article ("Failed Federal Housing—The U.S. as Slumlord") in a mid-December, 1971, *New Republic* emphasizes, they are confronting the Department of Housing and Urban Development with "the grim prospect of becoming the nation's No. 1 slum landlord."

Nor is it difficult to discern the ways in which this will come about. As we know the "partners" in these projects are absentee landlords with a vengeance. They don't really give a damn about the property in which they have "invested"; they probably don't even know in what city it is located—much less who lives in it. If the apartment complex sank into the muddy flats, tenants and all, these landlords wouldn't even know of it—and if they did, it would only accelerate their tax write-offs.

Thus, as soon as the property's operations show a negative cash flow the syndicate will walk away from the property, having already raped it for the tax benefits; the government (HUD) as the guarantor of the mortgage will thereupon become the owner of abandoned projects aggregating in the multi-billion dollar range (estimates of its guarantees range up to $80 billion, according to the article). The article ends by quoting an assistant HUD secretary, "We've got to look at a housing strategy real quick."

Invading the Insurance Domain

Even more daring was K&B's takeover of Sun Life Insurance Company. In this fashion K&B will really hit a bonanza for itself, judging from the ways in which the conglomerates of yore got into the fire and casualty companies they took over.

The acquiring companies derived important benefits from ingratiating themselves with accommodating investment houses and brokers through a deliberate diversion of business, and developing a corresponding cordial climate with selected banks to become the insurance companies' principal depositories and obtaining interest cost savings by using the insurors' cash balances as compensating balances for the parent companies, thereby deriving a free ride on other people's moneys. In addition, the new emperors were capable of directing huge dividend distributions to themselves, as in the case of Reliance and Great American to Leasco and National General. Then, too, very substantial portfolio-management fees may be burdened against the subsidiary; or the insurance company may be induced to make investments in securities which complement the corporate parent's program—Home Insurance buying General Development, in which Home's parent, City Investing, already held a major block—and in many other ways still not recognized by me.

Now, then, with K&B's control over Sun Life, with its "surplus surplus" accumulated over the years by the insurance company's management through the creation of reserves for their insurance contracts, or from its shareholders' undistributed surplus, the homebuilder could really have a ball. There could be dividends; there could be appreciable mortgage investments in K&B-built properties effected with the Sun Life resources.

Why my objections to the Sun Life move, probably even more than to the USF's incestuous excursion and the proclivities of the syndicates? First is my common indictment of the homebuilders' accountings based on my analysis—in my view they have not met the standards of visibility and accountability required before managements should be permitted to sit in judgment and control over huge pools of other people's money. This would apply to both the K&B and USF moves.

But then in the latter case I might say that the shareholders in USF Investors, those who provided the $50 million, were at least informed or forewarned as to what they were getting themselves into. Similarly, I must assume that the government has enough collective expertise to protect the public from injustice —if that's what it is. To shareholders and government, at least, we can say *caveat emptor*. But one cannot cop out as readily in the insurance-company situations—surely no one is asking the policy holders of Sun Life, for example, whether they concurred in this transfer of control over *their property* to the new management team. True, the insurance-company shareholders generally get a rich takeover package, at least initially—but are they the ones who are principally affected by the switch in heads?

I realize that the more aggressive, impatient breed of youth— the "go-go money managers"—will tell us that the old money managers had accumulated too much "fat" that needs to be drained off. But isn't this fat precisely what Adolph A. Berle, Jr., had in mind when he alluded to the "transcendental mar-

gin"—that which one generation bequeaths to the next to facili-
tate the objectives of these successive generations? Has not the
corresponding draining of fat from fire and casualty companies
by the conglomerates already had a serious and inimical impact
on our economic society? According to a *Best's* analysis, about a
billion dollars was thus drained during a single year, 1969. To
what extent has this contributed to the anemic state of insurance reserves in our country, with its resultant sharp rise in
insurance cost (assuming that coverage is even obtainable)?

It might be fairly said that Sun Life has already lost its innocence since, as K&B has stated: "For many decades, Sun Life has
had a substantial investment in mortgage loans." Also, through
a subsidiary, it "has more than 1,000 apartment units in various
stages of development in the Baltimore-Washington area." But
yet there is a critical difference between real-estate activities
which complement the life-insurance activities of the company,
and its becoming a reservoir of liquid resources for the real-
estate operator.

It may be true that my insistence on avoiding this potentially
serious conflict of interests would deny to Sun Life the potential
"benefits from involvement with Kaufman & Broad's mortgage
companies and with Kaufman & Broad Asset Management";
also, since "young homebuyers are an important source of purchase of life insurance . . . Sun Life could benefit from the
15,000 homes and mobile homes to be delivered in 1971" by
K&B.

It is true that I would thereby be denying to Sun and K&B
the benefits which the economists refer to as "reciprocity," or
feeder dynamics—that is the price we should be willing to pay
to maintain free competition and the vital constitutional process
of checks and balances. History has taught us that even the most
benevolent and most efficient of despots are despots nevertheless.
And our insurance resources, especially life-insurance resources,
are much too sacred a trust to be thus put into jeopardy.

Again, reverting to my special responsibility in this context,
I would be more sanguine about this new power thrust by the

homebuilders if their accounting standards produced important credibility and confidence—if they demonstrated greater visibility and accountability. Since they are not fulfilling these vital objectives, I respond most critically to these centrifugal moves by USF and K&B respectively—and who knows where the next "beehive takeover" move is being hatched?

Full and Fair Disclosure

This, then, leads to the second of my *Barron's* articles on the accountings by homebuilders, "Full and Fair Disclosure," which addresses itself to the problem of eliminating abuses.

Many of the proposals for reform contained in that article are equally applicable to other contexts in this work. Thus, there were recommendations regarding the accountings for business combinations. Regardless of the way in which the combination carves out year-to-year income, any and all sums should be spelled out which can be identified as "accounting-induced income"—amounts which get into the bottom line only because our pooling-purchase practices have permitted a suppression of the acquisition costs. It might be necessary to forgo proper recasting of the acquiring company's balance sheet to show the full cost, but there should be segregated from reported profit the portions which relate to the mere surfacing of values acquired (and paid for) on the acquisition.

Implicit in this proposal would be the charging to income, as the stock is disbursed, of any shares held in escrow or remaining unissued contingent on the earn-out or cash-flow formulas. Such shares are nothing more than an incentive to the old managements. Accordingly, they are essentially executive bonus plans. In fact, on close inspection it's evident shareholder-executives often agree to work for substandard wages since their compensation will come to them via capital gains or tax-free swaps. Further, these additional shares frequently are really little more than an additional payment on account of the values already implicit in the acquired assets.

Almost peculiar to the accountings by homebuilders is the accounting problem raised by their significant involvement in unincorporated entities—partnerships, joint ventures, syndications, limited partnerships. The preceding chapter pointed up the confusion in the U.S. Financial operating statements created by their mode of accounting for partnership profits, especially its 1970 gains on the termination of the Hallcraft partnership. That a great deal can be done to enlighten the reader of a company's financial statements regarding its partnership involvements is discernible from a reading of a prospectus filed during the fall of 1971 by Ernest W. Hahn, Inc. Ironically, that company's statements were certified by the very same accounting firm that attested to the aforementioned U.S. Financial statements. What do we find in these Hahn prospectuses which merits this invidious distinction?

To begin with, the company's share of joint-venture income, usually reflected as a single sum, is subdivided to show its share of the joint-venture rental income, separate from the venture's realty sales and gains on land sales; and the gain on sale of equity interests in joint ventures. If that wasn't enough to produce a hosanna, there is a five-year statement entirely devoted to the "Earnings of Joint Ventures." Deductions from rental revenues (payroll, interest, ground rent, taxes, maintenance, depreciation) all are detailed separately. There then follow the cost-revenue data on realty sales, producing the aggregate joint-venture income on which basis the reporting concern's participation is shown.

This joint-venture statement also carries its own set of rather detailed footnotes, which indicates right off: (1) the rules for capitalizing interest and taxes during the construction period; (2) when depreciation commences; (3) how expenses of obtaining leases are amortized; (4) how maintenance and repairs and expenditures for betterments are treated; and (5) that there may be "contingent interest" payable on certain of the mortgages—subject to the availability of gross income.

It also goes on to provide vital details with respect to each separate venture, including: opening date, joint-venture cost, original mortgage, current interest rate and maturity, annual debt service, the remaining mortgage balance, and the depreciated cost. The balance-sheet data are followed by the amounts for gross earnings, pre-tax earnings, cash flow, and finally, the reporting company's percentage share of the pre-tax earnings. All this is wrapped up in a "Combined Balance Sheet of Joint Venture," and a "Statement of Partners Capital of Joint Ventures" (indicating capital contributions, withdrawals, earnings added, and closing balances). A "Statement of Changes in Financial Position of Joint Ventures" accounts for the increase or decrease in cash for each of the three prior years.

This kind of detailed framework should smoke out those instances of front-end loading whereby a company is permitted to enjoy an inordinately rich mix of partnership income. But for good measure, the concern should be made to report separately: (1) income representing a return for a financing activity as distinguished from a continuing joint venture; (2) income from sales of land or improved property to syndicates where the reporting company or a finance subsidiary provided the financing (directly or through guarantees); and (3) income from transfers of land or "construction packages" to the syndicate where there is a continuing responsibility for the project's completion.

Flexible Alternatives

I turn next to the questions: When should revenues be reflected in the income statements? At what point of time does or should the company pick up the revenues from its operations, and consequently, the resultant net income? These are not questions peculiar to the homebuilder. We saw them raised for the land developers, the computer lessors, the computer peripheral manufacturer—it is, in fact, a pervasive theme. For the homebuilder the special accounting "thing" here in issue is the so-called percentage-of-completion method of accounting. This method seeks to attribute to a particular fiscal period the revenues and, probably more importantly, as the resultant net income, that amount which is the fair measure of the accomplishments of the enterprise during that fiscal period. This method is distinguishable from the completion and delivery assumptions for revenue recognition which prevail generally in our accounting theory and practice.

Under the "percentage" method, income is recognized as the work on the contract progresses; it is recorded in each accounting period over the life of the contract, rather than when the contract is completed. While this is understandable in theory, it raises serious misgivings regarding its implementation, especially because of the subjectivity implicit in making estimates of how much revenue and income should be picked up on work in progress.

The reader is now urged to go back to Chapter 5 where I described the ways in which National Student Marketing and R. Hoe & Co. were able to get away with their earnings exaggeration and asset inflation proclivities by using this frequently amorphous, invariably subjective and excessively flexible percentage-of-completion method, to see why I am unalterably opposed to its use excepting where it is unequivocally dictated by the prevailing circumstances. And even then I would condone its use only under the most severe constraints, requiring most competent and independent expertise to make the required evaluations or estimates.

Clearly, I consider these conditions to be inapplicable to the homebuilders—just as they were to National Student Marketing and R. Hoe & Co.

Another, possibly unavoidable, area of "accounting flap" for the homebuilder, as well as for the land developer, pertains to the mode of allocating land cost to particular parcels or projects where only part of the land is utilized or sold in a particular fiscal period. It is readily recognized that where an extensive parcel of land is acquired calling for development in stages or for multipurpose exploitation, each segment is not usually essentially equal to the other. For example, take a parcel acquired for $1 million to be developed into 1,000 equally valuable home sites, but where only 100 are developed and sold this year, and, let's say, a like number are to be sold annually thereafter.

This represents something of a capital-budgeting decision, calling for the application of the concepts implicit in the most recent Accounting Principles Board promulgation, Opinion 21, "Interest on Receivables and Payables." Thus, the $1 million total cost might be allocated in proportion to the *present discounted values* expected to be derived from net revenues from sales expected in the respective time periods (after taking into account future carrying charges for unsold land, on the one hand, and any reasonably foreseeable appreciation in sales prices on the other).

Closely allied to this problem is the bit of mischief involving land swapping. Sometimes the swap is "monetized" by providing for concurrent purchases and sales. These deals are remindful of the fellow who bragged that he sold a stray mongrel dog for $10,000. When his friend expressed delight and asked, "For $10,000 cash?," the animal fancier said, "No, for two $5,000 cats."

While the land swap might lead to a significant amount of numerical income, the auditor should be ever alert to the possibility of an Oxy–IOS–Macco–Great Southwest deal, and upon discerning such a phenomenon he should purge the accounts of such spurious income.

Sometimes the builder arranges a sale to a charitable foundation at an unrealistic amount of reported profit, coupled with an understanding that it would buy back the plot some years hence at an agreed price, leaving a substantial profit for the exempt entity. What we have is a financing or "warehousing" operation which should dictate the elimination of the specious profit from the homebuilder's accounts—at least those disseminated for public consumption.

Further, inventories should be categorized and detailed at

least along the following lines: land held for development incidental to homebuilding; land held for sale as such (corresponding to that held by the so-called land developers); land held for speculation; work in process, showing separately the direct costs, allocated overhead costs, and especially the profit allocation where the percentage-of-completion method is applicable; and finished homes (presumably apartment projects and commercial and other properties would have been excluded from inventories on completion under the usual terms governing their construction and sale). In addition, there should be an explicit statement as to the manner of determining the valuations, and an identification of any engineers who may have acted as independent experts in this regard.

Receivables, too, might be categorized to show the usual short-term customer receivables and mortgages, broken down to indicate FHA-VA mortgages already committed to lending institutions, and amounts owing by joint ventures, syndicates, and unconsolidated subsidiaries (with details to show if they are first mortgages or otherwise).

A similarly detailed breakdown should be given for the deferred taxes. For example, it should spell out how much comes from use of instalment accounting for tax purposes, separately stated for individual homes, apartments, commercial properties, recreational or other retail land, wholesale land sales, and the like. The breakdown should also detail the amounts derived from accelerated depreciation, capitalization of interest, taxes, start-up costs, and administration expenses.

The homebuilders' accountings should also be required to segregate the revenues and income derived from the programs which have been heavily subsidized by government funds. This point was made especially effectively in the February 28, 1972, *Quality of Earnings Report* where financial analysts T. O'Glove and R. Olstein first comment approvingly on the ways in which one homebuilder, Lennar Corp., discloses its operations under the so-called FHA section 235 programs. They then provide their "Interpretation" as to why this segregation is desirable:

It should be noted that the Federal Government is in the process of cutting back on its commitments to subsidized housing (under Section 236 of the National Housing Act) because of the growing difficulties occurring in the obtaining of proper construction, site-location, management and financial stability connected with the 236 programs. Section 236 provides for monthly interest reduction payments (multiple family housing) from the government to the mortgage lender. Section 235 is a similar program involving the purchase of single family dwellings.

Thus, it is highly important that a homebuilder reveal to the investor the amount of exposure it has under Sections 235 and 236 of the National Housing Act.

The O'Glove-Olstein recommendation can be seen to be especially timely in the light of a February 20, 1972, *New York Times* article, entitled "Drive to Reform U.S. Aid to Housing Gains in Congress." The article begins by observing that a bipartisan coalition is forming in Congress in an effort to reform a portion of the government's subsidized housing programs.

It then describes the reasons why these programs have become "a subject of rising controversy":

Last year, about one-fourth of the two million housing units built or rehabilitated carried Federal subsidies. In recent months, there have been widespread disclosures and charges of financial failures, poor construction, corrupt practices and mounting costs to the Federal Government in the subsidized projects.

The article continues by reciting testimony taken by a Senate Subcommittee on Housing under the chairmanship of Senator Harrison A. Williams, Jr., including:

1. Even though it would cost the government less to make direct loans for construction rather than follow the sections 235–236 route the Nixon Administration "wanted to hold down immediate Government outlays. . . ."

2. The Administration's estimates are that by 1978 all housing subsidies will be costing the government $7.5 billion annually. "Critics charge that much of the housing being produced will not last the life of the mortgage."

3. Citing the testimony of a "housing consultant for nonprofit groups who worked with both the direct loan and the [236] interest-subsidy group" the committee found that a particular project "would cost the Government almost $7 million under the Section 236 Program whereas the cost to the Government [under a direct loan program] would have been only $2.6 million."

4. And even this dramatic cost differential "does not include the revenue loss the Government undergoes by providing a tax shelter for high-income people who invest in Section 236 housing."

In sum, Senator Williams is quoted: "If that isn't a nuclear attack on fiscal responsibility, I never heard anything like it."

It follows that if our government were to create an effective defense against this metaphoric "nuclear attack," those homebuilders who had been deriving windfalls from our prevailing "Maginot-line defense" would be adversely affected. To provide a distant-early-warning system for analysts, O'Glove and Olstein are urging the segregation of these subsidized earnings. From the vantage point of full and fair disclosure by the accounting profession, I concur.

But probably of greatest significance is the recognition that a major homebuilder is really a diversified entity. As such, it should be made to spell out explicitly revenues and profits from all aspects of its operations—homebuilding (on site separate from mobile), land sales (retail and wholesale), land swaps, management fees of various kinds, financing, insurance, syndicated packaging, and the like. It is well known that the financial community "factors in" various earnings components in arriving at their value determinations. The independent auditor committed to the responsibility of reporting relevant and timely information should be aware of this fact of life, and, by anticipating the need, make certain the needed data are provided.

And while this description of accounting hangups and prescription for full and fair disclosure have been directed to homebuilding corporations as such, the challenges and recommendations for improvement are also relevant to corporations in other, seemingly unrelated lines of endeavor, but which have been taken on important involvements in the industry here under consideration. Thus, Chrysler, U.S. Steel, Philip Morris, to name a few, are involved. They should be made to segregate their realty operations and to conform to any stricter accounting standards which may evolve for homebuilders and land developers with respect to these operations.

Clearly, then, in this context, as in the others, I neither desire nor expect that my value judgments will prevail as to which industry will prosper and which will fail in the eyes of the gnomes of Zurich or their Western Hemisphere counterparts. To the contrary, I am committed to the complementary standards of visibility and accountability to avoid distortions and deceptions—to the end that our resource allocations will be predicated on a full and fair interpretation and communication of the facts concerning a particular entity or an industry.

Chapter 11

On Riding Two Horses with One Backside

At this time a critical question confronts the nation: a citizen's right to the facts of evolving history and of the forces shaping that history. Serious challenges are raised as to the right or privilege of statesmen, politicians, political leaders—the principal decision makers—to determine when and under what circumstances these facts and motivating forces are to be disclosed.

The question is not merely whether these statesmen are to have the privilege of controlling the release of the information, but extends also to the objectivity, independence, and reliability of those who gain access to these vital data, and who arrogate to themselves a special right to sit in judgment regarding these facts. In late June, 1971, Tom Wicker saw the Pentagon papers question as "whether the Johnson Administration lied to the people . . . or merely misled them artfully." Wicker was reminded of Stephen Potter's classic dissertation on gamesmanship —how to win without really cheating—"Government half-truths, cover-ups, obfuscations, sophistries, euphemisms and curve balls are permissible tools of the trade so long as a 'real lie' (meaning outright and provable) is not employed to gull the people." He then alludes to the prevalent view "that the faith of the American people in their government has been badly bent, if not broken, in the past decade."

After citing a roster of situations where the people "were lied to or misled or just held in such contempt that the whole truth was regarded as too fearful for them to accept," Wicker concurs in a conclusion to a *Foreign Policy* article: "The Government has been caught out in enough deceptions, even on the most important issues, to raise strong doubts in the minds of most informed Americans about the value of the official word."

It is this widespread loss of confidence in the credibility of their government and its leadership which may explain why so many Americans believe "a real breakdown in this country is impending."

The credibility gap which reached crisis proportions in the public controversy regarding the Pentagon papers has its parallel in the realm of the managed news created by corporate managements and their financial representatives. We have discerned in the preceding chapters the pattern of gamesmanship, with its panoply of cover-ups, obfuscations, sophistries, euphemisms, and curve balls (even without really cheating); we can also sense that the citizens in our corporate society, like their counterparts in the political universe, are "held in such contempt that the whole truth was regarded as too fearful for them to accept."

In earlier chapters I have emphasized the plasticity of our generally accepted accounting principles in describing the ways in which this gamesmanship and gulling were accomplished. This chapter will illuminate the circumstances which surround the supposedly independent audit function. I believe these circumstances inimical to the auditors' ferreting out and disseminating the real, hard truths.

I will describe the potential and frequently all too real conflicts of interest which arise when the independent auditing firm is concurrently engaged in management consultative services for the same corporate entity.

My colleagues in the accounting profession are quick to discern and condemn conflicts of interest in the acts of persons in other professions or callings. Thus, in an article by a past president of the American Institute of Certified Public Accountants we read about a member of the United States Supreme Court who entered into a contract providing payments to himself for life. The discovery of this conflict "produced a surge of indignation that obliged Mr. Justice Fortas to resign," triggering a long chain of historical consequences.

That article then observed: "The degree of opposition aroused by the nominations of Judges Haynsworth and Carswell to fill vacancies on the Supreme Court is further indication of public insistence that severe moral and professional standards be observed in selecting men for so important a post."

". . . Cannot See the Beam in Our Own"

According to Matthew, we can readily behold the mote that is in our brother's eye but cannot see the beam in our own.

But Leonard Spacek saw the beam in his Cambridge University lecture "What Is Profit?":

Management Services a Misleading Term: A word should be added here about the participation of the public accountant (or the chartered accountant) in the field of what is commonly called management services. This term is likely to mislead the public into thinking that we as professional accountants may be participating in the management of the business or that we may be monitoring managements' operating decisions on behalf of the public. We cannot do this. We do not have the competence; and even if we did have the competence, we could not do such work and at the same time pose as independent auditors.

While we may appropriately participate in designing and installing information systems and procedures, we must always remain verifiers and reporters of financial facts for those to whom management is accountable, not only the stockholders, but also labor, management, creditors and the public at large.

We cannot join in the responsibilties of management and at the same time measure the results of that management against accounting objectives without in the process measuring ourselves and thus being guilty of duplicity. In my opinion, the use of the word "management" in describing any of the services rendered by the public or the chartered accountants either disqualifies them as auditors or makes them guilty of misrepresentation to the public.

The AICPA a few years ago established an Ad Hoc Committee on Independence to study this problem. And the dimensions of the problem are indicated by John F. Lyons in an article entitled "The Big Eight Accountants—How Far Should They Go?"

... The Big Eight are going heavily into the long-range strategy of management. Methods such as simulation techniques are dramatic departures from traditional accounting theory and practice, because they essentially involve forecasting. . . . Companies know this, and they are hiring their accounting firms on the basis of what they can do beyond auditing. It's almost a public secret, for example, that Touche Ross landed the Litton Industries auditing job because Litton executives were impressed with a Touche Ross management advisory job.

Accountants now "counsel our clients on maximizing their profitability, spotting faulty operations and inefficiencies, and attempting to correct by management letter"; give "advice on industrial engineering, psychology, organization planning, marketing, personnel, systems design and production control"; arrange "mergers and conduct executive search programs," etc. (to quote some responses from partners in leading firms to Lyons' inquiries). What are my misgivings? Simply put, I believe, along with Spacek, that involvement in management consultative services may seriously impair the objectivity and independence of the firm when it proceeds to look back upon the year's transactions to develop the attested, certified, independently examined financial statements.

Possibly of even greater concern is that the public generally (and, I might add, much of my profession, as well as the Securities and Exchange Commission, and financial analysts) are not even aware of these services, subsumed under the title "management services" or "management consultative services" or any other euphemism. If the financial community (investors, analysts, financial writers) were aware of the nature and extent of these peripheral services being rendered by the supposedly independent attesting auditors, they would no more approve of these tandem involvements than the public approved the Fortas, Haynsworth, and similar conflicts.

Those who might be interested in a more detailed exposition of the problem of conflict of interest, and an analysis of the literature bearing on this problem, are directed to my *The Effectiveness of Accounting Communication*. For present purposes I will concentrate on a single theme: That the rendering of management consultative services by the same person or firm performing the audit function produces a conflict of interests, frequently in fact, and even more pervasively in appearance. The accounting profession is quick to discern, criticize, and condemn conflicts when they occur in other pursuits charged with a third-party responsibility; and yet we persist in our assertions that the individual or firm should have the almost exclusive responsibility for determining when he (or it) is vulnerable to a conflict of interests.

The traditional wisdom emanating from the hierarchy of the AICPA regarding the performance of management services by the attesting accounting firm would encourage this broadened scope of accounting services. Thus, the Council of the AICPA, in a formal 1961 resolution, has given this duality its *nihil obstat*, asserting that: "It is an objective of the Institute, recognizing that management services activities are a proper function of CPAs, to encourage all CPAs to perform the entire range of management services consistent with their professional competence, ethical standards, and responsibility."

As to the ethical standards, the Institute's Professional Ethics Committee (in its Opinion No. 12) ruled that while there is a need for the auditor's avoiding any "relationships which to a reasonable observer might suggest a conflict of interest, [yet] there is no ethical reason why a member or associate may not properly perform professional services . . . in the [area of] management advisory services, and at the same time serve the same client as independent auditor. . . ."

Mind you, neither the Institute's Ethics Committee nor its Council sought to define the term management services; nor did they seek to probe the way in which this duality would be viewed by the "reasonable observers," the vital parties in interest toward whom our audit function is oriented; instead, because we accept the fact that we are "basically honest" (as President Nixon's unconfirmed appointee Willie Mae Rogers put it), the outside world of "reasonable observers" is constrained to accept our conclusion that there is no conflict of interest.

Nor do we even generally tell these "reasonable observers" what management services are being undertaken; such a conflict as a result of performing a multiplicity of services is generally unnoticeable. Instead, we are comforted by the seeming lack of unrest directly attributable to management services; this calm confirms the self-serving declarations by Council, etc.

There have been other indications of a very special empathy on the part of the AICPA leadership for the management-services advocates; the following note appeared in the June, 1971, *CPA* (the Institute's newsletter): "In his report to Council [the] chairman of the committee on specialization presented the committee's preliminary recommendation for the possible creation of an associate status in the Institute for senior consulting personnel who work for CPA firms but who are ineligible to obtain the CPA certificate." We can see the handwriting on the wall: The Institute is on the road to becoming a trade organization and accordingly is preparing to admit paraprofessionals to membership.

The rendering of a broad spectrum of services concurrently with the performance of the audit can, of course, be justified on a number of grounds:

1. It's a most profitable pursuit. In some firms a third and even more of the personnel are involved in performing such

services, and the projections are that these personnel will grow in absolute number, but, even more significantly, in relative terms.

2. Its legitimacy is justified by history—we've done it right along.

3. These services flow directly from the audit function and are complementary thereto.

4. If the audit firm won't perform the services, someone else will; this someone else might be less competent and more costly than the audit firm.

5. Since the management-services consultant doesn't make the "final decision," but merely "recommends," his role hasn't merged him into management—the auditor has, therefore, retained his "independence."

6. Then we have what I call the "test-of-review argument." By this I mean that the management-service consultant–auditor is constrained to perform effectively in both areas since if he doesn't he may be subjected to exposure in a subsequent probe.

7. Some accountants believe that we may have made too much of the independence argument. In their view we've already lost our innocence through the very economics of the audit engagement, and our advocacy in tax matters. They assert that ultimately independence is a state of the auditor's mind, and the involvement in these peripheral services (or the lack of such involvement) should not affect the state of mind of a "basically honest" professional person.

8. There have been no cases reported, they say, where independence *in fact* had been impaired by the rendering of these peripheral services—or at least so the AICPA's Ad Hoc Committee on Independence asserted in its Report.

A Dissent to the Establishment

None of these rationalizations is sufficiently persuasive to justify the continuance, much less the extension, of this duality of services.

The fact that it is highly profitable for us to continue rendering this broad spectrum of services, or that it could cost more to get them done elsewhere, or that we can use the audit to ferret out the need for these peripheral services (which can then be performed by a branch of our firm), are not, to my mind, appropriate to justify an undertaking by a professional who is concurrently charged with a vital public third-party responsibility essentially rooted in independence.

Insofar as the "test-of-review" argument is concerned—I find it to be specious and utterly without merit in this context. Professional associations should anticipate major difficulties which may confront their members. And as has been pointed out in previous chapters, the Institute has presumably opened files on a significant number of *causes célèbres* in accounting practice; we have yet to see the ethics and practice review machinery move diligently and forthrightly to apply effectively this "test of review." Further, important sectors of our profession have expressed the view that Institute members should not bear witness against fellow members; there would then be no one to administer the test. (And if someone could be found, he would probably be ostracized a lot sooner than the CPA firm which is supposed to be tested.)

Regarding the "original sin" argument, that is, that we've already lost our innocence through the very circumstances of the audit engagement, my response is that we ought to move all the more diligently and conscientiously to avoid aggravating an already compromising situation. Thus, I believe that the rendering of these peripheral services produces an even more concentrated risk for the audit firm since it expands the revenues derived from the particular client. But more important, we will never achieve the standard expected of us by the users of financial statements unless and until the auditors make the "quantum leap" and recognize that while management may be signing the check, they're not really paying our fee; instead, we should know that the major portion of the fee is paid by the government through the tax deduction; the rest of it is paid by the shareholders and/or the customers for the entity's goods and services. In short, the corporation's management is doing nothing more than acting as the intermediary in behalf of the whole world of third parties to whom we are responsible.

Turning to the principal remaining arguments—that the management services consultant merely recommends but does not make decisions, and that there have been no reported cases demonstrating the embarrassment generated by this multiplicity of services. The first of these arguments makes the management consultant something of a eunuch—he gets things ready for someone else who makes the vital decisions. This argument might have been appropriate in some traditional, more bucolic era; in any event it is just not applicable to present-day complex corporate decision-making models. The *Statement of Basic Accounting Theory* (the 1966 statement by the American Accounting Association) shows how the several phases of the "planning and control functions of management" are inextricably interrelated —the *development* of data and setting forth of alternatives contributes importantly to the shaping of the decision.

The same point is effectively made by John Kenneth Galbraith when he describes the organization of "Technostructure" in *The New Industrial State*. This organization of group-think, of the decision-making apparatus, embraces "all who bring specialized knowledge, talent or experience to group decision-making. This, not the management, is the guiding intelligence —the brain—of the enterprise."

Even if the consultant would want to be self-effacing and assert that his own personality and ego and drives and urges are to be entirely submerged to the "decision maker," even if he were content to play the eunuch, the realities of corporate management and organization deny him such a sterility.

Further, even if such a submerged, sterile relationship were feasible, should we be making the determination for ourselves, and on our own terms?

It is arrogant to assert that we are the "chosen ones" and should enjoy a privilege of individual, subjective self-evaluation and self-discipline, which we extend to no other profession. We don't permit this unilateral judgment to the judiciary, administrators, or scientists; why should we be thus privileged?

The AICPA Ad Hoc Committee

The Ad Hoc Committee on Independence was constituted by the AICPA in late 1966 in response, as the Committee's report informs us, to "a number of articles . . . written raising questions as to the propriety of the rendition of management services by CPAs to companies for which they also perform the attest function." For the most part, the report continued, "the articles have been written by persons in the educational field. Moreover, in an address to the Institute's annual meeting in Boston in October 1966, Manuel Cohen, then Chairman of the Securities and Exchange Commission, also raised some questions in this area."

In going about its tasks the Committee undertook to read all the articles it found on the subject, held interviews with representatives of various user groups, and considered statements by the management-services committee of the AICPA. Also, "it was known that at least two of the writers had written articles based on surveys, namely, Drs. Abraham Briloff and Arthur Schulte, and so the committee arranged to have interviews with them."

The purpose of the interviews with Briloff and Schulte, the Committee said, was to learn firsthand of the concerns which they had expressed in their articles and to engage in dialogue for the purpose of clarifying viewpoints.

Also, according to the Committee, one particularly interesting point was developed in these interviews, namely, that neither of these two gentlemen knew of any situation where independence, in fact, had been impaired. Schulte stated that he had addressed inquiries to all of the state boards of accountancy asking if they had ever taken disciplinary action where the rendition of management services affected independence. He had heard from 44 of the state boards, and not one of them reported it had ever had such a case. The Committee recognized that this does not prove that no such case has existed but, on the other hand, they deemed it significant that the inquiry disclosed no evidence that audit independence had actually been impaired as a consequence of management services.

Both gentlemen, the Committee said, felt that the problem was not so much lack of independence, but the role of the CPA. They felt that the closeness to management, which they believe is involved in rendering management services, places the CPA in a position where outside observers would be concerned as to his independence.

I find utterly incomprehensible this repetition by the Committee of the comforting conclusion that "neither of these two gentlemen [Briloff and Schulte] knew of any situations where independence, in fact, had been impaired." Undoubtedly, whoever drafted this final report did not read the minutes of the meeting with the two doctors very carefully, at least not objectively. In any event, shortly after the Committee's Interim Report was released I wrote to the Chairman stating that:

> I believe that the minutes of our meeting would indicate that at that time I stated that the published disclosures regarding Yale Express, and American Express (insofar as Allied Oil was concerned), would indicate some serious contamination of independence flowing from "peripheral services." It may well be that the even more recent disclosures relating to the Westec litigation would add to my misgivings.

The Conflict at Yale

Let me elaborate on these misgivings. First, regarding the Yale Express fiasco.

My assertion that a serious breach of audit independence may have occurred in Yale Express is rooted in the various documents on file with the United States District Court (Southern District, New York) in *Stephen Fischer, et al. v. Michael Kletz, et al.,* especially in those pertaining to the motion of Peat, Marwick, Mitchell & Co. to dismiss parts of the complaint in the case.

In his 1967 decision denying PMM's motion, and ruling that the discovery proceedings be continued in anticipation of a definitive trial, Judge Tyler recited the background of the controversy: "Sometime early in 1964 PMM, acting as an independent public accountant, undertook the job of auditing the financial statements that Yale intended to include in the annual report to its stockholders for the year ending December 31, 1963. On March 31, 1964, PMM certified the figures contained in this statement."

Then, sometime "early in 1964," probably shortly after the completion of the audit, "Yale engaged PMM to conduct so-called 'special studies' of Yale's past and current income and expenses. In the course of this special assignment, sometime presumably before the end of 1965, PMM discovered that the figures in the annual report were substantially false and misleading."

Note that the new special-studies assignment undertaken by PMM was within the management-services ambit; it was in the course of this peripheral services task, and not as an incident to its audit, that PMM discerned the fact that they had been "had." Did they, then, "early in 1964" blow the whistle on Yale? I don't know whether the management-services partner told the audit partner (firms have been known to have an apartheid policy). In any event, PMM maintained its silence and it was not until May 5, 1965, when the results of the special studies were released, that PMM disclosed this finding to the exchanges on which Yale securities were traded, to the SEC, or to the public at large. This leads us to the critical determination by Judge Tyler:

> Strict analysis leads to the conclusion that PMM is attacked in the complaint because it wore two hats in conducting its business relations with Yale during the period in question. PMM audited and certified the financial statements . . . as a statutory

independent public accountant. . . . Following the certification, PMM switched its role to that of an accountant employed by Yale to undertake special studies. . . . In this sense, it can be seen that during the special studies PMM was a "dependent public accountant." . . .

The two-hat syndrome is again alluded to in the opinion:

It was, of course, during the conduct of the special studies that the inaccuracies in the audited and certified statements were discovered. . . . PMM maintains . . . that any duty to the investing public terminated once it certified the relevant financial statements. Plaintiffs, of course, contend to the contrary. Thus, the serious question arises as to whether or not an obligation correlative to but conceptually different from the duty to audit and to certify . . . arose as a result of the circumstances that PMM knew that investors were relying upon its certification of the financial statements in Yale's annual report.

Based on the foregoing, and other lines of reasoning, Judge Tyler denied PMM's motion and continued the controversy for further discovery proceedings and for trial—unless, as so regularly happens in matters destined to make history, a settlement is reached in the minutes before midnight.

Sure enough, we were denied the benefit of an adjudication of this vital professional issue on its merits. Pursuant to a Settlement Agreement among the parties, the defendants provided a Settlement Fund of $1,010,000 whereupon they were permitted "to put to rest all controversy and to avoid further expense, inconvenience and distraction of burdensome and protracted litigation, without in any way acknowledging any fault or liability." The Settlement Agreement goes on to say that the defendants "continue to deny . . . the charging allegations of the complaints . . . and in the Companion or Related Actions."

There will, of course, be the small matter of the legal fees for plaintiff's attorneys (Pomerantz Levy Haudek & Block) and accountants.

And so for $1 million plus Peat, Marwick, *et al.,* obtained absolution. In this we can all share their felicity, but the profession was denied an opportunity for a milestone judicial determination. Of course, the Institute's practice-review machinery might yet make a determination in this long attenuated and vital proceeding—but the reader is counseled not to await such a determination with bated breath.

National Student Marketing Again

In several previous contexts, reference was made to the February 3, 1972, complaint filed by the SEC in the Federal District Court for the District of Columbia, against National Student Marketing and Peat, Marwick, Mitchell, *et al.* The complaint is particularly relevant here since, to the extent the Commission's allegations are fair, they demonstrate the firm's determination to ignore its history and therefore, according to Santayana, is destined to repeat its mistakes.

Thus, in addition to setting forth the aberrations in the 1968 and 1969 statements, the Commission alleges (paragraph 48) that on October 31, 1969, at the closing of a merger between National Student Market ("NSMC") and Interstate National Corporation the principals of NSMC and their attorneys needed a so-called "comfort letter" from Peat, Marwick ("PMM") stating "that PMM had no reason to believe that unaudited interim financial statements of NSMC as of May 31, 1969 . . . were not prepared in accordance with generally accepted accounting principles and practices or required any material adjustments in order that the results of operations of NSMC be fairly presented."

Further, under the rules of the Commission, the comfort letter was to state that "NSMC had not suffered any adverse material change in its financial position or results of operations from May 31, 1969 until five business days prior to the effective date of the merger."

The complaint goes on to allege that the auditors were experiencing some difficulty in comforting those gathered for the Halloween, 1969, closing. Thus, the first such letter, "dictated over the telephone and unsigned," set forth some misgivings regarding the May 31, 1969, balance sheet and operating statement. While the closing was in progress [paragraph 48(b)] "PMM informed [certain other defendants named in the complaint] that PMM wished to add another paragraph to the comfort letter. . . ." This paragraph would state that if the statements were adjusted as PMM thought they should be, the May 31, 1969 report would have shown a loss rather than a $700,000 profit.

Later that same day (about an hour after the closing) PMM informed NSMC's counsel that they wished to add still another discomforting paragraph: "In view of the above-mentioned facts, we believe the companies should consider submitting corrected interim unaudited financial information to the shareholders prior to proceeding with the closing."

Despite these misgivings on the part of PMM, the attorneys for NSMC and Interstate determined that all signals were "A-O.K." and the closing was consummated without any further ado. The SEC now complains that [paragraph 48(d)]:

> As part of the fraudulent scheme, the defendant PMM, who assisted in the preparation of and reviewed the NSMC financial statements as of May 31, 1969 and who issued the comfort letter for the nine months then ended, failed in accordance with their professional obligation to insist that the NSMC financial statements be revised in accordance with the comfort letter, and failing that, to withdraw from the engagement and to come forward and notify plaintiff Commission or the NSMC and Interstate shareholders as to the materially misleading nature of the nine month financial statements.

Frankly, if the Securities and Exchange Commission is right in these assertions, then I must hold it to be *in pari delicto*. I say this most deliberately in view of its failure to act overtly in the wake of the "big skid" at Yale Express. Oh, it did file an *amicus* brief with the Court expressing disenchantment with the PMM "speak no evil" premise. But then the Commission failed, to my knowledge, to impose any sanctions whatsoever on the firm.

Going beyond the accounting implications and ramifications the "Third Claim" advanced in the complaint points an especially dismal picture of the ethics of the "executive suite," including the members of the learned and esteemed professions who are brought within its ambit.

Thus, the *dramatis personae* assembled for the NSMC-Interstate closing were (paragraph 50):

Marion Jay Epley, III, Esq., a partner of White & Case, counsel to National Student Marketing

Cameron Brown, Chairman of the Board of National Student Marketing

Paul E. Allison, William J. Bach, Robert P. Tate—all directors of Interstate National

Max E. Meyer, Esq. and Louis F. Schauer, Esq.—both partners of Lord, Bissell & Brook, counsel to Interstate.

Now what were the Halloween pranks which the SEC alleges were perpetrated by this distinguished assemblage? I'll let the complaint speak for the Commission:

50. In furtherance of a fraudulent scheme among the defendants NSMC, White & Case, Epley, Brown, Allison, Bach, Tate, Lord, Bissell & Brook, Meyer and Schauer, defendant Lord, Bissell & Brook, after having received and read the comfort letter, issued an opinion, dated October 31, 1969 and prepared by or at the direction of defendant Schauer and/or Meyer, stating in substance that certain NSMC shares acquired by certain Interstate shareholders pursuant to the merger between NSMC and Interstate could be sold. Such shares were sold on or about October 31, 1969 for approximately $3,000,000. The opinion of defendant Lord, Bissell and Brook was requested by defendants Epley and White & Case on behalf of defendant NSMC after they had received the comfort letter. The opinion made no mention of the need for adjustments in the May 31, 1969 financial statements or the need for public disclosure of the contents of the comfort letter before the shares could be lawfully sold.

51. As part of the fraudulent scheme on or about October 31, 1969, after having received, read and been advised of the contents

of the comfort letter, defendants Brown, Meyer, Allison, Bach and Tate and approximately seven other officers and directors of Interstate or subsidiaries thereof sold approximately 77,000 shares of NSMC common stock for approximately $1,900,000 without disclosing the contents of said comfort letter.

And finally after spelling out these most grievous causes of action (and there were more) what is it that "the plaintiff Commission respectfully demands"? It's rather lengthy so I won't burden this work by reproducing the material at pages 44 to 46 of that document. In essence the SEC is asking for a "final judgment of permanent injunction restraining and enjoining defendants" from again beating the same dead horse—at least in the same way and same place.

Distinguished members of the legal profession have expressed shock that the Commission has joined members of their profession in this most serious action. Is it because they believe that by their vows to "their mistress, the law" (to use the inspired phrase of Mr. Justice Holmes) they are put above and beyond it (her)?

My reference to Westec in the letter to the Chairman of the Ad Hoc Committee was predicated on articles in the *Wall Street Journal* which appeared over the past few years. Since my writing to the Committee we have been confronted with a sworn complaint in that major fiasco—much of it pertains to the role of the auditors in this messy situation. Reference was made to this complaint previously (Chapter 3); in addition to the assertions of negligence in the performance of their audit, the complaint describes the continuing and intimate involvement of partners of the auditing firm in management's most sensitive decision making as it pursued its objective of "firming up" the previously announced earnings figures. Also described in great detail are the ways in which the two-hatted firm was actively engaged in the determination of the acquisitions program, giving anticipatory, declaratory judgments regarding the effects of merger negotiations, particularly regarding the ways in which *nunc pro tunc* pooling could serve as a hypo for the prior-year earnings, and even in the development of the merger-magic calculus designed to achieve the earnings targets (or at least to develop the appearance of such achievement).

The document sets forth in great detail the many matters in which the independent auditors guided, or were much involved in, the nexus of transactions designed to produce this appearance of the target earnings. The curious will find this document in the files of the United States District Court for the Southern District of Texas, referred to as Action No. 68-H-378.

The Conflict in Wall Street's Back Office

Yet another dramatic, overt manifestation of the attest-function–management-services conflict surfaced even more recently than the Yale Express and Westec fiascos. This third grew out of the 1969–70 back-office mess in Wall Street, and reached a crescendo in mid-1971 with the filing on June 29, 1971, of a lawsuit by the New York Stock Exchange against Haskins & Sells, one of the Big Eight accounting firms, and the one responsible for many of the audits of major Wall Street brokerage houses. This particular action was tied to the financial difficulties of Orvis Bros., an old-line brokerage firm; however, Haskins & Sells were also the auditors for Hayden Stone, Francis I du Pont (there's a very extensive write-up on this foul-up in the July, 1971, *Fortune*), and Dempsey-Tegeler—all firms which came upon difficult times during 1970 requiring salvage operations by the Stock Exchange Special Trust Fund. The $5 million Orvis case may be something of a portent of bigger things to come.

On Monday, June 28, 1971, the lead editoral in *The New York Times* captioned "The Paper Jungle" began "Crime flourishes in Wall Street's paper jungle," and referred to the huge amounts of securities which just seem to evaporate. The editorial made reference to "the unrealiability of the accounts of many brokerage firms and of the auditing of public accounting

firms" and the "back-office disorder . . . untrustworthy accounting and auditing."

That editorial followed by a day a Sunday *Times* article entitled "Wall St. Audits Its Auditors," by Terry Robards. Among
the especially relevant statements:

> One of the great mysteries in the disastrous recession in Wall
> Street last year was how so many brokerage firms could suddenly
> find themselves in deep distress with scarcely a whimper of ad-
> vance warning.
>
> It has occurred to some Wall Street leaders that a few of the
> failures may have occurred because of inadequate auditing pro-
> cedures. . . .
>
> The New York Stock Exchange has quietly been delving into
> the accounting procedures used by its member firms and their
> auditors, and apparently has already concluded that liability in
> at least some of the collapses should be extended to the public
> accounting firms that audited the books and records.

The article then quotes from a letter from Felix G. Rohatyn,
of Lazard Frères and a governor of the New York Stock Exchange, resigning as Chairman of the Exchange's Surveillance
Committee, which was the key unit in the efforts to keep brokerage houses from toppling. From the letter:

> I have been disenchanted for a long time with the accuracy of
> member firm interim reports.
>
> I will now extend this to audited reports as well.
>
> The questions raised by the non-infrequent inaccuracy of both
> internal and audited reports will have to be studied by the Ex-
> change. . . . In my opinion they involve the entire concept of
> self-regulation since, if our tools are inadequate, we either have
> to get new tools or someone else should do the job.

These warnings were climaxed by the announcement regarding the lawsuit. Now what does all this have to do with the two-
hats syndrome? Simply, Haskins & Sells has for the past several
years been the recognized leader in the development of the data-
processing systems for stock brokerage firms and in offering the
services of their management-consultative services division to

these firms for the introduction and implementation of their systems. The auditing arm of an accounting firm would be hard-pressed to condemn the accounting system designed, installed, and "piloted" by their own management-consultative division. Surely, if even a minor fraction of the reports of defalcations and aberrations in "the paper jungle" are true, the independent auditors should have cried out loudly and clearly that the particular brokerage firm's internal control systems, the *sine qua non* of any accounting system, were in a state of disarray—and thereupon deny the statements their certificate. Auditors have appended their certificates in some instances after providing for reserves for unknown and uncontrolled losses, sometimes even tenuous in amount. Would the auditors have moved more forth-rightly if they were not concurrently involved with the manage-ment-consultative aspects of the brokerage firm's accountability process?

The Stock Exchange's complaint in the federal district court (71 Civ. 2912) makes repeated reference to the agreement re-quired to be signed by "all auditors selected by a member or-ganization . . . to submit certain information concerning the results of its audit to the Exchange." Among the explicit under-takings on the part of the auditors is to make a positive assertion, in their report to the Exchange, that they "have made a review of the [brokerage firm's] accounting system, internal control and procedures for safeguarding securities" and to "comment rela-tive to any material inadequacies found to exist in the account-ing system, internal control and procedures for safeguarding securities, and shall indicate any corrective action taken or proposed."

Here is the rub. On the one hand the accounting firm is re-sponsible for the development of the brokerage firm's "account-ing system, internal control and procedures for safeguarding se-curities," and on the other hand they are obligated to "comment relative to any material inadequacies found to exist" in that very same system.

Unquestionably, there may be those possessed of superhuman

integrity and objectivity who would be even more critical of their own left-handed practices than they would of the sinister acts of others. Unquestionably, there is a preponderance of such superhumans in my profession, especially among the major firms, but who outside our profession will accept this on faith?

That Haskins & Sells undoubtedly realizes the Orvis matter will become something of a landmark case is demonstrated by the fact that even though almost a year has elapsed since the suit was initiated, H&S has not yet filed its answer—having gotten successive month-to-month postponements to do so. In the meantime, judging from the docket sheets maintained in the court house, this matter is destined to become a federal case —literally and figuratively so; and judging by the number of H&S's co-defendants (partners in the defunct brokerage firm) who have entered cross-complaints against the auditors, the case is destined to become a Donnybrook.

Incidentally, there must be an Invisible Hand maintaining an equilibrium in my profession—at least for the major firms. At the very time when Haskins & Sells is feeling the "slings and arrows of outrageous fortune" resulting from the Wall Street accountings, they replace Peat, Marwick as auditors for the Penn Central complex. There must be an important moral in all this, and I'm certain that it is all most salutary for the profession and society generally—else I would lose faith in that Invisible Hand.

The back-office mess is not at an end with these civil proceedings. A *New York Law Journal* article of July 15, 1971, headlined "State Assails Stock Brokers, Auditors" begins "Stock brokerage houses and their independent auditors were accused yesterday by state Attorney General Louis J. Lefkowitz of keeping the investing public from 'important information.'"

The Attorney General's comments resulted from a six-month investigation into "the auditors of Wall Street." He cited a case that he claimed also "illustrates the prevalent practice by independent auditors of brokerage firms contrary to generally accepted accounting principles to conceal deficits of the brokers

in the capital section of the balance sheets . . . of such brokerage houses." In further criticism of the auditors Mr. Lefkowitz
said the auditors' opinions on balance sheets prepared for customers have "in many instances been deceptive, avoided essential
footnotes and been aimed more at showing a purported good
financial health . . . rather than a true financial condition consistent with the auditors' responsibility."

In the course of his indictment of the prevalent audit practices the Attorney General was especially critical of the Big
Eight firms' near-monopoly of brokerage-firm audits. According
to the *Law Journal,* "63 percent of the brokers who replied to
a questionnaire said they were audited by [these] eight firms."

In replying to these criticisms on behalf of the AICPA, Leonard Savoie asserted that the Attorney General was introducing
"a political ploy" and that he was manifesting "an inadequate
understanding of the auditing function. The main purpose of a
brokerage audit is to examine a firm's compliance with rules.
These rules are set by regulatory authorities, not the accounting
profession." Savoie's statement then made an invidious distinction between that which is required to satisfy the stock exchanges
and that which the stockbrokers' customers are privileged to see.
He insisted "that audits of brokerage firms furnished to the
stock exchanges provide full information . . . it is not the function of the independent auditor to relay conclusions from this
information to the broker's customers." (Maybe that's the reason
there are brokers' yachts and fast women but, as the saying goes,
"there are no customers' yachts.")

These comments from the chief spokesman of the profession's
Establishment are understandable as far as they go; they are, of
course, entirely consistent with the views of learned counsel for
one of the Big Eight referred to early in this work. Nevertheless
Savoie's remarks are unseemly strange coming so soon after the
New York Stock Exchange's complaint against Haskins & Sells,
which appears to contradict Savoie's sanguine air, since it is saying in effect, "the New York Stock Exchange was *not* provided
with full information." If, now, Savoie is right, then there are

some very serious questions that need to be answered by the Exchange and probably even agencies beyond them.

Independence: The Sine Qua Non

The sweeping observation by the Ad Hoc Committee that they knew of no "situation where independence, in fact, had been impaired" can no longer be fairly asserted—however true the Committee may have believed it to have been when it was pursuing its inquiry.

The Committee received my correspondence alluding to the inaccuracies in its report, because in its final report there is a rather curious paragraph which begins with what we already know: ". . . The committee addressed . . . inquiries to the authors of articles which had raised questions related to independence and management services. With one exception, none of them indicated that he knew of any cases of impairment of independence in fact." Whereupon the Committee determined: "The one exception described several cases, but on analysis they did not impress the Committee as exemplifying a lack of independence arising from the rendition of management services—rather they showed failure of CPAs to have observed generally accepted auditing standards in performing the attest function."

Since the Committee thus alludes to but a single "odd ball," and since I have already identified that character and his assertions, the foregoing paragraph leads inexorably to the following rather embarrassing question: Has the Committee thereby rendered its professional judgment that the auditors in the Yale Express and Westec cases failed to observe generally accepted auditing standards in performing the attest function?

It is unfortunate that the Committee did not develop a catalogue of the kinds of management services presently deemed fair game by our colleagues; we would then, at least, be in a position to judge whether the particular service or services are relatively innocuous or require the accountants to work cheek to jowl with management and should, accordingly, be proscribed if they wish to continue as independent auditors.

Nor did the Committee see fit to sponsor a research effort by academicians or other scholars capable of pursuing the subject objectively. Instead, the Committee limited its "research" to sixteen interviews based on the "Briloff questionnaire." And when the responses to the questions didn't suit them, the Committee changed the questions until they elicited a suitable response.

Even more seriously, neither did the Committee see fit at least to describe (even if it did not concur in) the recommendations made by any of their respondents for cutting this Gordian knot. If they had done so, the reader would have been able to judge for himself whether the Committee's conclusion that we pursue "business as usual, but do be a bit more careful" was necessarily the optimum response.

There is yet another unfortunate aspect to the AICPA's determination to probe the management services–audit independence controversy—the way in which the Institute structured the Ad Hoc Committee. Thus, it was comprised of five active practitioners, each a principal partner in his respective firm. The chairman was of Haskins & Sells, others were members of Arthur Young, Lybrand, Price Waterhouse—all prominent names, several associated with the very controversies described in this two-hats discourse. The choice of this committee was like sending a goat to guard the cabbage patch. There was, as a consequence, much disappointment, even with little surprise, at the essentially escapist, if not whitewash, report.

But moving positively—what needs to be done? Essentially and ultimately, let us proceed to dissociate our profession from the taxation and managerial functions in those situations and circumstances where such involvement might jeopardize our attest function. Only such a dissociation will permit our profession to fulfill its role as a surrogate or ombudsman in economic society—a role which becomes increasingly vital with the widening gulf between ownership and management in our larger business corporations today.

I recognize that the foregoing recommendation will not be speedily implemented by the AICPA; pending such ultimate dissociation, the following interim procedures should be instituted forthwith to correct the current communications and performance gap:

1. The American Institute of Certified Public Accountants together with the Securities and Exchange Commission should move to accumulate better and more definitive data regarding the kinds of services presently being performed by public accounting firms, and the revenues being derived therefrom.

2. The Institute and SEC should move to require all proxy statements requesting the shareholders' approval of management's engagement of independent auditors to describe in some detail any services performed during the preceding year by such audit firm other than the independent audit, per se, and the amounts paid for such peripheral services.

Finally, I envisage a dilemma in the future arising from the accounting profession's increasing commitment to the performance of management-consultative services for government and business. I am referring to our increasing involvement in the expanding military-industrial-scientific-educational complex. Here I am not declaiming against the power of the Pentagon and its constellation of corporate enterprise. (Professor Richard J. Barnet has done that most admirably in his *The Economy of Death*.) Nor am I considering the high concentration of the audit responsibility in the eight major national firms, with resultant concentration of information in the firms' data banks. Instead, I question the propriety of the same firms' undertaking any analytical or consultative services in behalf of government that could have an impact on their clients—whether the impact be salutary or inimical doesn't really matter in terms of the challenge to independence.

All one needs to do is to inquire regarding the accounting

firms' involvements in space, defense, aircraft, and other military programs under contract with various governmental defense agencies, and we begin to wonder whether they are CPA or CIA firms. And then we have the kinds of involvements alluded to by John Lyons in his prize-winning essay:

> Like many other industries, accounting has profited from great growth in government spending over the past 20 years. The profession's involvement with the government has reached the point where it is the accountants who are best able to advise clients on the bidding methods and cost-control preparations necessary to win government contracts. Some critics mutter darkly that the accountants are only selling their political influence. . . .
>
> But the real benefit for clients that comes from Big Eight's work with the government lies in the broad experience the accountants are accumulating. "In the management services area," says Peat, Marwick's Hanson, "we have done a tremendous amount of government work. We were involved in the Apollo program, and have done a lot of cost effectiveness work for the Defense Department." . . . Peat, Marwick's corporate pricing-and-cost techniques were developed from work that the firm did for the U.S. Navy.

One might then well make inquiry regarding the kinds of governmental security clearance demanded at various levels of our accounting firms, and we would be led to wonder how free we are in our freedom of disclosure to all those entitled to prompt, full, and unfettered knowledge regarding corporate histories.

A *New York Times* story, "Air Force Dismisses Consultant after Criticism of Industry Link," referred to the dismissal of a partner in Arthur Young who had undertaken an assignment as "part-time consultant on weapons procurement practice after questions of possible conflict of interest were raised over his relationship with a major aircraft company." The potential conflict arose because the firm is the auditor of Lockheed, the "producer of the controversial C-5A transport plane." His consultative assignment would have involved "reviewing costs and delivery schedule reporting procedures in major weapons programs."

Just as college students have insisted on knowing what relationships prevail between universities and the scientific-defense establishment, students in schools of business, and the investment community generally, might inquire regarding the nexus of activities of our major accounting firms. Because of their power (individually, but especially collectively) the profession might be considered a quasi-public institution—not unlike stock and commodity exchanges and the members thereof. This would demand of us much higher standards of visibility and accountability than are now deemed appropriate.

The conflict I have just described is, as yet, a shadow, a portent, rather than full blown. But unless this potential conflict is resolved—after full and open inquiry—it will, it is safe to predict, embroil our profession in serious controversy in the years ahead.

Thus, we may see increasing discussion, if not implementation, of Galbraith's suggestion that when a particular corporation becomes overly identified with the military complex—for example, when over 70 percent of its revenues are derived therefrom—the corporation should be deemed to be "really a public firm" as contrasted with private companies. I suggest that when accounting firms derive a corresponding inordinate percentage of their revenues from services to corporations thus identified as "public firms," and to the government, per se, that they also be deemed to be firms within the *public* sector of our society, as contrasted with the present presumption that they are as private and individualistic as the traditional individual practitioners or two-man partnerships.

The point regarding the accountant's role in the military-industrial complex is, as yet, somewhat tenuous. It is, however, a matter which will undoubtedly expose us to increasing challenges from the financial community, the academic realm, government, and the public. For the present I leave the question open-ended, to be pursued by the under-30 generation of scholars.

With all of these proposals for disengagement from relationships which involve present or potential conflicts of interest I sense something seriously missing. Thus, each of these proposals for dissocation has a negative, or at best a prophylactic, implication. There needs to be a more transcendent response to this most serious challenge. I believe that response must be rooted in the need for the profession to answer the questions posed in several contexts in this work, to wit: What is the independent auditor's role in our economic society, and in society generally? To whom is he responsible? When and for what are we responsible? Are our compensations to be measured almost exclusively in material terms, or should we endeavor to derive psychic benefits? In short, how will the profession resolve its current "identity crisis," which has generated so much criticism, mostly deserved in my view, from within and without the profession?

I would want future generations of auditors, committed to the independent audit function, to see themselves as historians of the economic microcosm, that is, of the corporate entity.

I would expect the accountant to "know himself" so that he can comprehend that no inquiry takes place in an intellectual vacuum—the historian is an actor and involved in the historical narrative. I would want such an accountant to grasp the implications of Mannheim's wisdom that the examination of an object "is not an isolated act" but instead "takes place in a context . . . colored by values, . . . collective-unconscious, [and] volitioned impulses." Nor should such a recognition of inexorable involvement lead us to despair regarding the quest for objectivity and independence. Quite the contrary. As Mannheim points up, by first understanding ourselves, our drives and impulses, we can ultimately hope to "control the unconscious motivations and presuppositions which, in the last analysis, have brought these modes of thought into existence."

In other words such awareness could bring forth "a new type

of objectivity—attainable not through the exclusion of evaluations but through the critical awareness and control of them."

This is consistent with the counsel of E. H. Carr, British historian and philosopher of history: "First . . . you cannot fully
understand or appreciate the work of the historian unless you
have first grasped the standpoint from which he himself approached it; secondly . . . that standpoint is itself rooted in a
social and historical background. . . . The historian before he
begins to write history, is the product of history."

A Postscript to Haskins & Sells

Haskins & Sells did file its "Answer to Amended Complaint
and Cross-Claims" in the Orvis Brothers suit on May 17, 1972.
Much of the answer repeats the litany for such documents, i.e.,
"Denies each and every allegation set forth in Paragraphs . . .";
or "Denies knowledge or information sufficient to form a belief
as to the truth of any allegation set forth in Paragraphs . . ."

But Haskins & Sells does make a most critical stab in several
contexts, asserting that if H&S had erred, the plaintiff (the New
York Stock Exchange) is not the one to cast the first stone. Thus
(Paragraphs 52-54):

> On information and belief, in derogation of its duties and obli-
> gations under the Securities Exchange Act of 1934 and its own
> constitution and rules, the Exchange has adopted a policy of not
> enforcing its own rules and/or selectively enforcing those rules.
> In particular, the Exchange adopted a policy of not enforcing
> Rule 325 [the one which requires that an Exchange member have
> an "aggregate indebtedness" of not more than 20 times its "net
> capital"] . . .
>
> The Exchange was informed, at least as early as December 1969
> . . . concerning violations on or about such date, of Rule 325 by
> Orvis, yet failed to take any action or any timely action with re-
> spect thereto.
>
> Plaintiffs are barred from any recovery in this action because of
> unclean hands and contributory foul or negligence.

But then, "Oh Wow!" Beginning with paragraph 56 and running through paragraph 89 we have woven for us a seamless and unseemly web of perfidious conduct which, if substantiated, will "one up" Clifford Irving for the "greatest story every fabricated." A capsuled version of the scheming which H&S attributes to the principal partners of the once-proud Orvis firm is included in the Notes at page 354.

Chapter 12

Quo Vadis?

W HERE then does this dismal saga lead us? How can we extricate ourselves from a condition where many of our publicly owned corporations fail their responsibility for full and fair and prompt accountability?

There is no panacea. The dilemmas are so pervasive, the burdens so overwhelming, that no one group, no one profession, no one sector, not even any one government, could possibly cope with them unilaterally. In fact, it is likely that unless there is a miracle, a "moral rearmament," an intensified commitment to make this Age of Aquarius something other than an Age of Deception in our private and public lives, the foregoing criticisms are idle jeremiads, and proposals for change mere platitudes.

But because there is hope that a new generation may be committed to Charles Reich's Consciousness III, and reordering of priorities, the following is offered as a program for action.

Consistent with the ubiquity of the problem, and the fact that no single group has the sole responsibility for effective response, these proposals for action are directed to different segments of society. Despite the fragmentation of this program, I want to reemphasize that the proposals are anything but mutually exclusive. In short, unless sophisticated financial analysts and the unsophisticated masses of investors, together with corporate managements, leaders in government and the legislatures, the law, the courts, and the accounting profession, and the individual professional accountant all collectively comprehend the implications of the crisis which this work has described, there is little hope for the survival of the corporation as a form of private enterprise.

To the Financial Analysts

I begin, then, with my recommendation to the professional financial analysts—those who are the most sophisticated users of the financial statements prepared under the CPA's aegis. The analysts might well assert that they just won't buy our product— either *in toto* or when peddled by firms associated with accounting fiascos, flip-flops, and other dénouements. Surely they would shun the product of a corporation or an industry or a governmental agency which asserted that it was dispensing a tested, safe product when in fact it was toxic, or even lethal. So should it be with the output of a profession. If the responsible analysts were to insist upon a safe product, released only after diligent and scrupulous labor, they would soon get a better product. These professional investors should bear in mind that they are the most important consumers of the output of the accounting profession.

The financial analysts should become better informed regarding the product they are buying. They should understand fully what accountants are saying, and the environment in which they work. The analysts should sponsor meaningful programs encouraging a vital dialogue between our professions, and not accept the traditional wisdom at face value. They should continuously challenge the answers they get—and not accept a situation as good, right, or fair because it's generally accepted. I am urging that the sophisticated professional investor get involved.

Similar counsel to the analysts was given by Robert Trueblood, a former president of the AICPA, when addressing the Los Angeles Securities Analysts, thus: "The great majority of corporate executives no doubt want sincerely to keep investors informed. But it is natural for them to want also to put their best foot forward. And no matter how many rules the accountants write, there will be some people who will find a way to circumvent them."

Trueblood then went on to describe a corrective measure: "When an analyst comes across something that is a bit too shrewd and tends to be misleading, I think he should speak up loud and clear. If he is unsure whether what he has discovered is right and proper, he should inquire of the American Institute as to the principle involved."

And because many of the analysts do not have the resources for reaching the public directly, Trueblood solicited the help of another group, namely, the business journalists: ". . . Some journalists . . . more or less specialize in trying to detect elements in annual or quarterly reports that appear to strain the facts. . . . A company tempted to some disingenuousness is likely to have second thoughts if the chances of being put in an unfavorable public view are high."

Trueblood reemphasized for the analysts the heavy responsibility vested in "anyone involved in supplying financial data to the public," and concluded:

> Information that is inaccurate, either through carelessness or culpable self-seeking, can have the most serious consequences. It follows, in my judgment, that all of us engaged in the process of financial communication should strive to understand the pressures and necessities of the other participants in our community. In that way, we can all cooperate most effectively in order to keep the process of financial communication at a high level of quality and integrity.

I grant that a critical attitude could have an adverse effect on the economics of analysts and their firms. The appearance-reality dichotomy may have helped, and in some instances may have been essential, to assure success in security underwritings. In other cases this dichotomy contributed heavily to the volume of trading on the securities markets, producing, at least for a time, prosperity and affluence. The financial analyst must understand what Leonard Spacek said several years ago: "A successful free enterprise system demands that men live up to standards of integrity and trust," and that a multiplicity of accounting standards is a license to mislead investors, which "will result in killing the kind of business system we would like to preserve."

To the Masses

At the other extreme of the statement-user spectrum is the great mass of investors—the 30 or more millions who have a direct ownership of the shares of publicly owned corporations. They must make unmistakably clear that they don't consider Wall Street an extension of the Las Vegas Strip; nor Dow Jones to be a roulette wheel to be manipulated for political advantage or private gain. Let these masses organize to campaign for greater corporate responsibility and stockholder and consumer protection. Let them exert pressure through their labor unions and pension trustees, possibly also managers of mutual-fund and insurance-company portfolios, to demand of corporate managements and independent auditors the standards of disclosure which are essential to integrity and trust.

Let these investors make clear to their state and national legislative representatives that they are not lemmings, willing to be led to economic turbulence and devastation without a whimper. Let them aggressively demand, at shareholder meetings and elsewhere, a full explanation of the "take a bath" accountings, so much in vogue during 1970—was this ablution and purging merely of dirt and fat taken on in the psychedelic '60s? And if the auditors and managements have survived the flip-flop, investors should ask them "How come?"; or if the old managements and their auditors were sent into the wilderness, investors should ask the present incumbents what actions are pending against their predecessors. Investors should make known their feelings about the revelations of the Penn Central trustees in a bankruptcy report where they advised that the current (1970) data were not comparable with those for the years preceding

". . . since the 1969 figures appear to have reflected a corporate policy at that time of putting the best conceivable face on the facts." Such a cosmetic process is not what shareholders and their advisors need to make decisions, and to avoid "killing the kind of business system we would like to preserve." Corresponding questions must be put to the Lockheed officials and other supplicants for a public bail-out.

The Responsibility of Government

Turning now to the challenges for government: First, the legislative branch should initiate a high-level inquiry into the factors which contributed to the state of disarray demonstrated by the cases spread on these pages. Such a legislative commission should pursue this problem as a critical, unitary matter—rather than tangentially to an inquiry into the monopolistic proclivities of the past decades, or as an incident to the disintegration of our transportation system, or insurance industry, or a particular political scandal.

But it's undoubtedly through the regulatory process that government should have its most direct and positive impact on the problem here under consideration—principally through the Securities and Exchange Commission and the Federal Trade Commission. The public generally, and even many with special expertise, presume that these agencies are, in fact, their guardian, if not avenging, angels. The realities are far from this myth, as amply documented by Louis Kolhmeier in *The Regulators.*

Federal Trade Commissioner Philip Elman, addressing the 1970 meeting of the American Bar Association, described the theory underlying the independent regulatory commission as "original and brilliant."

It emphasized the agency's independence; its ability to bring expert judgment to bear upon technical and complex economic issues; its insulation from political partisan control; its capacity

to provide both continuity and flexibility of policy; and its blend-
ing in a single tribunal of a wide range of powers and functions,
from general rule-making to case-by-case adjudication, permitting
the agency to exercise broad discretion in choosing the best tool
for dealing with a particular problem.

This original and brilliant theory notwithstanding, the agencies have failed principally because of their "chronic failure to
fulfill their unique quasilegislative function of developing and
implementing regulatory policies responsive to public needs
and the public interest."

This chronic unresponsiveness and the basic deficiencies in
agency performance are largely rooted in their organic structure
and will not be cured by minor or transient personnel or procedural improvements.

To remedy this unresponsiveness and other deficiencies, Commissioner Elman urged, first, that the regulatory commissions
be made less secure and less independent of the President—but
then to make it abundantly clear that the responsibility for the
fulfillment of the agencies' objectives is vested in the President.
Through such a clear attribution of responsibility Commissioner Elman would expect to obtain better appointments to
these commissions.

Elman would then "unhinge" the regulatory from its quasijudicial role, since "even the most conscientious regulator cannot, when he acts as judge, ignore the effect which the decision
will have on the agency's regulatory policies and goals. . . .
Agency members are not, and should not be, selected for their
judicial qualities; and the institutional environment in which
they work does not nourish the development of such qualities."
He then proposes the following *modus operandi* for the more
effective fulfillment of the regulatory function:

> Thus, while I have long held to the opposite view, I am now
> convinced that we will lose nothing, and gain much, by eliminat-
> ing from agencies like the Federal Trade Commission the func-
> tion of case-by-case adjudication of alleged violations of law. This
> function should be transferred either to the district courts or,

preferably, to a new Trade Court which is decentralized and holds hearings in every state, thus bringing the judicial phase of the regulatory process much closer to the people. The Trade Court could be given jurisdiction not only of complaints prosecuted by the agency, but also private class-action suits brought by consumers and competitors injured by the same alleged unfair trade practices. To permit full and comprehensive disposition of the case by a single tribunal, the Court should have authority not only to issue preliminary and final injunctions, but also, where appropriate, to award damages, civil penalties, and other equitable relief.

This trade-court idea could be especially appropriate for the accounting controversy which is the principal theme of this work. Such a court might well be the extension of the accounting-court concept advanced several years ago by Spacek. In brief, its judges would be expected to be far more knowledgeable of accounting principles and practices, both the "is" and the "ought," than the judges of the traditional civil and criminal law courts. I would expect the judges on this trade or accounting court to be independent, of judicial temperament, and in all aspects dedicated to the transcendent aims and objectives of the entire process of corporate visibility and accountability.

As I envision it, such a court would be in a position to encourage the best in the formulation of the corporation's and profession's rules and in adherence thereto. Further, such a tribunal could discern, and strike down, any conflicts of interest that arise in the conduct of our professional practice. A court so independently structured should be able, on the one hand, to avoid the quagmire in which the AICPA's Accounting Principles Board presently finds itself; on the other, it could provide the standards toward which the Board and the profession generally must adhere. In brief, the very existence of the court would, at least to an important extent, separate the quasi-legislative and quasijudicial powers which are presently concentrated in so few hands within our profession's Establishment.

These proposals, or even more inspired ones, may not prove

to be a panacea. Dean James M. Landis, in a 1960 report on the regulatory process to President-elect Kennedy, predicted that:

> Irrespective of the absence of social contacts and the acceptance of undue hospitality, it is the daily machine-gun-like impact on both agency and its staff of industry representation that makes for industry orientation on the part of many honest and capable agency members as well as agency staffs.

In their *America, Inc.* Morton Mintz and Jerry S. Cohen allude to that report and then, referring to the absence of an effective input from the public sector, state:

> The citizen comes to be regarded as an intruder, if he should attempt to participate at all. Over and over again, regulatory agencies have been discovered using secrecy as a device to make it impossible for representatives of the public to defend their interests, or even to know that their interests need to be defended.

A mere restructuring of the organizational chart of these agencies will not produce the vital changes required to make them regulate in the public interest. Such changes might produce an immediate jolting which could prove salutary, but very soon the process of entropy will take hold and the agencies will revert to their old habits—that has been the historical process thus far. To maintain a high level of excitement and ferment in the regulatory agencies, their activities must be continuously subjected to the visibility and accountability urged by Commissioner Elman. Conceivably, this could be accomplished either by a formal ombudsman system or, alternatively, by public-interest groups modeled after Nader's Raiders.

For a Federal Chartering System

The "primary recommendation" made by Mintz and Cohen in their concluding chapter could have a significant effect on corporate accountability and on the regulatory process. After describing the intense rivalry among the states for developing the most expeditious chartering scheme, the one with the least constraints on corporations, with the objective of garnering franchise fees and taxes, these authors urge "that federal chartering replace state chartering of corporations." Among the advantages accruing from such a shift, according to *America, Inc.,* might be the providing of the "mechanism to clarify the appropriate roles of the government and the corporation. . . . The legitimate government should set [the goals and priorities of the corporations] free from undue influence by the corporation."

Other advantages flowing from federal chartering might be the restructuring of "certain concentrated industries to introduce competition"; this might be achieved by limiting the business activities in which a business could engage—thereby halting and reversing the conglomerate tide. Such chartering could also "be the instrument to make management genuinely responsible not merely to itself but to a broader shareholder and public interest as well." In sum, "Federal chartering would allow the public government to regain its proper role as quarterback of the economy, without massive new bureaucracy and without that meddling which is rightly condemned." This would be done, according to Mintz and Cohen, by the government "utilizing its powers to grant, modify, and implement or revoke charters to achieve adherence to national goals and priorities as set forth in federal statutes, such as those intended to preserve the environment."

It may well be that even this proposal is now inadequate in terms of the evolution of our corporate society. Thus, the growth of multinationalism among corporations may call for some supranational chartering process, possibly under the aegis of the United Nations, or corresponding institution.

To Corporate Management

Now for my proposals for corporate managements—those who are at the vital center of the power sector of corporate society. This group not only has primary responsibility regarding the deployment of huge resources but, as I have emphasized, it is also responsible for determining the parameters of the writing of the history of its stewardship.

What then can I say to management in connection with this process of accountability, which goes far beyond accounting per se? Essentially, it is to forswear the gamesmanship to which Leonard Savoie referred in his Conference Institute address cited in the opening chapter. Let them understand that their "game plan" or "scenario" does not include the "now" alone, nor principally their own fate and destiny. Instead, that which they determine today may well affect the very nature of our economic and political society unto eternity.

This point is implicit in the discussions in the earlier chapters regarding Penn Central, Commonwealth United, Lockheed, Wall Street—and many more illustrations could be introduced to make the point.

It was stated especially vividly by J. K. Galbraith, possibly writing with tongue in cheek, in a *New York* magazine article, when he described the ways in which the fiscal dilemmas of Penn Central and Lockheed had brought them far along the road to a socialist takeover; and, as he saw it, these two companies were not the only two major American enterprises which will be moving along that *via doloroso*.

Recognizing, then, the total social involvement of the managerial responsibility I urge that management move to give their actions greater visibility—the handmaiden to accountability. George O. May suggested a solution almost forty years ago when he urged that each listed corporation be required to formulate a statement of the methods of accounting employed by it, and that the formulation be "in sufficient detail to be a guide to its accounting department, to have such statement adopted by its board so as to be binding on its accounting officers; and to furnish such statement to the Exchange and make it available to any stockholder on request. . . ."

Writing from the vantage point of the '70s, I think that there is an even more compelling need for just such a specific, detailed formulation to be filed with the SEC and the exchanges to serve as a covenant between the corporation and all the parties in interest. Such a formulation should be made responsive to the broad spectrum of present-day demands for fairer corporate accountability. Such a formulation should set forth not only the field rules for corporate accountability in general but extend to the requirements for divisional reporting which is presently in such confusion and controversy.

And because this formulation should not be known only to corporate management, this accounting book of rules for major public corporations (those with sales, say, exceeding a quarter of a billion dollars) should be promulgated by a consortium composed of representatives from management and their counsel and independent auditors, of course, but composed also of non-management-designated directors (to represent the shareholders), as well as representatives from the Federal Trade Commission, General Accounting Office (since government contracts would undoubtedly constitute a significant phase of the entity's business), and from the Internal Revenue Service. This consortium would develop the statement of methods of accounting to be employed by the particular corporation only after meaningful consultation with representatives from, for example, the Census Bureau (because of its responsibility for the standard industrial classification), the Department of Defense (to obviate any national security impairment), the Financial Analysts Federation, and the Department of Labor and organized labor (since the resultant formulation would undoubtedly affect future wage negotiations). Such consultation would also extend to representatives from the consumer sector as well as from society in general, since the process of corporate accountability will, in the foreseeable future, undoubtedly embrace the totality of the corporation's relationships with its total environment.

My omission of the Securities and Exchange Commission from the foregoing roster was deliberate. I would want it to be the independent agency of first impression—to receive from the

consortium the book of rules adopted for the particular corporation and to determine whether there are any gaps or other
inadequacies. The SEC might also act to mediate any differences
among the members of the corporate consortium, as well as
develop a file of accounting alternatives, and the circumstances
where they had been applied. I would hope that the Commission would avoid *ex parte* deliberations with any particular
segments of the consortium; instead, I would wish that all of
its proceedings would be formal and on the record.

Such an overtly formulated catechism of accounting assumptions for the entity would have the added virtue of objectivity
since the world would be let in on the corporation's specific
game-plan rules, and be capable of determining whether management *is* playing the game right down the middle of the field
rather than just inside the foul line.

Granted, I may here be infringing on the managerial prerogative as it is presently conceived; nevertheless, our corporate
society is too much a part of the totality of society to permit the
accounting formulation envisioned by George May to be left
essentially to a single sector (or a combination of only a few
such sectors) of our total society.

By way of concluding these words of brief counsel to management: Go back and review the roster of companies involved in
the foregoing retelling of the instances of abuse of fairness by
the use of "flabby GAAP." Note the once-proud names enu-
merated therein; go back and study the life cycles of each of
these bubbles; see what happened to their managements. In
some cases they're still with the corporations (in a few instances
they even enjoy some national prominence) but where are the
Lings, the Ackermans, the Levins, the what's his name who was
head of Commonwealth United? Read again the lamentable
piece in *Forbes* on Leasco's boy wonder. Study the roller-coaster
phenomenon of the land developers.

I would then add: Of what worth is it to live through a brief
psychedelic period, reading those beautiful market letters about

yourself, and then having to "mainline" in order to perpetuate the fiction?—always afraid that Wall Street will find out about how you cooked the books, in accordance with GAAP to be sure, with your auditors concurring in your recipes. Will you derive much comfort from the scrapbooks containing those words of high praise, frequently manufactured by your own public-relations staff (financial representatives, they call themselves), stuff which, unfortunately, you began to believe yourself?

To the Leadership of the Profession

Moving to the next inner circle, the organized accounting profession—the groups which have become the leading spokesmen for my profession, the AICPA, the CPA societies of the several states, the American Accounting Association, the National Association of Accountants, the Financial Executives Institute. To begin with, they must share with management the transcendent commitment to the total society and to posterity; they must manifest a realization that they are professionals, hence with the presumed commitment to an advancing body of knowledge, and a commitment to service—and thereby forswear the coloration of a trade association.

How should they proceed to fulfill these objectives which I believe to be so urgent? I shall address myself essentially to the AICPA, as the organization primarily charged with speaking in behalf of the accounting profession, and the one best endowed for self-regulatory commitment.

First, I ask that they free themselves from the identification hang-up, which produces conflicts of interest at every turn. As I have demonstrated in various contexts, we accountants don't know what we stand for, what our certificate means, to whom we're responsible, for what we are responsible, and how we are supposed to fulfill this responsibility.

Then, when we move to our distinguished elder statesmen, the Accounting Principles Board, we haven't seen evidence of sufficient judicial detachment from their world of partners and firm clients to permit them to measure the social implications of the serious matters on which they deliberate.

The Board has been receiving its "lumps" from all sides. A particularly stinging rebuke came from within the hierarchy of the profession itself, from among the very highest of its high priests.

A *New York Times* article of January 4, 1972, entitled "Rules Split Accountants," described the brewing of a major palace revolt in the following purple prose:

> . . . just a little over a year ago, Robert M. Trueblood, chairman of Touche, Ross & Co., and a former president of the American Institute of Certified Public Accountants, in effect threatened that his firm—one of the largest and fastest growing of the "Big Eight" national accounting firms—would bolt the Accounting Principles Board and deal directly with the Securities and Exchange Commission in the setting of accounting ground rules. . . .
>
> Mr. Trueblood charged that the business of establishing accounting principles was "dragging seriously," that there was a large question in his mind whether the present organization of the board was "efficient or even viable," and he said that Touche, Ross was reconsidering "its entire participation in the affairs of the board."
>
> Under the circumstances, he said, "I am sure you will understand that, as a practicing firm of some consequence, we will maintain our right of freedom with respect to direct contact with the S.E.C. on this and all other professional matters."
>
> The upshot of this and similar outcries from several major firms . . . was a gathering of the elders of the profession, and, subsequently, the appointment of two study groups to appraise the work of the board.
>
> One, headed by a former S.E.C. commissioner, Francis M. Wheat, is to analyze the machinery for rule-making, while the other, chaired by none other than Mr. Trueblood himself, will look at the philosophical underpinning (or lack of it) in the setting of accounting rules.

Neither study has yet been completed, but they seem certain to provide plenty of fireworks when they are. . . .

Last fall, at a public hearing held by Mr. Wheat's committee, Mr. Defliese [Chairman of the APB] called for only relatively minor changes in the board's membership and procedures, though he did recommend that the chairman's job be full-time, rather than part-time as at present.

By contrast, Mr. Trueblood, and several other dissidents as well, called for the replacement of the present 18-man part-time board with a relatively small full-time highly paid board completely divorced from the pressures of day-to-day business.

I might observe, in passing, that I agree in essence with everything Mr. Trueblood is quoted as having said in this connection; in fact I am an avid reader of his many profound articles urging our profession on to higher commitments and greater accomplishments. I have been much informed and inspired by his precepts. But when I reflect on the fact that it was his own firm that was responsible for the Litton, Perfect Film, Leasco, and U.S. Financial accountings which were the subjects of serious criticisms in these pages, I cannot help but feel that Mr. Trueblood might have given our profession an even greater jolt, and would have had a far more salutary effect, if he "threatened that his firm . . . would bolt" those among its clients who did not adhere to the standards so effectively articulated by him, rather than to bolt the APB.

As of this writing the prestigious Wheat and Trueblood studies referred to in the *Times* article are still in gestation. There are, of course, rumors with varying degrees of reliability as to what they might determine and recommend. And then there are varying predictions as to whether any important proposals could ever be implemented in practice—given the present constraints on the profession.

Being thus deprived of the benefits of the Wheat-Trueblood wisdom we are thrown back on to our own resources and must proceed to develop our own proposals for change at the Accounting Principles Board.

When addressing an American Petroleum Institute convention meeting in mid-1971, I included counsel along the following lines to the APB (under the title "Will the Real APB Please Stand Up?"):

I suggested, first, that the APB be disbanded forthwith; and because I have no personal animus toward its members I would immediately reconstitute them as a new APB. This time, however, to call a spade a spade, APB would stand for the *Assiduous Plumbing Board*. Now, I want to make it abundantly clear that I am not thereby denigrating plumbers and plumbing—to the contrary, I find a wrench to be a lethal weapon, and changing a washer a traumatic experience.

Instead, I want the world to know just what the APB is really up to. We know it hasn't discovered or even discerned a single principle in the over a decade of its existence; all it has done was to tinker with the plumbing of our profession.

A case in point was the mandate laid down by Savoie in his 1969 speech cited in Chapter 4. Remember how he asserted that a "forthright solution" to the business combinations issue was a premise upon which his other forecasts for accounting viability were predicated. This forthright solution would have proscribed pooling accounting; and "anything less," he said, "will mean simply a 'repositioning' of the abuses which have become so rampant in recent years."

We now know that a year later the Board ended up with just such a "repositioning" in the form of its Opinions 16 and 17. This "repositioned plumbing" took the form of a Rube Goldberg creation—with pipes, wires, gadgets, levers, balls, alarms, valves, spigots, and the like. That the system has built-in leakage was clear to the Board—this was the price they had to pay to get the politicized two-thirds vote. That the leakage is being exploited by the users of the system is already discernible to most of us—certainly to all of us in practice.

Even more recently this Plumbing Board, in its wisdom, determined that it was desirable to hook up the principal entity's reservoir of accounting principles (already seriously contaminated, as we are all painfully aware) with the smaller reservoirs of the "investees"—hence the Equity Method of Accounting prescribed by Opinion 18. Now, if these secondary waters were comprised of clear, fresh springs gushing forth purified waters, this would most certainly have a salutary effect on the investors' reservoir. But the APB could not wait to test these new waters—1971 had to be a year for earnings improvement— and so the valves from the potentially even more polluted waters of the investees were opened wide, and already I can see some raw sewage flowing into the main reservoir of the investors' accountings.

My next recommendation for the APB is that it be disbanded, and the same persons be reconstituted as another APB—this time as an *Anti-Pollution Board*. Here, in all seriousness, they could perform an extraordinarily vital function. In this guise I would expect them to say to corporate managements whenever this APB discerns a potentially polluting process: "This has to stop and stop peremptorily. We don't yet know the right answers but we sure can see the wrong ones. We're not going to string along with your managerial proclivities until the right ones come along. Period." In other words, "We're just not going to associate our reputation with financial statements contaminated by 'Cleverly Rigged Accounting Ploys'."

Let management then commit itself to developing the approved practices at higher levels of meaningful communication. If the Board had moved in this vein, the profession would have had a lot less agony over such problems as earnings per share, pooling-purchase, marketable securities, accounting for the land-office business, leases, and so forth, than it has experienced over the past decade. By so doing, corporations and their auditors would not develop a vested interest in a particularly perverse practice—which can be exorcised only after a long struggle and an attenuation of principle.

At present, "go-go," aggressive, "swinging" management has a distinct advantage because the APB (here, the *Accounting*

Procrastination Board) spends so much time determining how to avoid devious reporting in a particular context that by the time they define their position the swingers and hustlers have done their thing and departed.

Enough of this berating of the APB—in truth and in essence I would like to see the APB become an *Accounting Philosophers Board*. The members thereof would be persons of the highest personal integrity and wisdom in accounting practices and procedures, of course. But in addition, they should evidence a vital comprehension of the total environment in which the financial-reporting process is pursued, and of the total universe which is affected by the consequences of the historical narrative of the corporate entity.

I assume strict detachment of the members of the APB from any involvement in accounting practices; nor would I condone persons taking an interim leave from their firms with the contemplation of returning after their period of service *pro bono publico*.

Further, I would not designate members to this Accounting Philosophers Board without open inquiry into their credentials; this would give the profession and the public the opportunity of interrogating, or even challenging, the candidates on any questionable involvements on their part, or on the part of their respective firms.

You can see that I am here analogizing the circumstances for appointment to this APB with appointments to the judiciary— at the least, for candidates for important legislative or regulatory posts. Such a standard is, in my view, absolutely essential if my profession is to earn the confidence of the society in which we function. Failing such a standard, and a correspondingly high level of performance, we will continue to be dogged by a credibility gap, a crisis in confidence, and the indictments of creeping irrelevance so prevalent today. In such a dismal circumstance accountants will have forsaken any valid claim to professional stature and status—and in such an environment our corporate society, and with it our capitalistic economy, will have been made seriously vulnerable.

This conflict of interests can be discerned in another dimension of our profession's responsibility—that of the disciplining of our members who may have erred grievously. The past decade has produced what I described as a veritable "roll of dishonor," including: (1) Continental Vending; (2) Bar Chris; (3) Yale Express; (4) The "stinking salad oil spillover on American Express"; (5) Westec; (6) Pioneer Finance; (7) The "Mess in Wall Street"; (8) R. Hoe; (9) Belock Instruments; (10) Commonwealth United; (11) Penn Central; (12) Mill Factors; (13) Liberty Equities; (14) Lockheed; (15) Investors Overseas Services; (16) Black Watch Farms; (17) Major Realty; (18) Ecological Sciences; (19) National Student Marketing; (20) etc., etc.

How has the profession's disciplinary machinery moved into action? Not even with "all deliberate speed"—it just hasn't as far as the outside world could discern.

What do we find in the recorded actions of our Institute's Trial Boards—the Boards which administer disciplinary proceedings against members? All one need do is analyze their determinations as published in *The CPA* (the Institute's monthly newsletter) over the past dozen years and he will there find some of the "most serious" professional aberrations described for public censure. The reported disciplinary actions involved breach of our rules of ethics (advertising, client piracy, dual listing in a telephone directory); most involved transgressions *vis-à-vis* tax laws (including inordinate propinquity to Internal Revenue agents); others involved prior conviction of crimes (using mails to defraud, conspiracy to commit murder, and moral turpitude—whatever that might imply). Then there were some 12 cases that go to the heart of our professional commitment—to audit the books and records of business entities and to report fearlessly and fairly to all those entitled to know. Do we find any of the major fiascos involved in any of these proceedings? Not so that you'd recognize it. There are, in addition, the culprits who trafficked in CPA exams, failed to review inventories, or certified a statement they knew to be false, or used their letterheads for a statement without disclaiming an opinion. In short, except for someone called Homer E. Kerlin who got his lumps for the Olen–H. L. Green mess, and possibly the defendants in the Continental Vending case who appear to have been censured anonymously in the October, 1971, issue, the Boards can be seen to be moving in the manner of the false guides referred to in the Scriptures—"those who swallow camels yet strain at gnats."

Nor would this cynic have expected anything different after looking at the composition of the Trial Board complex. Of the twenty-one members presently on the Board, six are from the eight largest accounting firms—this cynic could well hear the words of the Great Teacher echoing through the Trial Board's halls when a major fiasco is presented for their awesome deliberations: "Let him who is without sin cast the first stone." Since writing this I have learned that the Institute does "open files" on these *causes célèbres* when they learn of them, but as with classified documents in the Pentagon, they remain in such a state perpetually—or at least until they will no longer embarrass anyone important.

Let's leave the pathological aspects of our professional organization's responsibility. What should the AICPA do to advance the body of knowledge which we profess, our accounting philosophy and precepts of practice?

This body of knowledge within the special realm of the profession's expertise cannot be static; this was asserted unequivocally by A. N. Whitehead, when defining a profession as "an avocation whose activities are subjected to theoretical analysis, and are modified by theoretical conclusions derived from that analysis."

The analysis and criticism required by a profession must, he said, be relevant "to the purpose of the avocation and to the adaptation of the activities for the attainment of those purposes." It must be "founded upon some understanding of the nature of the things involved in those activities, so that the results of action can be foreseen." In brief, a profession must be possessed of "foresight based upon theory, and theory based upon understanding of the nature of things."

Foresight and Research

Failing such foresight and the forward thrust of theory, Whitehead concluded, we have but a craft, the antithesis of a profession. In his view, "Pure mentality easily becomes trivial in its grasp of fact." The craft is an "avocation based upon customary activities and modified by the trial and error of individual practice." This act of creation, this advancement of the frontiers of theory, this better comprehension of the nature of things, this anticipatory foresight, is generally considered to result from research dedicated to the fulfillment of these lofty objectives.

That there is a serious anemia in research in all areas of knowledge is evident from Pierre Teilhard de Chardin's lament that though we exalt research and derive enormous benefit from it, yet "with what pettiness of spirit, poverty of means and general haphazardness do we pursue truth in the world today." To emphasize this point Teilhard continues: "We behave as though we expected discoveries to fall ready-made from the sky, like rain or sunshine. . . ." If, he went on, we were to relate the proportion of our nation's revenue allotted to research, "we should be staggered." We are so parsimonious in this respect that "surely our great-grandsons will not be wrong if they think of us as barbarians."

Let's back up a bit to consider briefly the present entirely inadequate research apparatus within the accounting profession. There is, of course, a great deal of so-called research being carried on within the major accounting firms in our midst. However, this kind of research might be said to correspond to the research and development activity conducted by a major corporation incident to its creation of new products and the improvement of old products in order to enhance its sales and profit position. Research under such conditions has to be characterized as useful or within a company's field of interest to be considered desirable. Research so conceived and pursued may have a salutary effect for the scientific community (the accounting profession, for present purposes); this is, however, tangential since "basic research holds an unstable position in the laboratory." In brief, the most effective utilization of research in the corporate laboratory (and the firm) is in applied research. While the corporation (like the firm) needs and depends upon basic research, it looks to the university for much of it.

The foregoing observations, based on a study of research in industry, are consistent with the conclusions found by G. Edward Philips in his study of "Research in Major Public Accounting Firms." He there found that:

> The research department . . . performs as a staff function. It accumulates, analyzes, and summarizes information and ideas as a service to the operating sections of the firm. . . . It does not appear likely that public accounting firms will devote much formal effort to constructing an accounting theory which can be used as a basis for evaluating the soundness of alternative accounting practices. [Research activities actively pursued by the firm are] oriented toward keeping the firm aware of current practices and developments, providing a basis for establishing policies in accounting and auditing matters, and resolving urgent questions that arise in the course of practice.

By far, though, the most ambitious single venture in accounting research was undertaken in 1959 when, faced with growing discontent over current financial-reporting practices, the American Institute created its Accounting Research Division, and concurrently formed the Accounting Principles Board to supersede the Committee on Accounting Procedure which had theretofore been responsible for promulgating Accounting Research Bulletins.

This new program was launched with much fanfare and high hopes. Prof. Maurice Moonitz was designated as the first Director of Accounting Research, whereupon he proceeded with an ambitious agenda aimed to provide a theoretical infrastructure for accounting. In the fulfillment of this endeavor professors in various universities undertook to develop research studies under contract with the Research Division. It might well have been presumed that the Division would pursue its studies independently and diligently and, in turn, that the Accounting Principles Board would promulgate their Opinions as a consequence of the deliberations of the research scholars. The expectations for this program at its launching are evidenced by the following prediction by Weldon Powell, the first chairman of the APB:

> [We] shall try to do some bold thinking about our problems. If we are to succeed, we shall have to be willing to consider new ideas in developing theory, and to reach out towards new methods not tried before in developing relevant practices and procedures. There are those who think we need a major overhaul, not a minor repair job. George O. May in writing to me recently, said: "It is no time for patching up; it is time for viewing the system as a whole and developing, if not a philosophy of accounting, at least a mode of thought that visualizes the problems as a whole.

Alas, these high hopes were dashed very early—undoubtedly because the studies promulgated by the Research Division were too abstract to solve the profession's concrete problems. The recommendations were far too radical for early implementation —and the leaders of the profession were reluctant to give change a chance. Whereupon Paul Grady, a retired partner of a major accounting firm, replaced Moonitz as Director of Accounting Research; Grady immediately set out to develop the catalogue of all the "is's" he could find in our profession's practice, which he published as another research study (No. 7, *Inventory of Generally Accepted Accounting Principles for Business Enterprises*).

Essentially the studies which have subsequently issued from the Research Division, including those under the aegis of Grady's successor, Reed Storey, have been essentially pragmatic —given to the resolution of a particular problem of common concern (goodwill, extractive industries, pension plans)—and even these have been pursued by practitioners who were continuously and concurrently identified with their firms (from which they presumably continued to draw their usual compensations).

The Accounting Principles Board, in the meantime, has gone its own way—issuing Opinions generally without prior formal research, at the least without any published studies; and where there was such research, the APB paid mere lip service thereto—but otherwise followed its own proclivities.

The foregoing is a brief historical, and somewhat critical, background. What are my proposals for a restructuring of our research endeavor?

First, the manner of financing research in accountancy needs to be changed. The accounting research in the universities is suffering from the anemia alluded to by Teilhard—both in the degree of responsibility of the programs for effecting the breakthroughs in knowledge, as well as in the available financing. Who is to pay for this research? How should the funds be administered?

The answer to these queries might well be, principally the accounting profession. However, to assure the pluralistic support required to permit greater independence, support should also be forthcoming from the securities and commodities exchanges, labor unions, chambers of commerce, associations of financial analysts, from the government, and possibly also from consumer groups and broad-based organizations like Common Cause.

The kinds of research which I envisage for the accounting profession involve value judgment and must, accordingly, be insulated from the unwarranted and frequently inimical influence and control of government, labor, industry, as well as the profession. In brief, a Foundation for Accounting Research would give to the scholars the maximum assurance of freedom of intellectual pursuit, the *sine qua non* of creative research.

Of course, no categoric assurance can be given that such a pluralistically supported and structured research program will succeed, even if launched and implemented under optimum circumstances. However, it stands a better chance than the present program centered in the Institute; the circumstances of the founding of such a Foundation for Accounting Research, the pluralism of its support, and the manner in which the research programs are launched should have a positive impact on the acceptance of the results of such research.

For a Corporate Accountability Commission

At the Institute level, I recommend the creation of a "Corporate Accountability Commission." Such a commission would be comprised of certified public accountants in practice as well as those in teaching and research. In addition the Commission would include representatives from the banking, labor, investment, consumer, and governmental sectors of society, and from other relevant disciplines in universities. Such a body would be charged with the special responsibility for anticipating the evolution of our corporate state and determining the kinds of information and disclosures required to permit such evolution to be consistent with the goals and objectives of a democratic, capitalistic society. The Commission would be continuously apprised of aberrations in the stewardship and accountability process of corporations, and in general to judge how effectively the modern American corporation is fulfilling its economic and social responsibility.

This proposal parallels one expressed by Edwin D. Etherington, a former president of the American Stock Exchange, when addressing the 1971 G. M. Loeb Awards convocation. He spoke principally of the need for restructuring the governance of the New York Stock Exchange. He expressed his conviction that "the problems confronting the Exchange are not ones which can be solved as long as there can be legitimate doubt concerning the perspective of those who must develop solutions." He then spoke of the need to eradicate the present mood of treating the Exchange's "public business as a family affair," thereby making it "more a bastion against change than a bulwark for strength." But then, Etherington said, there is a "second problem—the lingering implication of unacceptable self-interest summarized by the 'private club' label first pasted on the Exchange by an SEC official," adding that the Exchange's Board of Governors should move "to blot out that insulting phrase" by "realizing that the policy-making structure of the Exchange invites the accusation."

He then urged the Big Board to consider surrounding a full-time paid chairman and a president to function as the head of operations "with a Board made up largely (but not exclusively) of people who are not members or allied members of the Exchange. It should be a balanced Board whose members are justly respected in their own field." Etherington's hope for the Board, like mine for the Commission, is that "Such a structure, energized by the acknowledged economic power of the Exchange, would give it the basis for a leadership role. A lot of action would follow."

If the AICPA Fails

But to return to the mainstream of these concluding remarks, if the AICPA fails to move vigorously to meet its responsibilities to statement users—responsibilities which it has either assumed for itself or had delegated to it by the essential abdication of the accounting-principle promulgation responsibility by the SEC—or having thus moved, fails in its mission, then what? Here I can see a close parallel with the crisis which confronted the New York Stock Exchange in mid-1970. The Exchange, like the AICPA, asked government and public to entrust them with setting high standards for the members of the "club," and disciplining erring members. Both the Exchange and the AICPA assert that they are self-regulatory bodies.

When it became apparent that the Exchange wasn't really

disciplining the practices of its members and/or the standards were not adequate to protect the interests of society, the Exchange had to assume the financial burdens of the aberrant members. This assumption was voluntary at first but soon threatened to be compulsory, in the First Devonshire and Robinson litigations. This traumatic era brought the Exchange to importune Congress hat in hand, sacrificing its autonomy and freedom of action. A governmental assistance program was evolved for these stalwart symbols of free enterprise—with the resultant blow to the egos of the "club members," who must have realized that they had thereby moved themselves along the road to socialism.

The AICPA will find itself in a similar vulnerable position, given an epidemic of successful lawsuits against accounting firms. Some firms might not have $5 million to placate the Mill Factors creditors; $40 million was sought in the Continental Vending lawsuit, although it was settled for "but $4 million." The Institute itself may become the "defendant of last resort." This could be justified by reference to the AICPA's openly professed vows—a covenant that the Institute is fulfilling inadequately. And then we will find that the accounting profession has joined the stock exchanges, Penn Central, and Lockheed and other defense contractors on the sad trek to Washington, and socialism.

The New York Stock Exchange's current lawsuit against Haskins & Sells adds another dimension to the foregoing observations regarding the AICPA's vulnerability to becoming a defendant, as was the Exchange during 1970. Suppose, *purely hypothetically,* that the Orvis Bros. action mushrooms to embrace the Hayden Stone, Du Pont, and Dempsey-Tegeler matters, and that the single accounting firm cannot meet judgments against it. Will the Exchange then move against the American Institute of Certified Public Accountants on the ground that the latter self-regulatory body contributed to the Exchange's losses through the Institute's failure to maintain standards of performance by its members?

An affirmative answer to this hypothetical question is suggested in the New York Stock Exchange complaint, which reads: "As a result of the expending of approximately $5,000,000 by the Trustees of the Special Trust Fund in order to safeguard the public customers of Orvis . . . the plaintiffs are subrogated to the rights of the public customers of Orvis in said amount."

Now, just as the swordfish concentrates mercury ingested when it swallows smaller poor fish, so it is that ultimately the Stock Exchange will accumulate enough stuff to make it potentially lethal to other organisms or organizations.

This suppositious chain of occurrences can have awesome implications. But the solution in an age of increasing complexity and specialization of function is for the leadership of each profession claiming to be self-regulatory to maintain standards at the highest, and to discipline aberrations vigorously. This is an essential precondition to a profession asking that "it be trusted."

As aggrieved parties press their claims against the authoritative body of a particular profession, it in turn may accuse another profession which might be guilty of "contributory negligence." This could, ironically, prove salutary, since we would have another manifestation of "countervailing power"— whereby various major groups, with equal gravitational pull, somehow maintain themselves in an effective orbit.

To the Alpha and Omega

Finally, I turn to the alpha and omega, the first and the last, of this preachment segment of "Unaccountable Accounting." I of course mean the individual accountant, the first person singular, involved in the fulfillment of our professional commitment. It is only if the individual "I" can sense the pervasive implications and ramifications of his professional commitment that any of the foregoing high horizons can be reached. It is only if the individual accountant comprehends the meaning of the poignant counsel of A. Whitney Griswold that we can hope to attain what otherwise would be an impossible dream; his essay on "Society's Need for Man" concluded with this plain moral:

> To do good we must first know good; to serve beauty we must first know beauty; to speak the truth we must first know the truth. We must know these things ourselves . . . and wish to do so, when no one else is present to prompt us or bargain with us. We must hold true to that purpose. No price, no mess of pottage, can equal its value to our country and ourselves, its citizens.

We will attain our objectives only when there are enough of the "I's" to comprehend the meaning and significance for our profession of the philosophy of history: Fact, theory, and interpretation form a closely knit complex in the historical (and accounting) narrative. The simple facts of history (and accounting) are not simple at all; or insofar as they are simple and elicit universal agreement—names, dates, places—they seem to be trivial and only reinforce the need for interpretation. The facts of history (and accounting) invariably appear in a context of interpretation; and there is no interpretation without theory. In brief, we cannot disentangle this complex web of facts and theory, narration, and interpretation.

With the foregoing in mind (and equally essential in heart) we must commit ourselves to perfecting our special language so that the interpretation and the narrative regarding the economic microcosm (the corporate entity) will be fully comprehensible to all who depend on us. The "I's" would be constrained to comprehend their absolute requirement for freedom and independence for the narrative and interpretation to fulfill the expectations of society for the independent attest function.

Our alpha and omega must understand that his values, emotions, and ideological concepts will invariably enter into his analysis and interpretation—he cannot dissociate himself from the preconceptions of his age, class, or personal *Weltanschauung*. Knowing all this, he must be diligent in avoiding entangling alliances; correspondingly, he should be zealous in disclosing all material facts known to him so that persons who have different values or ideological concepts could determine for themselves whether the particular auditor's interpretation of the facts was fair.

In essence I am seeking to impose a "Nuremberg Code" on each of us engaged in our professional pursuit, a code whereby we commit ourselves to implement a standard of fairness, even though a contrary result could well be subsumed under GAAP. And we should adhere to the code in spite of "superior orders" or clients' directives. This is an awesome burden which I am imposing on the individual—but it is only through the acceptance of just such a burden that accountants will have a fair claim to professional recognition.

In thus returning to the individual accountant and his sense of the fair, the good, and the right, I am repeating the saga of Hermann Hesse's literary character, Siddhartha, who set out on a long quest in search of the ultimate answer to the enigma of man's role on earth. After a tortuous road he discovers that the answer was always within the self, and it is there that one is constrained to search for it.

Notes

Preface

page xv: Mr. Justice Douglas's quotation: Foreword to Abraham J. Briloff, *Effectiveness of Accounting Communication,* New York: Praeger, 1967.

Chapter 1: 2 Plus 2 Equals . . . ?

page 3: Hot-pants reference: An extensive discourse on this recent trend is presented in an interview by Ray Brady in *Dun's,* October, 1971, pp. 8–13.

pages 3–4: "Taken off LIFO" reference: Considered in some detail in Chapter 2 when discussing the 1970 accountings by the Chrysler Corporation.

page 4: "Market Place" article: The New York Times, May 1, 1971, p. 40.

page 6: Reich quotation: Charles A. Reich, *The Greening of America,* New York: Random House, 1970, p. 129.

page 7: Reich's discourse on Consciousness III: Reich, *ibid.,* Chapter IX, "Consciousness III: The New Generation," pp. 217–264.

page 7: Medical Committee case: Officially cited as *Securities and Exchange Commission v. Medical Committee for Human Rights.* The decision of the United States Court of Appeals, District of Columbia, 432 F. 2d 659 (D.C. Civ. 1970).

pages 7–8: Shanahan article: Eileen Shanahan in *The New York Times,* May 11, 1971, p. 43.

page 8: Medical Committee case: The decision of the United States Supreme Court mooting the Medical Committee case is reported at 404 U.S. 403 (1972).

page 8: Closing Circle *references:* Barry Commoner, *The Closing Circle,* New York: Knopf, 1971. Professor Commoner's discussion of "externalities" is in Chapter 12, "The Economic Meaning of Ecology," pp. 250–292. For Commoner's quotation from K. W. Kapp, see pp. 256–257.

page 9: Casey's address: Address by Chairman William J. Casey, delivered in New York City on November 18, 1971, entitled "Responsibilities and Liabilities in Corporate Life."

page 10: Saul references: Speech delivered by Ralph S. Saul in Washington, D.C. on January 26, 1970, entitled "Some Fundamental Changes in the Securities Industry."

pages 10–11: Lufkin references and quotations: Speech by Dan W. Lufkin before the Connecticut Chapter of The New England Council, September 22, 1970, entitled "Is the Corporation Dead?"

pages 11–13: Eckstein quotations: Statement by Otto Eckstein entitled "The Astonishing Revisions of Corporate Profits," July 21, 1971.

page 13: Galbraith, et al. references: John K. Galbraith, *The New Industrial State,* Boston: Houghton Mifflin, 1967; Wilbert E. Moore, *The Conduct of the Corporation,* New York: Vintage Books, 1962; Andrew Hacker, "Corporate America," in Andrew Hacker (Ed.), *The Corporation Take-Over,* New York: Anchor Books, 1965, pp. 1–17; Eugene V. Rostow, "To Whom and For What Ends Is Corporate Management Responsible," in Edward S. Mason (Ed.), *The Corporation in Modern Society,* New York: Atheneum, 1966, pp. 46–72; Carl Kaysen, "The Corporation: How Much Power? What Scope?" in *ibid.,* pp. 85–105; and Adolf A. Berle, Jr., *Power Without Property,* New York: Harcourt, Brace & World, 1959.

pages 13–15: Savoie references and quotations: Address by Leonard M. Savoie, delivered in New York City, November 20, 1970, before The Conference Institute, New York City, entitled "Game Plans and Professional Standards." In concluding this address, Savoie urged the business leaders there assembled to "take a more constructive role in seeing that the game plan of corporate reporting is played according to fair and reasonable standards." This, he said, was essential since "if they are not developed through the existing machinery, it is almost certain that they will be imposed by some other authority." In that event, "the game will certainly be played according to different rules. . . . This, in turn, will cause the game to change into one of less appeal and less reward to the public in general." In retrospect, it may well be that by this despairing speech Savoie anticipated his resignation from his position as Executive Vice President of the American Institute of Certified Public Accountants as of June 30, 1972.

page 15: Spacek quotations: Address by Leonard Spacek delivered on September 19, 1970, pp. 5–6. (Privately printed by Arthur Andersen & Co., File Ad 7910–Item 126.)

page 17: The Effectiveness of Accounting Communication: Abraham J. Briloff, *The Effectiveness of Accounting Communication,* New York: Praeger, 1967.

pages 17–19: AICPA's Select Committee report reference: Report of Special Committee on Opinions of the Accounting Principles Board, as presented to Council of the American Institute of Certified Public Accountants, Spring, 1965, pp. 6, 12, and 13–14.

page 19: AICPA's Committee on Accounting Procedure pronouncement: APB Accounting Principles—Current Text as of December 1, 1971, Volume One, New York: American Institute of Certified Public Accountants, 1971, § 510.13. Henceforth this will generally be cited as *APB Accounting Principles*.

pages 19–20: Ethics seminar article: The New York Times, November 22, 1971, p. 63.

pages 20–21: "Continental Vending Machine Corporation fiasco" reference: Litigation officially captioned *United States of America against Carl J. Simon, Robert H. Kaiser and Melvin S. Fishman;* quotations are from the opinion by Circuit Judge Henry J. Friendly, reported at 425 F.2d 796 (United States Court of Appeals, Second Circuit, 1969) certiorari denied 397 U.S. 1006.

pages 21–22: Petition for a writ of certiorari: Filed with the Supreme Court of the United States on February 7, 1970. The quoted material is at pp. 14 and 15 of the petition.

pages 22–23: Sommer quotations: A. A. Sommer, Jr., "Survey of Accounting Developments in the 60's; What's Ahead in the 70's," *The Business Lawyer,* November, 1970, p. 209.

Chapter 2: Alice in GAAP Land

pages 24–25: Loeb Article: G. M. Loeb, *Financial Analysts Journal,* May/June, 1971, p. 28.

pages 25–26: Forbes *reference:* "Just Grab the Nettle," editorial, *Forbes,* June 1, 1971, p. 15.

pages 28–29: "Keys to Successful Data Communication": Reported in John L. Carey (Ed.), *The Accounting Profession—Where Is It Headed?,* New York: American Institute of Certified Public Accountants, 1962, p. 54.

pages 29–30: Staggers' dialogue with Messrs. Barr and Cary: U.S. Congress, House Subcommittee on Commerce and Finance, of the Committee on Interstate and Foreign Commerce, Hearings on H.R. 6789, H.R. 6793, S. 1642, 88th Cong., 1st and 2d Sess., p. 1298.

page 30: Carey quotation: John L. Carey, "The SEC and Accounting," *The Journal of Accountancy,* December, 1963, p. 50.

pages 30–31: Patman's remarks: Reported in the *Congressional Record,* January 29, 1971, p. H-239.

pages 31–32: Storey, et al. references: Reed K. Storey, *The Search for Accounting Principles,* New York: American Institute of Certified Public Accountants, 1964, pp. 1–2; Thomas Henry Sanders, Henry Rand Hatfield, and Underhill Moore, *A Statement of Accounting Principles,* New York: American Institute of Certified Public Accountants, 1938, p. xii; and Adolf A. Berle Jr., and Gardiner C. Means, *The Modern Corporation and Private Property,* New York: Macmillan, 1932, p. 202.

page 32: Andersen "Postulate": The Postulate of Accounting—What It Is, How It Is Determined, How It Should Be Used, privately printed monograph by Arthur Andersen & Co., p. 9.

page 32: Anthony quotation: Robert N. Anthony, "Showdown on Accounting Principles," *Harvard Business Review*, May/June, 1963, p. 99.

pages 32–33: Hawkins quotation: David F. Hawkins, "The Development of Modern Financial Practices Among American Manufacturing Corporations," *Business History Review*, Autumn, 1963, p. 168.

page 33: Special Committee's catechism: Report of Special Committee on Opinions of the Accounting Principles Board, New York: American Institute of Certified Public Accountants, 1965, p. 15.

page 33: Maryland court opinion: Burroughs International Co. v. Datronics Engineers Inc., 255A 2d 341 (Md. Ct. App. 1969).

pages 33ff: Accounting Principles Board Statement No. 4: Incorporated into *APB Accounting Principles,* December 1, 1971, as Sections 1020 through 1029. Henceforth in this chapter, this compendium will be cited as 1971 APB followed by the paragraph (§) number.

page 34: Spacek criticism: Address delivered by Leonard Spacek to the Conference Institute in New York City on November 19, 1970, entitled "The Significance of Recent and Pending Opinions of the Accounting Principles Board," p. 16 (privately printed by Arthur Andersen & Co., File AD 7910—Item 130).

pages 34–35: "Relevance" reference: 1971 APB § 1024.16.

page 35: Whitman-Shubik article: Martin J. Whitman and Martin Shubik, "Corporate Reality and Accounting for Investors," *Financial Executive,* May, 1971, p. 52.

page 36: "Understandability" reference: 1971 APB § 1024.17.

pages 37–38: Internal Revenue Service Revenue Procedure 69–11: Service's Cumulative Bulletins, vol. 1969–1, p. 401.

page 39: Internal Revenue Service Revenue Procedure 71–16: Internal Revenue Service's Bulletin, 1971–2, p. 26.

page 39: "Verifiability" reference: 1971 APB § 1024.18.

page 40: Oppenheimer quotation: Robert J. Oppenheimer, *The Flying Trapeze: Three Crises for Physicists,* London: Oxford, 1964, pp. 52–53.

pages 40–41: Monod quotation: Jacques Monod, *Chance & Necessity,* New York: Knopf, 1971, p. 174.

page 41: "Neutrality" reference: 1971 APB § 1024.19.

page 42: "Timeliness" reference: 1971 APB § 1024.20.

pages 42–43: The New York Times *quotations: The New York Times,* June 19, 1971, p. 33.

page 43: Babson article: David Babson, *Financial Analysts Journal,* September/October, 1967, p. 129.

page 44: Kripke references: Homer Kripke, "The SEC, The Accountants, Some Myths and Some Realities," *New York University Law Review,* December, 1970, pp. 1151–1205. See also his "Is Fair Value Accounting the Answer?" in *The*

Business Lawyer, November, 1970, pp. 289–295, and his address entitled "The Objective of Financial Accounting Should Be to Provide Information for the Serious Investor," before a conference at Northwestern University, October, 1971. Included in Alfred Rappaport and Lawrence Revsine (Eds.), *Corporate Financial Reporting,* New York: Commerce Clearing House, 1972, pp. 95–119.

page 44: "Comparability" reference: 1971 APB § 1024.21; also §1024.23–.33.

pages 45–46: Wall Street Journal *article: Wall Street Journal,* February 16, 1972, p. 23.

pages 46–47: "Completeness" reference: 1971 APB § 1024.22.

pages 48–49: So-called "Equity Method of Accounting for Investments in Common Stock": Integrated into 1971 APB § 5131.01.–.21.

page 49: Atlantic Acceptance Corporation, the Canadian "bust" reference: Report of the Royal Commission, under the Honorable S.H.S. Hughes, 4 vols., gives a thorough analysis of what went awry up there. For the accounting implications, Chapter XVII, "The Riddle of the Accounts," is especially informative. I cannot avoid making the invidious distinction between the "sweeping under the rug" syndrome which prevails here and the "full ventilation" approach taken by the Canadians and the British (e.g., in their inquiry into the Pergamon Press fiasco).

This Atlantic Acceptance mess was the subject of a most probing article by Professor A. Beedle in *The Accountant* (England) December 10, 1970, pp. 801–805. The article entitled "Atlantic Acceptance Corporation—A Sorry Affair" carried the following headnote:

> In Canada the name "Atlantic Acceptance" lies heavily on the collective mind and conscience of the accounting profession for, even with the greatest indulgence, it was a very sorry affair.
>
> Four chartered accountants were expelled by their professional institute; a fifth, the prime mover in the débâcle, was described in the investigating Royal Commissioner's report as "inventive, ingenious, incompetent and corrupt," and was saved only by death from charges which in all probability would have sent him to prison for many years; the actions and work of other firms of auditors was described as "servile complicity" and involving differences "so startling as to provoke disbelief in the existence of any audit worthy of the name." Companion to the patent dishonesty which was revealed so many times in the Commissioner's report is the breakdown of the quality of independence on the part of certain of the auditors.

Interestingly, this article was reprinted in our *Journal of Accountancy* with the foregoing lead omitted. Did our *Journal's* editor feel that this summing up was too gory for American tastes?

page 52: Stabler reference: Charles N. Stabler, "Heard on The Street," *Wall Street Journal,* June 24, 1971, p. 29.

pages 53–54: "Bar Chris" reference: Officially cited as *Escott v. Bar Chris Construction Corporation,* 283 F. Supp. 643 (United States District Court, New York, 1968).

pages 55–56: "Revenue" and "Realization" references: 1971 APB § 1026.14; the requisite "Exchange" is considered at § 1026.15.

pages 57–58: Revenue-Cost association precepts: Included at 1971 APB § 1026 .20–.24.

Chapter 3: Dirty Pooling and Polluted Purchase

pages 60 ff: Accounting Principles Board Opinions 16 and 17: Integrated into *APB Accounting Principles* as Sections 1091 and 5141 respectively. Henceforth in this chapter this compilation will be cited as 1971 APB.

page 60: Pooling of interests: 1971 APB § 1091.12.

pages 60–61: Purchase method of accounting: 1971 APB § 1091.11.

page 64: Penn Central merger: It should go without saying that if I were writing this article today I would not use the Pennsylvania Railroad-New York Central merger to exemplify the underlying theoretical justification for a "clean pooling." In fact, as of this writing, I just could not conjure up a particular case to substitute for what I believed, in 1968, to be the particularly appropriate illustration.

page 77: Leasco-Reliance acquisition: The original "Exchange Offer to Holders of Common Stock of Reliance Insurance Company" was made by a prospectus dated August 19, 1968.

page 83: Notre Dame Lawyer *reference:* Abraham Briloff, "Accounting Practices and the Merger Movement," *Notre Dame Lawyer,* Summer, 1970, pp. 604–628.

pages 85–86: Westec litigation: Officially cited as *Orville S. Carpenter v. E.M. Hall, Jr., et al.,* C.A. No. 68–H–738 in the United States District Court for the Southern District of Texas, Houston Division.

Chapter 4: The APB and the "P" in the Pool

pages 88–89: Savoie speech: Speech by Leonard Savoie, entitled "Our Profession Looks Ahead to the 1970's," delivered before the 15th Graduate Accounting Conference, The Pennsylvania State University, at University Park on September 8, 1969. In retrospect, this speech was a most momentous one, since it foretold most precisely where and how the Accounting Principles Board would be heading toward its nadir.

pages 90–91: "Trinity of conditions precedent to . . . pooling accounting" reference: Based on the "conditions for Pooling of Interests Methods" spelled out in *APB Accounting Principles,* § 1091.45–.48.

pages 91–92: Cost allocation on a purchase transaction field rules: Suggested at *ibid.,* § 1091.88–.89.

pages 92 ff: APB's beliefs regarding the value of intangible assets: Spelled out at *ibid.,* § 5141.27–.29.

page 99: March 1971 complaint: Filed with the United States District Court for the Southern District of New York on March 12, 1971; it is captioned: *Mollie Nussbacher against The Chase Manhattan Bank (N.A.), Trustee, Continental Illinois National Bank and Trust Company of Chicago, et al.,* 71 Civ. 1153.

pages 99–100: Gunther article: Samuel P. Gunther, "Poolings-Purchases-Goodwill," *New York Certified Public Accountant,* January, 1971, p. 250. As a postscript to the Gunther article and the V-F fulfillment of his prophecy we have a U.S. Home Corporation prospectus dated December, 1971. This document describes three poolings (Witkin, Norwood, and Paparone) which were yet to be consummated (p. 11); it then refers to the offerings by "Selling Stockholders" of substantial (in some instances, major) portions of shares which were to be concurrently acquired on the pooling (p. 40). As Gunther envisaged, all vestiges of the standard of continuity of interests, theoretically required for a pooling, have been stripped away by APB's "sweet sixteen." Maybe it is just as well that a process of deception has been eliminated by a permissiveness to perpetrate in the open the hitherto clandestine act.

pages 105–107: Baker speech: Speech delivered by Richard T. Baker on August 24, 1971 (privately printed by Ernst & Ernst; the material quoted herein is from the 2nd and 3rd pages of the unnumbered text).

Chapter 5: A Look at Some Inflated Bosoms and Big Busts

page 109: SEC and AICPA committee meeting: Reported in a November, 1970, draft of a Peat, Marwick information letter on accounting for franchising companies. According to that letter, at a meeting of the Institute's committee, on August 1, 1969, Andrew Barr, the SEC's Chief Accountant, indicated that: "The [SEC] staff is concerned that some of the situations where franchises are sold and income recognized upon sale of the franchise, that such recognition of income often may not be justified."

pages 109–110: AICPA release: Dated November 19, 1969, the day following Leonard Savoie's address before the joint meeting of the Atlanta Chapter of the Georgia Society of CPAs, the Atlanta Society of Financial Analysts, the Financial Executives Institute, the National Association of Accountants, and the Planning Executives Institute. The address was entitled "The Business Community and the Public Interest."

pages 115–116: Cost–plus–fixed-fee contract accounting method: Integrated into *APB Accounting Principles* as § 4041.01–.22. Excepting that the "Government Contracts" caption has been deleted, the pronouncement remained unchanged.

pages 116–117: National Student Marketing demise: "National Student Marketing Stock Slide Hits Many Investment Firms, Institutions," *Wall Street Journal,* March 12, 1970, p. 36.

pages 117–119: SEC complaint: Captioned *Securities and Exchange Commission v. National Student Marketing Corporation,* et al., was filed with the United States District Court for the District of Columbia (Civil Action No. 225–72).

page 120: APB Opinion No. 7: "Accounting for Leases in Financial Statements of Lessors" is incorporated into *APB Accounting Principles* as Section 4051.

page 121: Standards for adopting the financing lease method: Set forth at *ibid.,* § 4051.17.

page 121: Special conditions precedent to the use of the financing lease by manufacturers: given at *ibid.,* § 4051.12.

pages 121–122: Memorex action by the SEC: Entitled *Securities and Exchange Commission against Memorex Corporation,* filed with the United States District Court, Southern District of New York (71 Civil Action No. 2812).

page 127: Telex "less than five percent" assertion: The New York Times, February 11, 1970, p. 16. This assertion was reiterated in *Barron's,* June 15, 1970, p. 3.

page 128: Auditors' settlement with the Mill Factors' creditors: The New York Times, September 23, 1970, p. 65.

page 129: Mill Factors' insolvency going back to 1965: The New York Times, December 17, 1969, p. 93.

pages 129 ff: McDiarmid article: F. J. McDiarmid, "Blow to Confidence," *Barron's,* May 12, 1969, p. 1; it carried the subtitle, "Financial Companies Will Suffer from Mill Factors' Disaster."

Chapter 6: Some More "Flap in GAAP"

page 134: Leasco and Saul Steinberg article: "How's That Again?" *Forbes,* January 15, 1971, p. 14; it carried the subhead, "For eight years Leasco has reported that it was making money in computers. Now, after a sudden write-off, Leasco has wiped out those years of profits."

page 152: Leasco's refinancing: Wall Street Journal, December 1, 1971, p. 27.

page 152: Revised configuration," based on Leasco's September 30, 1971, financial report, was as follows:

ASSETS	Leasco's Fully Consolidated Balance Sheet (1)	Reliance Insurance Company (Including its Life Insurance Subsidiary) (2)	Leasco Excluding Reliance Insurance (col. 1 minus 2) (3)
	(All amounts in millions)		
Common and preferred stock at cost	$ 184.	$183.	$ 1.
Bonds at amortized cost	382.	382.	–
Cash and certificates of deposit	59.	13.	46.
Accounts and notes receivable	109.	68.	41.
Finance lease receivables	52.	–	52.
Rental equipment (depreciated cost)	243.	–	243.
Prepaid expenses	53.	50.	3.
Policy and first-mortgage loans	39.	39.	–
Real estate—at cost	25.	17.	8.
Computers, furniture, and equipment (depreciated cost)	14.	4.	10.
Goodwill	16.	–	16.
Other Assets	26.	36.	(10.) *
Total Assets	1,202.	792.	410.

LIABILITIES

Unearned insurance premiums	207.	206.	1.
Unpaid insurance losses	246.	246.	–
Life policies and reserves	96.	100.	(4.) *
Notes payable	253.	–	253.
Accounts payable and accruals	80.	28.	52.
Federal and foreign taxes	28.	31.	(3.) *
Subordinated and convertible debt	98.	–	98.
Minority interests	7.	–	7.
Total Liabilities	1,015.	611.	404.
Equity	$ 187.	$181.	$ 6.

* These incongruous balances undoubtedly result from differences in classification and nomenclature used by Leasco, *et al.,* in their statement presentations.

page 158: President Nixon's decision to salvage Lockheed: The New York Times, May 7, 1971 p. 1. The story was headed: "President to Ask Congress to Back Lockheed Loans—Connally Reports Nixon will request $250 Million—Approval is Uncertain."

pages 158 ff.: SEC report: Promulgated on May 25, 1970, by the Commission's Division of Trading and Markets. In transmitting the report, the Division's Director stated: "The sheer dimensions of this report bespeak the scope of our investigation. The fine efforts of the Division's staff deserve special mention; all worked tirelessly in bringing to completion in a timely manner a most difficult and complicated investigation." One can only hope that their arduous efforts (and the collateral efforts of the staff of the SEC's Corporation Finance Division) will have a salutary effect on the standards of disclosure and accountability for defense contractors.

pages 160–161: Lockheed financial statements: Quoted from, or based on, the disclosure section of the SEC staff report, pp. 54–61. Also included, under "Involvement of Other Parties," are references to the role of Arthur Young, the company's auditors, especially their equivocation regarding the loss reserves required to be established in view of Lockheed's serious production problems.

Chapter 7: Accounting for the Land-Office Business

page 163: "Castles of Sand" article: Subtitled, "An Expert Questions the Accounting Practices of Land Development Companies," in *Barron's,* February 2, 1970, p. 3.

pages 164–165: GAC story: The feature article of the *Wall Street Journal,* March 3, 1972, p. 1.

page 166: Amrep letter: Letter from Howard Friedman, Amrep's President, in *Barron's,* February 9, 1970, p. 16.

page 172 ff.: Commonwealth United proxy statement: Related to a special meeting of stockholders scheduled for December 29, 1969; this meeting was finally held on March 23, 1972. It was a stormy one judging from the report in *The New York Times,* March 24, 1972, p. 55.

Because the trail through the CU proxy statement may be somewhat treacherous, here is how I marked it: The opening gambit regarding the "two real estate transactions" is reported at p. 15 under "Transactions With and Fees to Kleiner, Bell"; the shift is then to pp. 48–49, to review the "Year End Transactions—Sale of Hawaiian Land" story; then back to p. 47 for the Hawaiian Properties" story.

pages 175–176: SEC's allegations against Major Realty: The allegations on which the Commission based its order, are detailed in a "Statement of Matters by the Division of Corporation Finance to be Considered at a Public Hearing . . . ," and summarized in the Commission's September 18, 1970, press release.

page 176: Commission's order: This terminated its proceedings against Major Realty, dated April 8, 1971.

page 177: Liberty Equities proceedings: Initiated August 6, 1970, were docketed as Civil Action No. 2351–70.

pages 178–180: Auditors' answer to the SEC's Liberty Equities complaint: Filed on November 16, 1970.

pages 180–181: Termination of the Liberty Equities proceedings: Wall Street Journal, May 7, 1971, p. 30.

pages 181–183: Occidental Petroleum land saga: Retold officially in the action referred to as: *Securities and Exchange Commission v. Occidental Petroleum Corporation and Armand Hammer,* United States District Court, Southern District of New York, Docket No. 71 Civ. 982. For the expurgated version see "Occidental Issued False Profit Data, SEC Says; Injunction Is Accepted," *Wall Street Journal,* March 5, 1971, p. 3. The conclusion to that article served as the basis for my sardonic observations regarding the SEC's consent decree process, thus:

> In Los Angeles, Dr. Hammer said: "As our consent states, Occidental and I in consenting to the injunction don't concede that we have violated any regulation of the SEC or any rule of law whatsoever or any proper accounting practice."

> · · ·

> "However, as our consent states, we are desirous of avoiding costly and protracted proceedings. We also seek to save the time of our executives in vindicating our position by formal legal proceedings."

> · · ·

> He added that "the financial aspects of the complaint have been discussed with Occidental's independent auditors, Arthur Andersen & Co., and Occidental's financial statements for the years 1969 and 1970 have been audited."

> The company's 1970 earnings, released Feb. 22, 1971, were based upon such audited financial statements, he said.

> "No changes will be made in those statements or in the company's quarterly interim statements for 1969 and 1970 since none will be appropriate," Dr. Hammer said.

"Occidental and I have in the past complied and will continue in the future to comply with SEC laws and with generally accepted accounting principles consistently applied," Dr. Hammer said.

pages 186 ff.: Arctic land write-up: Retelling of the negotiations and related arithmetic are based, in good measure, on Charles Raw, Bruce Page, and Godfrey Hodson's *Do You Sincerely Want to Be Rich?*, New York: Viking, 1971, especially pp. 295–301.

Chapter 8: Great (and Not So Great) Southwest Land Deals

pages 193 ff.: "Six Flags" article: Reprinted in the *Congressional Record*, January 29, 1971, pp. H–239–241.

page 194: Fortune-*Penn Central reference:* The colloquy between the editors of *Fortune* and the auditors of Penn Central began with a feature story entitled "The Penn Central Bankruptcy Express," tied in tandem with an editorial "It's Time to Call the Auditors to Account" in the August, 1970, issue, pp. 104 and p. 98 respectively. It ended with a letter to *Fortune* from the auditors, published the following month (p. 87) and a postscript expressing the editors' regret for "any implications in [the August story] that the Penn Central's auditors, Peat, Marwick, Mitchell & Co., performed their duties in any way or manner that violates professional accounting standards and practices."

page 203: "Series of Staff Reports": Promulgated for the Committee on Banking and Currency of the House of Representatives, these reports have since been consolidated into a single volume, *The Penn Central Failure and the Role of Financial Institutions*, Washington: U.S. Government Printing Office, 1972.

pages 203–204: Great Southwest loss and lawsuit: Wall Street Journal, June 21, 1971, p. 11.

page 205 Peat, Marwick reference: To my knowledge Peat, Marwick's "Analysis of the Accounting Aspects of the Sale by Great Southwest Corporation of Six Flags Over Texas" has not been formally published. It may be that a copy could be obtained directly from the firm.

page 210 ff.: Interstate Commerce Commission reference: The Commission's over 1,500-page compendium "Investigation into the Management of the Business of the Penn Central Company and Affiliated Companies (Docket No. 35291)" has not, to my knowledge, been published for general dissemination. However, copies may be studied at the offices of the Commission.

pages 210–214: Deller findings: George K. Deller's findings are contained in Verified Statement No. 13. The statements excerpted by me are from p. 6 (profit history); pp. 7–8 (on the euphemism "Great Southwest deals"); pp. 8–14 (the Bryant Ranch chronology); and pp. 14–15 (the other real-estate deals by Macco and GSC).

pages 214–215: Russo affidavit: The assertions in the affidavit of Thomas J. Russo included, *ibid.*, as Verified Statement No. 9, were introduced into this chapter as follows: p. 2 (re: Maximization of Reported Earnings); and p. 3 (re: Earnings Improvement Opportunities).

pages 216–218: Williams action: In the United States District Court for the Northern District of Texas, Dallas Division; it carries the docket number: Civil Action CA–3–4859D.

page 219: Statement of matters reference: The "Statement of Matters By the Division of Corporation Finance to be Considered at [the] Public Hearing" which accompanied the order for the proposed GSC probe is also informative regarding the two Six Flags deals in Georgia and Texas, as well as those pertaining to the Bryant Ranch.

pages 220–221: Patman's questions: Congressman Wright Patman's "lines of questioning" were set forth in a January 3, 1972, letter to SEC Chairman William J. Casey. The letter was the subject of a *Wall Street Journal* article, "Acounting Inquiry Is Asked in Hearings on Penn Central Unit," January 4, 1972, p. 7.

Chapter 9: A House Is Not a Home

pages 224–225: Barron's story: The references to the repercussions following the unfounded rumors of an imminent *Barron's* story on homebuilders are to: "Stock Prices Slip As Rally Fizzles," *The New York Times,* July 15, 1971, p. 42; "Market Surges Then Edges Off," *The New York Times,* July 16, 1971, p. 32; "Abreast of the Market," *Wall Street Journal,* July 16, 1971, p. 25; and "Heard on The Street," *Wall Street Journal,* July 29, 1971, p. 29.

pages 225–226: Newsletter reference: ERA Accounting Review, August 15, 1971, published under the aegis of a major brokerage firm, and written by Professor Lee J. Seidler.

pages 243–244: Regarding U.S. Financial's Front-End Loading of Income: The corporation's 1971 report, promulgated April 21, 1972, indicates that it took cognizance of the criticisms in the *Barron's* article. Thus, under Note A the auditors inform us:

> For 1971, the Company adopted the more conservative policy of deferring fees from joint ventures and recognizes such fees as income as the project is completed and sold. In prior years, such fees were recognized as received. As a result of this change in accounting policy, net earnings for 1971 are approximately $2,500,000 ($.50 per share fully diluted) less than they would have been if the policy in effect prior to 1971 had been continued.

This is, of course, all to the good. However, I cannot reconcile this $.50 a share suppression with one of the assertions by U.S. Financial in an "Information Bulletin" which followed by four days the "Gimme Shelter" article. Thus, in responding to a rhetorical question as to the effect which an elimination of unrealized profits from transactions with its joint ventures would have, the corporation replied: "We have just completed an analysis showing it would reduce this year's after-tax earnings by approximately $400,000 or 8¢ a share fully diluted."

That U.S. Financial was experiencing serious difficulties with its 1971 audit is evidenced by its form 8-K filed with the Securities and Exchange Commission for the month of January, 1972. We there learn that on October 21, 1971, Touche, Ross (TR) was superseded by Haskins & Sells (H&S) as the firm to audit USF's 1971 accounts. No sooner had H&S taken a look at the books than "at a meeting of the [USF] Board on January 21 [1972], Mr. Walter [the Board Chairman] informed the Board that he had terminated the engagement of H&S and re-engaged TR to audit 1971."

There were some "potential disagreements as to accounting principles between the management of USF and H&S [involving] the question of when income should be recognized by USF." These questions were not among those which I had discerned in my "Gimme Shelter" article, written on the basis of the public record available to me at the time of my writing. According to the 8-K, these income-recognition controversies pertained to:

a. Commissions, fees, and financing-type income received in cash by USF in 1971 from joint ventures or partnerships in which USF had an interest, where the cash received by USF came out of moneys loaned by USF.

b. Gains, profits and commissions income received by USF in 1971 where USF's profit or gain was represented at the end of 1971 by notes rather than cash, or where USF had a continuing cash investment in the transaction or had a contingent obligation to supply funds.

c. Gains or profits realized by USF out of sales of secured notes by USF to USF investors, a real estate investment trust.

We were then informed that Touche, Ross was willing to accept the income recognition on the USF-USF investors' transactions. Reciprocally, U.S. Financial's management was willing to defer the recognition of the income from the joint venture fees until they were *really* realized. Similarly, USF would refrain from picking up anticipatorily mere paper profits or profits from sales to purchasers where "USF had a continuing cash investment in the transaction or had a contingent obligation to supply funds."

It should go without saying that had I recognized the existence of the (a) and (b) situations—the (c) type transaction was not relevant when my article was published—in the USF-TR game plan for the 1970 and prior accountings, I would have been quick to expose them as further manifestations of rigged incestuous accountings for the homebuilding industry.

Chapter 10: Is There a Termite Nest in the House?

pages 253 ff.: USF Investors prospectus: Dated June, 1971; the preliminary "red-herring" copy from which I quoted was dated May 25, 1971.

pages 253–254: Schulkin article: Peter A. Schulkin, "Real Estate Investment Trusts," *Financial Analysts Journal,* May/June, 1971, p. 33.

pages 255–256: Schwartz article: Sheldon Schwartz, "How to Find Tax Shelter As a Limited Partner," *Real Estate Review,* Summer, 1971, p. 54.

page 258: Kaufman & Broad prospectus: Promulgated for the Sun Life acquisition, dated November 19, 1971.

pages 258 ff.: American Housing Partners prospectus: Promulgated under the aegis of Kaufman & Broad and E. F. Hutton & Company, Inc., dated August 31, 1971.

pages 265–266: Berle reference: Adolf A. Berle treats this "Transcendental Margin" theme with special importance in the concluding Part Three–"Value," *The American Economic Republic,* New York: Harcourt, Brace & World, 1963.

page 266: Regarding Kaufman & Broad's acquisitive pattern: It is interesting to observe that the K & B evolution parallels the "three stages of conglomerate expansion" described by John M. Blair in his *Economic Concentration: Structure, Behavior and Public Policy* (New York: Harcourt Brace Jovanovich, 1972), thus (from pp. 293–300):

> In the first stage, as they are making their initial acquisitions, the conglomerates, either by accident or design, are able to secure high P/E ratios. A high multiple of market price times earnings is a *sine qua non* for the investor approval needed for future expansion.
>
> .   .   .
>
> . . . because of their high P/E ratios, the new conglomerate achieved the ability to make instant "merger profits" by taking over firms with low ratios. It was this type of activity that occupied the second stage of their history. . . . The conglomerates . . . become attracted to firms possessing large reserves of liquid assets that could be used to shore up their . . . financial structures. . . . It is more than coincidence that the conglomerates directed their acquisitive bent towards these insurance companies. They coveted their huge pools of liquidity, their cash flow. . . . There was, then, a symbiotic relationship formed between the conglomerates and insurance companies.

page 266: Best's Analysis reference: "Corporate changes–1969," *Best's Review: Property Liability Insurance,* March, 1970, p. 10.

pages 272–273: O'Glove-Olstein analysis: T. O'Glove and R. Olstein, Quality of Earnings Report, February 28, 1972, pp. 3–4.

Chapter 11: On Riding Two Horses with One Backside

pages 276–277: Wicker column: Tom Wicker, "A Man to Be Trusted," *The New York Times,* June 29, 1971, p. 37.

pages 277–278: Article by the "past president of the American Institute of CPAs": Robert M. Trueblood, *Journal of Accountancy,* December, 1970, pp. 35–38.

pages 278–279: Spacek quotation: Address by Leonard Spacek, September 19, 1970, pp 8–9. (Privately printed by Arthur Andersen & Co., File Ad 7910, item 126.)

page 279: Lyons reference: John F. Lyons, "The Big Eight Accountants—How Far Should They Go," *Corporate Financing,* January/February, 1970, p. 94. That article begins at p. 21 with the lead: "The Big Eight accounting firms are becoming the design consultants of finance," and poses a series of rhetorical questions, concluding with: "Is it wise to allow a Big Eight firm to act as both architect and building inspector; and at the same time determine the building code?"

page 280: The Effectiveness of Accounting Communication: Abraham Briloff, *The Effectiveness of Accounting Communication,* New York, Praeger, 1967. Chapter 6, "The Proliferation of Services to Management," is especially relevant.

page 281: Rogers quote: This Willie Mae Rogers *bon mot* was reported in *The New York Times,* February 16, 1969.

pages 281–282: "AICPA's Ad Hoc Committee on Independence Report": Published in *The Journal of Accountancy,* December, 1970, pp. 51–56.

page 283: Ostracize a CPA reference: That there may be substance to my assertion that the profession would move to ostracize a CPA who dared to judge his colleagues harshly, however fairly, is discernible from a section entitled "Testimony" in John L. Carey's compilation, *The CPA Plans for the Future,* New York: The American Institute of CPAs, 1965. This strongly worded section relates to testimony by CPAs against defendant CPAs. While Carey agrees that no profession should conspire to deprive the public of expert testimony needed in the punishment of wrongdoing, yet: "It may be questioned whether it is proper for a professional man to testify against a colleague when there is real doubt as to whether he failed to conform with professional standards or not." (p. 417.)

To emphasize his strong beliefs on this score, Carey suggests that a rule of ethics be adopted to implement them; and if such a rule be deemed unlawful (as a "restriction of free speech") he would circumvent the Constitution by an "admonitory resolution" so that the testifying CPA will know that his "conduct is regarded as unprofessional and is disapproved by the membership."

That Carey's counsel might not yet be the established norm might be evidenced by the following statement included under "Concepts of Professional Ethics" in the *Proposed Restatement of the Code of Professional Ethics,* New York: American Institute of Certified Public Accountants, 1972.

Although the reluctance of a professional to give testimony that may be damaging to a colleague is understandable, the obligation of professional courtesy and fraternal consideration can never excuse lack of complete candor if the CPA is testifying as an expert witness in a judicial proceeding or properly conducted inquiry.

A CPA has the obligation to assist his fellows in complying with the Code of Professional Ethics and should also assist appropriate disciplinary authorities in enforcing the Code. To condone serious fault can be as bad as to commit it. It may be even worse, in fact, since some errors may result from ignorance rather than intent and, if let pass without action, will probably be repeated. In situations of this kind, the welfare of the public should be the guide to a member's action.

page 284: American Accounting Association Statement: Published by the Association, Evanston, Ill.: 1966.

page 284: Galbraith reference: John K. Galbraith, *The New Industrial State,* Boston: Houghton Mifflin, 1967, essentially chapter VI. Especially relevant: "It will be evident that nearly all powers—initiation, character of development, rejection or acceptance—are exercised deep in the company. It is not the managers who decide. Effective power of decision is lodged deeply in the technical, planning and other specialized staff." (p. 69.)

page 286: Yale Express litigation: Docket number 65 Civ. 787.

pages 286–288: Tyler opinion: Judge Harold Tyler's opinion on this vital procedural question is reported at 266 F. Supp. 181 (U.S. District Court, Southern District, New York, 1967).

pages 289–292: SEC complaint: The "News Report" column of *The Journal of Accountancy,* March, 1972, refers to this SEC complaint (pp. 10–13). Then, the *Journal* reproduces a statement made available by "Victor M. Earle III general counsel of PMM & Co. . . . which had been distributed within the firm" (p. 12). After taking issue with the "fraud" assertion and the booking of NSMC's contracts the statement concludes:

> Perhaps the most startling allegation has to do with the comfort letter cited in most newspaper accounts. During the course of its annual audit the firm came into possession of information which cast doubt on the nine-month unaudited figures being used in proxy material in connection with an acquisition. Accordingly, the firm withdrew its draft comfort letter and so notified the parties to the merger and their counsel.
>
> The merger went ahead nonetheless, following which the firm notified each member of both boards of directors, including the outside directors, of its revised comfort letter including the recommendation that the closing be postponed in order to issue revised financial information.
>
> Nevertheless, the Commission is claiming that the firm should have gone even farther and notified the SEC or the shareholders of the two companies. The plain implication of Statement on Auditing Procedure No. 41 is that client confidences and state law and Rule 1.03 of the AICPA Code of Professional Ethics can be breached, if at all, only where the auditor has subsequently acquired information affecting his previously issued expression of opinion on audited financial statements.
>
> Here, the information acquired related to the company's previously issued unaudited financial statements as to which the firm had not expressed an opinion.

I could not help but react to this statement with a feeling of *déjà vu.* It was all too remindful of the rhetoric used by the firm in its abortive attempt to avoid its burdens in the Yale Express litigation. But even taking all of the statement's assertions at face value should not this irresponsible act of suppression of vital information have demanded that the auditors set forth this serious managerial dereliction in the financial statements to which the auditors certified within a month after this act of deception?

In brief, on the basis of the material published thus far (Spring, 1972), it would appear that the firm has forgotten nothing since its Yale Express trauma; but then, has it learned anything?

page 293: New York Stock Exchange litigation: Docket number 71 Civ. 2912.

page 293: "Paper Jungle" editorial: The New York Times, June 28, 1971, p. 30.

page 294: Robards story: Terry Robards, "Wall St. Audits Its Auditors," *The New York Times,* June 27, 1971, section 3, p. 2.

pages 296–297: Attorney General's report: A 54-page document, entitled *The Auditors of Wall Street.* Among the report's specific conclusions are the following:

> Independent accountant-auditors have been part of an arrangement whereby the public is told a tightly lidded story about the financial condition of broker-dealers.
>
> Accounting techniques . . . abetted by minimum standards of regulatory and self-regulatory rules, have cloaked by sophisticated language . . . the regular and systematic and habitual misuse and misappropriation . . . of fully-paid securities . . . of members of the investing public.
>
> The stated opinions of auditors . . . have, in many instances been deceptive, avoided essential footnotes, and been aimed more at showing a purported good financial health of a client rather than a true financial condition. . . .

pages 297–298: Savoie comments: Leonard Savoie's comments on the Attorney General's report appeared in the *Wall Street Journal,* July 15, 1971, p. 4, in an article entitled "Securities Firms' Public Financial Reports Assailed by New York State's Lefkowitz." This article makes frequent reference to a statement from the American Institute of CPAs on this issue. It is not entirely clear whether Savoie was there putting forth his own views or acting as the Institute's spokesman. To the extent he promulgated the AICPAs statement this becomes a distinction without a difference.

page 300: Barnet book: Richard J. Barnet, *The Economy of Death,* New York: Atheneum, 1969.

page 301: Lyons quotation: From his "Big Eight" article, *Corporate Financing,* January/February, 1970, p. 92.

pages 301–302: Air Force dismissal: The New York Times, November 8, 1969, p. 66.

page 302: Galbraith suggestion: John K. Galbraith suggested the nationalization of "really public firms" in a *New York* magazine article, September 21, 1970, entitled "Richard Nixon and the Great Socialist Revival," pp. 24–29.

page 303: "Mannheim wisdom" reference: The writings of the noted sociologist, Karl Mannheim, for example: *Ideology and Utopia,* New York: Harcourt, Brace & World, 1936.

page 304: Carr reference: E.H. Carr, *What is History?,* Harmondsworth, Middlesex: Penguin Books, Ltd., 1964, originally published 1961.

page 304: The Postscript: In the cross-claims section of their answer, Haskins & Sells makes the following most serious allegations against a number of Orvis Brothers' partners, especially two with the Dickensian names Kilduff (the Financial Partner) and Eucker (Partner in Charge of Operations):

1. (Paragraph 67): Orvis's accounts showed a balance owing to the firm of $880,000 by the "Clinton Oil Pension Fund." This balance arose from a sale by Orvis's "trading accounts" to the pension fund of 80,000 shares of Clinton Oil Company. (Paragraph 70): ". . . no such entity as Clinton Oil Pension Fund existed and . . . the sale of the 80,000 shares of Clinton Oil . . . was fictitious." (Paragraphs 71–72): The principal Orvis partners named in this cross-claim suppressed evidence regarding this fraudulent scheme.
2. (Paragraphs 74–75): An account with Clinton Oil was used as the receptacle for carrying "underwriting commissions receivable by Orvis in connection with its sale of participations in the oil and gas development program of Clinton." Then "Orvis improperly transferred securities [which were] . . . subject to a subordination agreement . . . to such account in order to make [the account] . . . appear properly secured."
3. (Paragraph 77): Orvis "improperly failed to accrue approximately $400,000 of commissions payable to registered representatives in connection with the sale of the Clinton Oil participation units.
4. The principal Orvis partners knew that the firm had sustained a loss of over $1.6 million during the eight months ended August 31, 1969, yet they perpetrated a hoax on H&S by having their books reveal a loss of only $718,419.
5. (Paragraph 79): A check for $500,000 which should have been credited to a customer's account went, instead, to the credit of Orvis's trading account.

And so this tale of deception, fact distortion, "falsity" and "fiction" is un-raveled for us; even someone whose stomach has been conditioned by cor-responding tales finds himself distressed by it all. When and how will it end? Who will be brought to judgment?

Chapter 12: Quo Vadis?

pages 307–308: Trueblood speech: Address by Robert Trueblood, delivered before The Los Angeles Society of Financial Analysts on October 9, 1969, entitled "Corporate Reporting—and How it Grows."

pages 309–310: Penn Central Trustees: These acerbic comments by the Penn Central trustees were included in testimony before the Committee on Com-merce of the United States Senate on November 23, 1970, p. 9 (of the trustees' statement). That this kind of an assertion did not thereupon trigger some senatorial gasps and moral indignation is incomprehensible to me.

page 310: Kohlmeier book: Louis Kohlmeier, *The Regulators*, New York: Harper & Row, 1969.

pages 310–311: Elman address: Address by Commissioner Elman, delivered in St. Louis, Missouri, on August 11, 1970, entitled "The Regulatory Process: A Per-sonal View."

page 313: America, Inc., *reference:* Morton Mintz and Jerry S. Cohen, *America, Inc.,* New York: Dial, 1971, pp. 237–238.

pages 313–314: Federal chartering recommendation: Made in *ibid.,* pp. 339–363.

page 315: Galbraith article: John K. Galbraith article in *New York* magazine, September 21, 1970, pp. 24–29.

page 315: May proposals: The George O. May proposals published in P. Grady (Ed.), *Memoirs and Accounting Thought of George O. May,* New York: Ronald, 1962, p. 68.

pages 319–320: Split within the hierarchy of the profession: The New York Times, January 4, 1972, p. 45.

page 320: Regarding the Wheat Committee: The Committee did complete its task and render its report on March 29, 1972. The report, entitled *Establishing Financial Accounting Standards,* made four principal recommendations; from pp. 8–10 of the report:

A Financial Accounting Foundation

We propose that a new foundation, to be called the Financial Accounting Foundation, be established, separate from all existing professional bodies. It would be governed by a Board of Trustees composed of nine members, whose principal duty would be to appoint the members of the Financial Accounting Standards Board and to raise the funds for its operation.

A Financial Accounting Standards Board

We propose that a Financial Accounting Standards Board be established with seven members, all fully remunerated and serving full-time. The function of the Standards Board would be to establish standards of financial accounting and reporting. The Board of Trustees would appoint members of the Standards Board and would also designate one of them to serve as chairman at the Trustees' pleasure. During their terms of office, the members of the Standards Board would have no other affiliations. Four of them would be CPAs drawn from public practice. The other three would not need to hold a CPA certificate but should possess extensive experience in the financial reporting field.

A Financial Accounting Standards Advisory Council

We propose that the Board of Trustees of the Foundation establish a Financial Accounting Standards Advisory Council, with approximately 20 members, to work closely with the Standards Board in an advisory capacity. Members of the Advisory Council would be appointed by the trustees to serve one-year terms which could be renewed indefinitely. They would be entitled to reimbursement of expenses, but no remuneration. They would be drawn from a variety of occupations, although not more than one-quarter of the members should be drawn from any single sphere of activity. The chairman of the Standards Board would also be, ex officio, chairman of the Advisory Council.

Financial Accounting Research

We urge that the Standards Board structure its research activity with its needs and objectives clearly in mind. It must first determine the type of research needed to complement the public testimony and position papers which the Board will receive in the course of its proceedings, as well as the abundance of published research prepared by academics, professional and business associations, and the like. In our view, research performed by the staff of the Standards Board should be analytical, empirical, evaluative, and directed toward systematically dealing with the topics before the Board. For example, it should deal with such questions as:

What are the issues?

What are the alternatives?

What theoretical and practical support exists for alternative solutions?

What are the practical effects and implications of the alternatives?

pages 325–326: Whitehead quotation: A. N. Whitehead, *Adventures of Ideas,* New York: New American Library, 1955, originally published 1933, p. 64.

page 326: Teilhard quotation: Pierre Teilhard, *The Phenomenon of Man,* New York: Harper & Row, 1961, pp. 278–279.

page 327: Philips article: G. Edward Philips, "Research in Major Public Accounting Firms," *The Journal of Accountancy,* June, 1964, pp. 37–38.

page 328: Powell speech: Speech by Weldon Powell, entitled "Report on the Accounting Research Activities of the American Institute of Certified Public Accountants," published in *The Accounting Review,* January, 1961, pp. 29–30.

pages 330–331: Etherington address: Address by Edwin D. Etherington, delivered at The University of Connecticut, Storrs, on May 27, 1971.

pages 332: First Devonshire and Robinson lawsuits: Respectively: In the matter of the First Devonshire Corporation, United States District Court, Southern District of New York, 70 b 739; Robinson & Co. litigation, United States District Court, Eastern District of Pennsylvania, 70–518.

After first resisting the claims of the customers of these two bankrupt stock exchange firms, the New York Stock Exchange agreed to compensate the customers for their losses. The Exchange's reversal was, it appeared, a condition precedent to the congressional enactment of the securities investor's protection (SIPC) legislation. (*Wall Street Journal,* November 18, 1970, p. 4.)

pages 333–334: Griswold quotation: A. Whitney Griswold, *Liberal Education and the Democratic Ideal,* New Haven, Conn.: Yale University Press, 1959, p. 136.

Index

AICPA, *see* American Institute of Certified Public Accountants

AMK, 101–102, 104; *see also* United Fruit Company

Accountant's report, *see* Auditor's certificate

Accounting Court, Leonard Spacek proposal for, 312

Accounting Principles Board, *see* American Institute of Certified Public Accountants

Accounting profession, responsibility of, 318–332

Accrual, 50

Ackerman, Martin, 317

Agro Resources Inc., Occidental Petroleum and, 183

Allied Oil, American Express and, 286

Allied Radio Corp., *see* LTV–Ling Altec

Allison, Paul E., 291

American Accounting Association
responsibility of, 318
Statement of Basic Accounting Theory, 284

American Express, 324
and Allied Oil, 286

American Housing Partners, Kaufman and Broad and, 257–263

American Institute of Certified Public Accountants, 17
Accounting Principles Board, 17, 312, 318
crisis at, 88

criticism of, 320–324; by Trueblood, 319

franchisor accounting, 110

pooling-purchase controversy, *see generally* Chapters 3 and 4

and research, 327–329

Opinion No. 7: 120–121, 138–139

Opinion No. 9: 178, 194

Opinion No. 16: 89–92, 241; *see generally* Chapters 3 and 4

Opinion No. 17: 92–93; *see generally* Chapters 3 and 4

Opinion No. 18: 48–49, 243; *see also* Equity method

Opinion No. 20: 230–231

Statement No. 4: Basic Concepts and Accounting Principles, *see generally* Chapter 2

Special Committee to Study Opinions of, 17–19, 33

Accounting Research Division, 327–329

defendant of last resort, 332–333

responsibility of, 318

Long Range Objectives Committee, keys to data communication, 29

on management services, 300

Committee on Accounting Procedures

on the company and its auditors, 19

on cost-plus-fixed-fee accountings, 115–116

Committee on Cooperation with the SEC and Stock Exchanges, 109

73 74 75 10 9 8 7 6 5 4